CORPUS DELICTI

CORPUS
DELICTI

DIANE WAGNER

ST. MARTIN'S / MAREK
NEW YORK

Design by Mina Greenstein

Library of Congress Cataloging-in-Publication Data

Wagner, Diane.
   Corpus delicti.

   1. Scott, Leonard Ewing—Trials, litigation, etc.
2. Trials (Murder)—California.   I. Title.
KF224.S33W34   1986   345.73'02523   85-25061
ISBN 0-312-17016-5   347.3052523

First Edition

10   9   8   7   6   5   4   3   2   1

To WALTER WAGNER,

who inspired dreams;

to MAXINE WAGNER,

who made them possible.

Acknowledgments

This note is a brief thanks to the men and women I interviewed for the story that follows. Though many others contributed their memories to these pages, some individuals were especially generous with their time: J. Miller Leavy, Arthur Alarcon, Adolph Alexander, Gene Blake, Herman Zander, Nick Cimino, George Putnam, Seth Hufstedler, Al Matthews, Lewis Watnick, Dorothy Mumper, and yes, L. Ewing Scott.

—DIANE WAGNER
Los Angeles, 1985

□ □ □

Keep in mind, the *corpus delicti* of murder is not the actual *body* of the deceased, like detective magazines tell you with those so-called pictures of the "corpus delicti!" That's a lot of bullshit. The corpus delicti is the *body* of the *crime*. You only have to prove—even in a circumstantial evidence case—two elements: first, that death occurred, and second, by some criminal means.

—J. MILLER LEAVY

There was no witness, no confession, no smoking gun. There wasn't even a corpse. But J. Miller Leavy is still certain there was a murder, a deliberate, clever killing that left no earthly trace of Evelyn Scott, save her husband's scandalous eulogy. "I know he killed her," Leavy says firmly this summer afternoon almost thirty years later. "There's not an iota of doubt in my mind."

Leavy is no stranger to his convictions. For forty years, Leavy tried some of Los Angeles' most memorable death penalty cases. He sent Barbara Graham, the doe-eyed murderess who inspired Susan Hayward's Academy Award–winning performance in *I Want to Live,* Caryl Chessman, the so-called Red-Light Bandit, and others to that small green chamber just inside the walls of San Quentin State Prison.

To colleagues, Leavy is the quintessential prosecutor, with a brilliant memory for detail and law, absolute faith in the integrity of his evidence, and a courtroom showmanship that keeps every eye riveted on him. Even defense lawyers admiringly call him the best trial attorney ever to prosecute in the city's storied courtrooms. Yet, Leavy's biggest case, a landmark, precedent-setting circumstantial murder with no corpse, no indisputable proof of death, and no legal precedent was a challenge he almost didn't get.

"I wasn't on the case at the start," Leavy tells me now, as we sit comfortably in the den of his San Fernando Valley home. At seventy-nine, he is a tightly built man of eager, intense energy, dark-eyed, with thinning silver hair. "Ernie Roll and I were good friends, you know, and we'd tried a number of cases together before he was the district attorney. But he was quite jealous of the publicity I used to get, and he didn't want me in the Scott case—at least, that's the story I got." So Leavy, a master at circumstantial evidence case law, sat on the sidelines, playing only a small, behind-the-scenes role as

1

the strategy to snare a shrewd murderer was formulated. Not until the chief of police personally asked for him was Leavy assigned to the case.

"It wasn't the first 'no body' case. No," Leavy says, pushing his thick black-rimmed eyeglasses back into place with quick, stubby fingers, "there were five or six other ones before it. In every other case, though, the killer confessed or acknowledged that his victim was dead. But you have to remember that he's got almost as much ego as I've got. L. Ewing Scott has never even admitted that Evelyn Scott is dead. To this day, he insists she's alive."

The Mercedes-Benz climbed easily up North Bentley Avenue, a thin ribbon of road unwinding gently through the Bel Air foothills. From the driver's seat, all Ulrich Quast could see at first were high hedges hiding long driveways and big houses. Then he passed an oriental gardener, serenely rooting spring-colored slips of flowers, and two giggling Mexican girls—maids, probably—but no one who looked rich enough to belong in Bel Air.

To an immigrant like Quast from war-wasted Germany, this oasis was mesmerizing, a mecca built by movie stars and self-made millionaires. With Beverly Hills to the east and Brentwood to the west, Bel Air was centerstone to a necklace of nouveau riche neighborhoods strung together near southern California's cool Pacific coastline. Though lacking the bloodlines and breeding of its old-line cousins, such as Pasadena, Bel Air nevertheless was an unequaled address for the newly arrived.

Quast slowed. He glanced at the address jotted in his appointment calendar: *217 North Bentley Avenue, above Sunset.* A solid Bel Air address all right, but on its less spectacular and more modest western border. Underneath Quast had added, *2:15 P.M. SHARP.*

He was habitually on time, and this Monday afternoon, May 16, 1955, was no exception, despite the steady stop-and-go traffic along Sunset Boulevard. Clients didn't like to be kept waiting for a car salesman, and these small details of customer service were as critical as the car's performance. "Both must be superior," the Mercedes-Benz representative had stressed during Quast's training. "Two minutes late might cost you the sale." Quast looked at his watch. It was 2:12.

Number 217 North Bentley was to his left, an inconspicuous two-story house almost hidden in the hillside. Dense shrubbery concealed all but sedentary rows of ash-colored shingles lying on the flat roof.

Quast swung the Mercedes onto the flagstone driveway and parked. A stone path, flanked by a covered wood-louvered walkway to the garage, led to the front door. Quast rang the doorbell and waited. His watch read 2:15 P.M.

"Mr. Quast?"

The door was opened by a wide-shouldered man with fluid, easy features and silver hair. He wore a tailored suit, a crisp, white shirt, and neatly knotted tie. Next to him stood a gray-haired woman—legs too spindly for a still-thin torso, Quast thought fleetingly—dressed in the same elegant, conservative style.

"I'm Ewing Scott and this is my wife," the man said, one arm placed loosely around Evelyn Scott's shoulders. With his other arm, he gestured toward the driveway. "Let's take a look at that car you've got there."

Quast waited until they had passed him on the stone porch before he followed the Scotts toward the cream-colored four-door sedan. Scott walked with the stiff, straight-legged steps of an old man, even though Quast judged him to be still in his mid-fifties. Evelyn, in her fashionable yet sensibly moderate heels, walked a few clipped steps in front of her husband.

They circled the Mercedes once, Scott scrutinizing the paint job, Evelyn peering inside at the matched leather interior. She glanced up as Quast approached and smiled pleasantly. Scott looked up too.

"Well, now, that's a very nice car. But as you can see"—Scott pointed toward the open garage—"we already have two cars, a '40 Ford and a '48 Dodge, and they're both in very good condition. I never drive over thirty-five miles an hour." He looked from the garage to the new Mercedes-Benz parked in the driveway. Evelyn was admiring the car's exterior, an expertly executed finish of paint and polished chrome. "All right," he said indulgently. "Let's go in the house and talk about it."

Inside, the air was cool and still. Venetian blinds covered most of the windows, filtering out all but tiny seams of sunlight. Scott led Evelyn and Quast past a formal living room on the left into the den, an intimate room more casually furnished with a couch and several high-backed chairs. Scott seated Evelyn and gestured at a chair for Quast.

4

A simple gold jewel case filled with Evelyn's cigarettes decorated a tabletop.

"Now, before we go along any further with this thing, I want to know just how much that car is going to cost me," Scott said. "We want a good, solid car to drive in Europe—my wife and I are considering living in Spain for a period of time and that can get rather expensive. We don't want to go into too much money."

"The Mercedes-Benz 220-S sedan costs $2,975," Quast answered. His German accent, unexpectedly thick, magnified Quast's blond Teutonic good looks. He continued cautiously, clearing his throat. Few clients focused so quickly on the Mercedes' not inconsiderable cost. "If you take delivery of the car at our factory in West Germany, there will be some additional expense to bring the car back to Los Angeles."

"Oh, I know all that," Scott interrupted. "What I want to know is how much money it's going to run into and I want it in writing."

Quast nodded patiently. "Of course, Mr. Scott. The shipping cost will be approximately two hundred dollars. Depending on how long you are gone, you may have to pay a used-car or a customs tax. My office can put these estimates in a letter for you."

"All right," Scott said, apparently satisfied. "Now, which one of our cars are you going to take as a trade-in?"

"We usually suggest to our customers to sell their other car outright," the salesman said quickly, sensing that Scott would not be pleased by this company policy. "The customer is in a much better position than we are to dispose of a used car."

"Well, now, I don't know if I like that. We're talking about a lot of money here, which I intend to pay in cash. Your cooperation in this matter would be appreciated."

"Oh, Ewing, we'll just sell one of the cars when we get back," Evelyn said, breaking into the men's conversation. To Quast, she added, "We'll only be gone a few months. We love Spain, but I don't think I could stand to be away from Los Angeles for very long. We have so many friends here."

Quast nodded his head eagerly, relieved at her interruption. "Yes, yes, Spain is a very beautiful country. Almost as lovely as *mein Deutschland*," he said.

"Well, why can't we just pick up the car in Spain?" Scott asked.

"Spain would not permit it—they have certain customs regulations against it there," Quast said.

"Now, everything I want to do, you tell me I can't," Scott said loudly, complaining, Quast guessed, mainly for benefit of his wife. "I don't think I like that very much."

Evelyn looked at her husband. "Maybe you should see how you like the car before you make up your mind."

"All right, sweetie," Scott said, grandly giving in to her. "Let's take it for a little test drive."

"Very smooth ride." Quast demonstrated with an even stop where North Bentley Avenue crossed Sunset Boulevard. A stream of cars flowed down Sunset, a major east-west artery through Los Angeles. The new San Diego freeway under construction a few blocks away would be a more efficient route to the city's downtown district, but this Monday afternoon, the roadway's grading was still waiting for its first coat of concrete. Although Quast was driving, Scott asked him to turn left, heading east on Sunset toward Beverly Glen.

To the south of Sunset Boulevard, UCLA and Westwood Village formed a red-tile-roof mosaic, the university and its Mediterranean-style commercial district, culled by savvy developers from barley fields in the 1920s as a cultural drawing card for the mansions that soon dotted the foothills nearby. The best addresses were above Sunset, amid Bel Air's eclectic collection of mock-Tudor estates, colonial castles, and low-slung western ranch houses. Hollywood's "First Lady of Song," Jeanette MacDonald, and her producer-actor husband, Gene Raymond, were among Bel Air's celebrated dwellers, and Evelyn and Ewing visited the couple in their sumptuous home here.

In 1955, the Mercedes-Benz was a classic make, known—if at all in America—just to racing enthusiasts who would recite its long list of championships: Le Mans, Grand Prix, the Monte Carlo Rally. A few Americans already drove special models, Clark Gable among them, but Daimler-Benz, the automobile's West German parent company, had only just begun to export its cars to the United States three years earlier. Mercedes-Benz considered this model, the 1955 220-S sedan, a solidly designed car with remarkable handling, ideal for the frugal well-to-do.

6

"We Germans have a very fine reputation for our cars," Quast said. Scott's directions were taking them north on Beverly Glen now, a canyon road that curved past more architecturally extravagant homes. "Mercedes-Benz has designed this car to be very safe. You have seen in the papers the stories of accidents, people killed by the steering column in a collision?" Quast twisted to look at Evelyn, sitting alone behind her husband in the right-hand corner of the back seat. He wanted to be sure she heard him. "In a Mercedes-Benz, the steering column goes away from you, like so." Quast's hands pantomimed an imaginary steering column thrust away from his chest and toward the dashboard.

"That's good to know," she murmured, the feats of German engineering of uncertain value to her. "I do like this back seat," she added, running her hand across the vanilla-colored leather. "I hardly feel like we're moving."

At Mulholland Drive—named for William Mulholland, the land developer whose waterways made arid southern California fat with subdivisions and swimming pools—Scott asked Quast to turn left. The hilly, two-lane thoroughfare was intersected intermittently by anonymous driveways and roads, but Quast thought that Scott seemed to know his way here well.

"You see here on the side of the road—it is gravel. This is what we have in Europe," Quast said, swinging the Mercedes off the paved road and onto the gritty shoulder where he stopped the car and turned off the engine. "See how well the Mercedes handles? No problems for you. In just a moment, if you wish, you may drive. But first, may I show you how to change a tire?"

The two men got out, the salesman dwarfed by Scott's six-foot-four frame. Quast walked to where Scott stood, an arm's length from the open door of the passenger's seat. Inside, Evelyn leaned forward. "Ewing, I'm cold," she said. "Okay, sweetie," Scott said amiably, and he pushed his car door shut.

"Mercedes-Benz has designed a frame jack, not a bumper jack like your American cars. It goes here, you see," the salesman said, pointing to one of four holes in the chassis near each wheel. Squatting in the dust, Quast, gesturing as he spoke, inserted the jack into the opening behind the front passenger's seat. Scott, still standing, watched as the salesman expertly changed the tire. Evelyn sat quietly in the back seat, staring out absently at the brushy hillside and the skyline of the distant city.

Scott drove the Mercedes home. He must be telling the truth about those two cars in the garage, Quast thought. The man really did drive no faster than thirty-five miles an hour.

As they neared North Bentley Avenue, Scott turned to Evelyn in the back seat. "Now, do you want to drive it?" She smiled and shook her head no. "Okay," Scott said. Quast's watch read 4:21 P.M.

"Well, I think it's a very nice car," Scott said as he parked the Mercedes in the driveway. "But I want to know exactly what it's going to cost me before I'll agree to any of it."

"Why don't I put those estimates together for you, Mr. Scott, and call you later in the week?"

"That'll be just fine." Scott opened his car door. Quast got out too, and pulled open Evelyn's door for her. "Thank you for bringing the car out to show us," Scott said. "I'll expect to hear from you Thursday."

"Yes, Thursday, very good. I'll do that. Good-bye, Mrs. Scott," Quast said, shaking hands with her.

"Yes, thank you very much," Evelyn said pleasantly, and she started toward the house with her husband.

A sale looked good, despite Scott's niggling over money, Quast thought, pleased with his afternoon's efforts. He backed out of the driveway as the Scotts reached the front porch; for an instant, they were framed together by their doorway in an impromptu snapshot. Evelyn turned around and waved good-bye to the car salesman with a warm, wide smile.

Other than her husband, Ulrich Quast was the last person known to see Evelyn Scott alive.

□ **2**

In 1949, Evelyn Throsby Mumper, at fifty-seven, looked fifteen years younger. She took impeccable care of herself and it showed. She was no more than five feet six, very slender, and she dressed elegantly in a quiet, classic way. Blue-eyed, with graying hair swept up into her customary pompadour, Evelyn was quintessential society in the best of Pasadena's silk-stockinged style.

But Evelyn Mumper was hardly the stereotypical society widow. She was canny about money and investments, and kept her own meticulous records in a six-by-six-inch black notebook. Notations in Evelyn's graceful, looping handwriting listed holdings worth not quite $1 million: a nine-sixteenth interest in The Edgewater, a $600,000 Milwaukee apartment house that netted her $1,400 or $1,500 a month, a $220,000-plus stock portfolio, bank accounts totaling almost $200,000, and a sumptuous Pasadena home, valued in 1949 at $45,000. Still, Evelyn's penny-wise sensibility kept her driving in her 1948 blood-red Dodge Deluxe Coupe for blocks just to find a free parking place on the street.

Evelyn's life-style was compatible with that of Pasadena's conservative and self-indulgent well-to-do. She pampered herself with weekly beauty treatments, an exquisite wardrobe, and furs that were more decoration than necessity in southern California's temperate climate. Her full-time household staff included a cook, a gardener, a handyman-chauffeur, a maid, and a secretary-companion, all of whom freed Evelyn for planning her garden soirees or for attending charity affairs.

Yet Evelyn considered her chief treasures to be her friends of many years, the living threads of a shared lifetime woven through four marriages and a cross-country move from her native New York City to Los Angeles. She entertained them richly at dinner parties in her home or in intimate groups at exclusive restaurants or clubs; her most frequent guests were Gertrude and Bill Brawner, Mildred and Bill Schuchardt, Gladys and Arthur Baum, and Opal and Hewlings Mumper, her brother-in-law and his wife. Evelyn, whose sole living relative was a younger brother, Raymond Throsby, loved her friends dearly, and remembered each one's birthday, anniversary, or celebration with a note, telephone call, or gift. Her friends, just as devoted to Evelyn, reciprocated her invitations and gestures in kind, spanning over twenty years—thirty years for some ties that reached back to Evelyn's East Coast roots. Evelyn was particularly close to Mildred Schuchardt, an arthritic shut-in with whom she visited by telephone

9

every day. Mildred, along with next-door-neighbor Gertrude Brawner, and Gladys Baum, who also lived nearby in Pasadena, were Evelyn's most trusted and cherished friends.

Evelyn's table talk, punctuated by long draws on the sleek black cigarette holder she favored, ran to pleasant generalities, the light witticisms or unremarkable observations that were neither offensive nor remembered. On politics, Evelyn was a bellwether of her sex and times, sincerely concerned about a postwar world of which she had only a naive understanding. She read news stories and editorials dutifully and wondered over the one, perhaps two, old-fashioneds or highballs she might nurse all evening if maybe Eisenhower couldn't do a little more to balance the budget at home and thaw the cold war abroad.

But Evelyn's passion was traveling, and she constantly scoured guidebooks for new ways to see the Old World. Evelyn was no daydreaming voyager either: her passport already carried stamps from across Europe, Mexico, South America, and the Caribbean. Periodically, she swept into New York City for brief reunions with old friends. Evelyn traveled locally too, the way other wealthy southern Californians did—perhaps a brunch in Santa Barbara two hours north of Los Angeles or a weekend in La Jolla, an hour and a half to the south. Wherever she went, however, Evelyn delighted in finding mail from home waiting for her, and she always made sure to leave her itinerary with Gertrude, Mildred, Gladys, and her other friends. Without fail, a copy of Evelyn's schedule always prudently went to Jim Boyle, her attorney, "just in case" some urgent business required her immediate attention.

But even her closest friends, the confidantes with whom she lingered over long lunches at the Brown Derby or Perino's, knew little of the private Evelyn, the woman behind the wide smile and the generous checkbook. She seldom spoke about herself—her childhood, her parents, or her four husbands. Yet, if Evelyn—energetic, easygoing, and ebullient—had voiced her private heartbreak, her bitterest disappointment, it would have been another thread winding through her life: men. From its beginning with an absent father, the course ran through her four marriages, the first two aborted mismatches to alcoholics, the second two happier unions that had left her twice a widow.

*   *   *

She was born Evelyn Throsby in New York City on May 11, 1892. Her father, a marine engineer, deserted his small family, which by now included her younger brother Raymond, for the lure of Alaskan mining adventures. Although their subsistence was modest, the children later remembered their youth as satisfactory. They shared the same wide, broad facial features, but Evelyn, four years older than her brother, would be the stronger, more ambitious, and ultimately more successful of the Throsbys throughout their lives.

Evelyn worked from an early age, starting as a stenographer for the Thomas Flying Automobile Company in New York City. It was the first of a succession of secretarial jobs that Evelyn would hold until she married in 1916, the same year that her mother died of a liver ailment. Twenty-four-year-old Evelyn wed Walter Kiernan, son of a wealthy Staten Island coal merchant, in St. Agnes Church in New York City. In place of their errant father, twenty-year-old Raymond gave Evelyn away.

But her union with Kiernan ended less than two years later with Evelyn's demand for a divorce. Kiernan, a stock broker, was a chronic alcoholic, and his excesses repulsed his young bride. Evelyn's friends made sure her evenings were filled with bridge games, parties, and dinner invitations. No one, least of all Evelyn, mentioned her divorce.

In 1920, with her brother Raymond once more at her side, Evelyn married again, this time to Dr. Myrnee Lewis, a gifted New York City surgeon. But this union, too, was a failure: Like her first husband, Lewis was an alcoholic. He spent months, year after year, seeking sobriety in sanatoriums, yet Lewis' cravings still left him thirsty. After seven years, the couple separated at Evelyn's request.

Unhappily contemplating her second divorce, Evelyn went back to work in the closing years of the twenties. With two partners, she opened a women's specialty shop on Madison Avenue in Manhattan, a store where moneyed matrons shopped for one-of-a-kind ball gowns or finely tailored dresses. Within six months of the shop's opening, Evelyn met the man who would eventually become her third husband.

Clement Pettit was a wealthy, divorced Manhattan land developer and scion of a rich Milwaukee banking clan. Pettit was also a severe arthritic, so crippled by his disease that he walked haltingly even when bolstered by two canes. He was charmed by this vivacious beauty, with her quick wit, sunny personality, and self-possessed bearing, and around Evelyn, his friends saw that Pettit was noticeably brighter.

Evelyn waited patiently for another two years as Lewis continued his constant—and ultimately unsuccessful—clinical treatments. Finally, she went alone to Reno, Nevada, and obtained her second divorce on June 10, 1929. She was thirty-seven. With the dissolution of her second marriage completed, Evelyn spent a month visiting her brother to rally her spirits. Raymond, now living in Los Angeles, was just starting up a business venture of his own, a tire manufacturing concern called the Transportation Guarantee Corporation.

Almost immediately upon her return to New York, Pettit asked Evelyn to marry him. But she demurred, preferring instead to keep her newly acquired independence and the small apartment she had taken during her separation. Sixteen months later, however, Evelyn did marry Pettit in his apartment overlooking Central Park, and for the third time, Raymond Throsby gave his sister away.

Pettit was generous to Evelyn, presenting her with valuable blue-chip stocks and bonds, a majority interest in The Edgewater, a Milwaukee apartment house that he had inherited from his father, and exquisite jewelry that included several ropes of luminescent pearls, two diamond-encrusted cameos, and a brilliant star-sapphire-and-diamond ring.

But Pettit's health, always uneven, was worsening. Evelyn began graciously declining invitations from friends, choosing instead to remain at home to care for her husband. By now, she had given up her interest in the shop to be with Clem, to read him the morning's business news or to fuss over him with tenderhearted attention. When the couple did venture out, Evelyn was never far from Pettit's side. Finally, on the advice of Pettit's doctors, Evelyn and Clem moved from Manhattan to Los Angeles, where a more benign climate might ease Pettit's suffering. Evelyn looked forward to seeing more of Raymond too, who was working as a supervisor for the State Emergency Relief Association after the Depression had squeezed his fledgling manufacturing company out of business.

The Pettits were the kind of settlers Los Angeles wanted, not desperate dust-bowl migrants hoping for work but wealthy easterners with ample resources of their own. Evelyn and Clem fell in love with Pasadena, the sunny, orange-scented city founded by East Coast financiers and midwestern manufacturers, many of whom, like Pettit, came seeking the warmth of California's health-giving sun. It was 1932, and the couple and their wealthy, politically right neighbors blended together comfortably in a city that was already the nucleus of an elite suburban enclave. Evelyn and Clem, sociable, Republican, and rich, fit in very well in Pasadena.

The Pettits built a one-story, three-bedroom white wood house at 261 South San Rafael Road in 1935, among the city's most desirable addresses. They developed a warm, close friendship with neighbors Bill and Gertrude Brawner. Brawner, a prominent Los Angeles attorney, watched Evelyn and Gertrude grow especially close, with almost daily chats over their shared backyard fence. Raymond, now a safety engineer for the federal government, visited the Pettits' home often. In 1941, when a doctor recommended a sanatorium stay for Raymond's health, Clem Pettit willingly paid his bill.

Despite the distance, the couple maintained the friendships they had left behind in New York City. Evelyn mailed periodic, chatty notes, filled with tidbits about their last party, their next trip, or the pleasant weather. Among those friends to whom Evelyn wrote regularly was Marguerite Watson, since fallen into genteel poverty with the burden of a family member's illness. Evelyn sent occasional modest checks with her letters to Marguerite, and, as World War II came to an end, two boxes a year of the previous season's gowns, suits, hats, and shoes. Evelyn told Marguerite to keep whatever she wanted and suggested sending on whatever was left to the needy in war-torn Europe. For ten years, those packages arrived regularly every six months or so, unfailingly preceded by a note from Evelyn.

As the war continued, Evelyn volunteered, serving at Pasadena's USO Hospitality House until Pettit's frail health, complicated by heart disease, forced her to put aside her charity work. On January 18, 1944, Pettit died at home, leaving a grieving—and wealthy—widow.

Friends again came to Evelyn's rescue, among them architect Bill

Schuchardt and his wife Mildred. Pettit and Schuchardt, childhood friends, had met again after a lapse of many years aboard a transatlantic cruise in 1936, a chance meeting that rekindled a warm friendship. Over time, Evelyn and Mildred grew close too, much more than an agreeable complement to their husbands' friendship. Like Clem, Mildred was a severe arthritic, and later, when Mildred's crippling disease left her largely housebound, Evelyn took up her convalescence with understanding. They spoke daily by telephone, a bittersweet ritual for Mildred, as Evelyn described the galas and party-goers that Mildred's illness prevented her from enjoying firsthand. They celebrated their birthdays together too: Mildred's birthday, May 12, was just a day after Evelyn's. Remembering Evelyn's love of travel, the Schuchardts invited her along on a month-long visit to Mexico City and Acapulco shortly after Pettit's death. As usual, Evelyn dropped a note to Jim Boyle with her schedule.

Almost two years after Pettit's death, Evelyn, still attractive and desirable at fifty-four, was wed a fourth time, to Norris McAllister Mumper, whom she had met once briefly, years earlier, at a party in Palm Springs. Mumper was a retired engineer who served as an aeronautics consultant to the U.S. State Department at the request of a member of New York's Rockefeller family. Divorced, Mumper had resisted the idea of remarriage until he met Evelyn again at the home of a friend. They married in a quiet garden ceremony at the Schuchardt's Bel Air home in December 1946.

The Mumpers lived in Evelyn's house on South San Rafael Street, by now given over to dark green ivy twining across the house's white wood slats. They entertained frequently in Evelyn's formal backyard garden, a flagstone terrace graced by four spreading elm trees that met over a star-shaped fountain. A full-time gardener made sure the grounds were beautifully kept.

The house was only one of the assets Evelyn had acquired over her fourteen-year marriage to Pettit, and Mumper, who had no wish to involve himself in her separate property matters, suggested that Evelyn hire a professional investment counselor to manage a stock portfolio worth $183,000. In April 1947, Evelyn selected J. Smith Miller of Willis & Christy as her broker. Although her husband was present during some of her consultations with Miller, Mumper made no effort to influence his wife's decisions. For his part, Miller found Evelyn an ideal client: attentive, interested, and capable of making her own business decisions.

Soon after Evelyn's marriage to Norris, his son and daughter-in-law began house-hunting in Pasadena. But prices were steep even then for a young couple just starting out, and Evelyn enthusiastically suggested that Bill and Dorothy Mumper build a home of their own on her acreage: Evelyn's lot was deep enough to accommodate two houses yet ensure each family's privacy. Although she never seemed to regret not having any children of her own, Evelyn was already a willing baby-sitter to the young couple's two toddlers. Bill and Dorothy accepted Evelyn's generous offer happily, and both families excitedly planned their future as neighbors while the house was being built.

But the young family moved into their new home just a few days before Norris Mumper died of a heart attack in the early morning hours of September 3, 1948. Devastated, Evelyn cried for days, taking what comfort she could from Opal and Hewlings Mumper, the brother and sister-in-law by marriage to whom she would always remain close. Although the bulk of his estate went to his family, Norris left Evelyn over $30,000 in cash.

Evelyn stayed with Opal and Hewlings for several days after Norris' funeral. She then moved to Pasadena's gracious old-line Huntington Hotel for several weeks, reluctant to return to the house on South San Rafael where Clem Pettit and Norris Mumper both had died. Raymond, employed as an insurance agent now, kept a close, protective watch over his sister, often stopping by Evelyn's hotel suite to offer what comfort he could.

The deaths of her two husbands frightened Evelyn and left her with a vague uneasiness about her own health. She had had a slight brush with a superficial skin cancer in 1947, which required the removal of two small moles underneath her right eye. Although the treatment was successful, Evelyn still religiously visited the Pasadena Tumor Institute every six months for checkups. When routine tests showed only that her health was excellent, Evelyn's physician suggested that she consult a psychiatrist, Dr. Purcell Schube of Pasadena. Dr. Schube pinpointed the deaths of Pettit and Mumper as the source of Evelyn's anxieties, and after several months, her worries were eventually quieted. Gradually, Evelyn's life settled back into its familiar routine of parties, charity affairs, and dinner engagements.

When Evelyn moved back to her Pasadena home in late 1948, she was not alone. She brought Olive Wright, a woman she knew casually from her wartime volunteer work, with her. Olive had helped acknowledge the flowers and notes that arrived after Norris' death, and Evelyn hired her as a full-time secretary-companion. For $200 a month, Olive answered Evelyn's mail, paid her bills, and did her banking and marketing. Olive, who was married with two grown children of her own, drew her salary even while her employer traveled—Evelyn spent Christmas in Hawaii that year, followed by an eight-week cruise to South America in the spring of 1949.

Evelyn was financially secure for the rest of her life: Pettit and Mumper had seen to that. But childless, twice divorced, and now twice widowed, Evelyn at fifty-seven faced an unwelcome solitude in her autumn years. Evelyn's friends filled as much of her time as possible with dinner invitations, cocktail parties, and shopping excursions to Beverly Hills. Yet Evelyn knew, as many widows discover, that they could do little to fill a house empty of all but memories.

Then, in the early summer of 1949, Bill and Gertrude Brawner escorted Evelyn to a dinner party at the home of the Roy Wilcoxes. The only other guest that evening was Evelyn's dinner partner. His name was L. Ewing Scott.

□ **3**

A successful marriage, Scott decided at an early age, was no more than a sales contract: goods ordered, goods delivered. All it took, he believed, was a shrewd salesman who knew how to package whatever his prospect could be sold. Scott had been waiting a lifetime for an opportunity like Evelyn, and at age fifty-three, he knew he had found her.

* * *

During dinner, Ewing pressed Evelyn to talk about herself, drawing her out with a word or a question as if she were the most important person in the room. Her late husband worked in Washington? Scott had worked there himself—but Norris Mumper? No, Scott didn't think they had met, but, of course, doing *classified* government work, he'd hardly had time to meet anyone. Pettit was in real estate? Why, he was a land developer too, Scott said, that is, when he wasn't busy with his investment business. "You know, don't you," he interrupted himself, "that's a very lovely perfume you're wearing."

Evelyn was captivated. Her dinner partner lit her cigarettes, even though he said he didn't smoke them himself, charming her with Old World manners that served as the basic currency of any upper-crust drawing room. He was well traveled, handsome as a movie star, a Scheherazade conversationalist. He studied her features appreciatively with the cool, admiring eye of a man who always looked for quality, and before the evening ended, Evelyn invited Ewing to her home for dinner. Almost overnight, he became her steady gentleman caller.

Ewing quickly established himself as Evelyn's chief suitor. Throughout that summer, he interrupted her afternoons with sentimental telephone calls or spontaneous lunch dates. In the evenings, Ewing courted Evelyn with quiet dinners at the prestigious Jonathan Club, capped by moonlit small talk and hand-holding in the handsome gardens of Evelyn's Pasadena home. Before each evening ended, Ewing always asked Evelyn when he would see her again, and, enchanted, Evelyn never turned him away without the promise of another date.

In August, Scott proposed a leisurely drive through northern Mexico, and Evelyn accepted his invitation enthusiastically. Once there, Scott had another proposal, this one a suggestion of marriage, and Evelyn impulsively said yes. Evelyn and Ewing said their vows twice, first on September 3, 1949, in Mexico, and again two weeks later in an American civil ceremony in Carson City, Nevada.

Their courtship, the classic whirlwind affair, was initiated, proposed, and consummated over the briefest of seasons. But within weeks of her sudden remarriage, Evelyn found herself isolated from her friends of a lifetime and alone with a stranger, a man four years

17

her junior whom she had known for a matter of months. Unlike her own friends, longtime Pasadena neighbors who handled each other's business affairs and socialized together, Ewing's past was a mystery to Evelyn. She soon learned how little she really knew about her handsome new husband.

Leonard Ewing Scott was born September 27, 1896, in St. Louis, Missouri, to Margaret Clara and Leonard Wright Scott. His mother's family, the McDonalds, were Irish immigrants, and his father's family, also immigrants, were Scotch and Irish. Although Ewing was raised as an only child, he had a wary, chilly relationship with a half-brother and half-sister, George and Lucy Scott, from his father's first marriage.

Leonard Scott was a failed wildcatter who worked only sporadically in the oil business, chasing the elusive gusher he dreamed would pay off big. But as one well after another proved dry, Leonard Scott drank a little more and stayed away from home a little longer. When his business prospects were bleakest, sometimes a morose Leonard Scott would take Ewing, still a child, along to some saloon for sympathetic companionship. At a very young age, Ewing learned to loathe alcohol, cigarettes, and the streetwise barroom women who diverted his father's attention from his strong-willed, devoutly Catholic mother.

Margaret Scott, worried that her husband's drinking might affect their young son, sent Ewing off to stay with her relatives. At least part of his childhood was spent first with an aunt, then with his maternal grandmother. Although he was raised in his mother's faith—Margaret Scott was educated by nuns—Ewing claimed later that he rebelled against Catholicism and chose instead to attend a Presbyterian church where he received a Bible bound in red morocco leather for a year's perfect attendance.

At nineteen, Scott moved away from home to Chicago, where he passed World War I clerking for an import-export firm. For a few months, he even erratically attended business classes and lectures at a local university, but Scott never formally registered for a disciplined college education. He kept to himself mostly, making only nodding acquaintances of his fellow workers and students, and later recalled a perfunctory coupling with a streetwalker he hired one night for a dollar as his first sexual encounter.

In 1919, Scott, now twenty-three, returned to St. Louis to live with his mother, the same year that his father died of liver disease. He went to work as a bookkeeper for a St. Louis stock brokerage, where Scott first met the conservatively suited, prosperous salesmen in whose image he would dress himself for the rest of his life.

Scott liked the way these investment counselors were treated by their moneyed clients, with the deference and respect he believed a man of substance should enjoy. Discreetly, Scott studied them, slowly cultivating their style and mannerisms as his own. At home alone, he dressed and redressed himself in their sober uniform—starched white shirts and muted dark wool suits—and turned himself around and around before a mirror to study each minute fashion detail for flaws. In time, Scott built his confidence enough to add the slight flairs that would catch a woman's eye: a silk handkerchief nattily tucked into his breast coat pocket or a polished pocket watch and chain.

With his handsome, tailored appearance eventually came a promotion to stock salesman, and Scott began learning to speak the language of his colleagues, using the newspapers and magazines they read as his textbooks. He spent his free time reading aloud to himself, always seated before his mirror, refining his voice and vocabulary until each was faultless. Scott paid particular attention to articles on music, art, travel, sports, business, and politics, repeating key passages to his reflection again and again, so that their content might be spontaneously regurgitated as his own opinions. He invested no similar effort in any sort of formal study of business, however.

Perhaps in one of the publications he perused Scott found the creed he adopted for himself, a brief quotation that he wrote out in his slanting, exacting handwriting and left pinned over his desk: "Never be associated with failure. Never defend the weak, even when he is right. Never attack the pillager of the treasury, if he has great power. He may crush you and there is no use being a martyr."

As a stock salesman, Scott soon calculated the value of an extensive network of acquaintances, the social connections who could be transformed into business contacts. He joined every civic, business, or social group he could, including the Masons, a Presbyterian church, and a local men's athletic club. Scott tried to capitalize on this network of contacts when he opened his own small St. Louis investment firm, the L. E. Scott Company; the business failed but records show that he attempted at least one transaction. In the summer of 1934, Scott negotiated to buy a $25,000 life insurance policy from Perry Pasmezoglu, a representative of the General American Life Insurance Company. In return, Scott offered the insurer Triple A-rated Canadian bonds worth the value of the annual $1,000 premium. Missouri's Commissioner of Insurance refused to approve the transaction, however, and the trade was never consummated.

Soon after, Scott and Pasmezoglu considered going into business together, though they never did. Pasmezoglu stayed in the insurance business and Scott moved west to Los Angeles, followed soon after by his mother. The two men met again accidentally five years later in 1939, in the heart of the Los Angeles financial district. Pasmezoglu, impressed by the rich cut of Scott's clothes, was certain that his old friend from St. Louis had done quite well for himself.

Indeed, Scott *had* done well. In 1937, he managed to meet and marry Alva Gagnier Brewer, the daughter of a rich Canadian publisher and heiress to a family mining fortune. Although he told Pasmezoglu that he was still an investment broker, Scott was in fact no longer actively pursuing his career. His champagne marriage had offered him other options instead.

His wife's fortune provided Scott with an entrée to the Jonathan Club, an exclusive private club that listed among its members some of Los Angeles' most ambitious and powerful men. Scott lived half the year on a sixty-acre walnut farm in the San Fernando Valley paid for by his bride's father—Scott did dutifully dally at harvesting the crop one season—and he traveled the rest of the year with Alva by cruise ship around the world. Their marriage was less than idyllic, however. After five stormy years of bitter and abusive fights, some of which were over money, Scott was persuaded to divorce his wife with a substantial financial settlement from her family. Later, Scott said that *he* insisted on the divorce, once he learned his wife was "sleeping around" with men she met in the bars Scott said she frequented.

Despite his divorce, Scott remained a member in good standing of the Jonathan Club. But he soon discovered that the wealthy circle of associates acquired during his marriage were Alva's friends really, and Scott bitterly resented their indifference to him. Proudly, Scott avoided all but the most superficial questions about himself and

20

adopted a defensive conversational style that was usually a wordy, evasive amplification of his own accomplishments. Scott hinted meaningfully at his highly successful—but very secret—deals, boasting of transactions that sometimes sounded too good to be true.

In Scott's eyes, World War II and a government job in Washington, D. C., offered escape and exoneration from the humiliation of his divorce. He told his associates that his work for the federal government's Office of Price Administration, finagled through a childhood friendship with Bob Hannegan, a former Democratic party chieftain and postmaster general under President Truman, was top-secret stuff, requiring classified negotiating with the wartime British and Russian allies. In truth, however, Scott's job was a glorified clerk's position, from which he was quickly dismissed without prejudice. Government records show, in the only written employment evaluation that exists on Scott, that he was fired for his "lack of cooperation and dependability, and for antagonizing other workers." So Scott went home to Los Angeles, telling anyone who asked that his work for the government had been completed even though the war still raged abroad.

Scott returned just as southern California's latest real estate boom was heating up, with acres of farmlands being transformed almost overnight into housing tracts such as Hawaiian Gardens, Lakewood, and Bellflower. With funds in part contributed by his mother, Scott invested in a development in 1948 in Santa Ana, near what later became Knott's Berry Farm. The project netted a profit for a company Scott set up called the Cardinal Construction Corporation, largely due to the efforts of Carl Vernell, a glib, good-looking, part-time movie extra, dance instructor, and construction worker. Vernell, who was promised by Scott a handsome fee and a construction superintendent's job on the building site, "facilitated" approval of the previously rejected Federal Housing Administration loan Scott needed through his friendship with a fellow rumba enthusiast who happened to be the FHA's top West Coast official. Later, Vernell called on Scott at the Jonathan Club to collect his fee, but he always wound up waiting in the lobby for Scott, who never materialized.

Scott's interest then wandered away from housing tracts; instead, he conducted a few rather unscientific chemistry experiments. Scott concocted a hair restorer and tested the product with a promise to pay

21

a reward for the most improvement to one of five bald men who agreed to use it daily for six weeks. Neither hair nor payment ever materialized. Scott similarly experimented with a pesticide spray he developed, which he tried out by inflicting it on a neighborhood tree. Neither product was ever commercially developed.

With the skill and style polished in front of his own mirror, Scott, a handsome older bachelor, managed to move in Los Angeles' most moneyed circles as a sort of socially acceptable gatecrasher. Yet, at fifty-three, his entire fortune consisted of a nine-year-old Ford automobile, some $3,000 in joint bank accounts with his mother, and a temporary modest room at the Jonathan Club. He was working as a house-paint salesman, showing up at his sales calls in the custom-tailored three-piece suits he favored.

But one summer morning in 1949, Scott abruptly quit his job and boasted to his co-workers about the biggest sale of his life. He was marrying a rich old widow, he bragged, and from now on, he would be managing her money as his own.

□ **4**

As soon as he could, Scott moved Evelyn away from her familiar Pasadena life-style. A month after their marriage, Evelyn sold her South San Rafael home for $45,000 to Opal and Hewlings Mumper and used part of the proceeds as a down payment for the $75,000 seven-room, white stucco house at 217 North Bentley Avenue, built eight years earlier by comedian El Brendel. To Evelyn, the move was a gesture of faith in this—her fifth—marriage. But the two-hour round-trip drive from Bel Air to Pasadena and the separation from her friends left Evelyn terribly vulnerable when her romance ended after a few months. Vera Landry, Evelyn's live-in maid, was an unwilling witness to the Scotts' first private battles, one of which woke Vera from a sound sleep.

* * *

Vera opened her eyes. What was that noise? A huge WHUMP! as though something large upstairs had crashed to the floor. Vera listened drowsily to the now-noiseless night, heard nothing more, and soon slipped back to sleep.

Vera was still asleep in the tiny maid's room near the kitchen when she awoke to another noise, this time the soft scrape of bedroom slippers across a linoleum floor. Vera pulled on a robe and eased her door open cautiously until she saw Evelyn in the kitchen.

"Why, Mrs. Scott," Vera said, pulling her door wide open, "can I—?" Vera caught her breath. Evelyn's cheek bore an angry welt, a blue-black bruise straight across the bone. "What happened?"

"I'm afraid I fell," Evelyn mumbled. "I thought some ice might help."

"Was that what I heard?" Evelyn looked up sharply but the maid was already bustling into the refrigerator, hunting for a slice of raw meat. "Oh, I thought I heard something, like somebody took a real hard spill. There you go," she said, pressing a cold steak to Evelyn's cheek, "you don't want ice. This is what'll remove the blood."

In the morning, Evelyn slept late. Scott stopped Vera in the kitchen for a moment.

"Did Mrs. Scott tell you what happened?" he asked.

"No, sir, she didn't," Vera lied. "Did she fall?"

"No, she didn't fall," Scott said. "I just slapped the wind out of her, that's all there is to it."

After that argument, there were more fights that Vera overheard. Although Evelyn never mentioned those battles to Vera, retreating instead to the separate bedroom she maintained after her marriage, Scott did. "You know," Scott told Vera on one occasion, "I didn't marry Mrs. Scott for love—just for her money."

A month after the household's move to Bel Air, Vera returned from her day off to find her employers already waiting for her in the kitchen. Although Scott said nothing to her, he watched Vera expectantly. After a moment's awkward hesitation, Evelyn spoke. "I'm afraid, Vera," she began, "that you'll no longer be with us. Mr. Scott—and I—have decided to let you go."

23

Vera was only mildly surprised at her dismissal. She didn't like Scott and she didn't trust him—not since he'd ordered her to eavesdrop on Evelyn's telephone conversations and to watch her mail for him. Indignant, Vera had refused to spy on Evelyn and Scott then threatened to fire her. A few nights later she awoke to find her bedroom door tightly shut and her unlit gas heater hissing. A repairman told her that the gas valve could only have been turned on by human hands, and with just the three of them in the house that night, Vera had her ideas about how the heater had been turned on. She liked Evelyn, though, and wondered idly to herself how Scott had persuaded his wife to let her go. Evelyn, her cheeks coloring, looked uncomfortable. "I have your check ready," she told Vera. "When you have your things packed, Mr. Scott will drive you home."

But Scott didn't take Vera home. He simply drove her to an isolated city street corner where he dropped her off, alone with a heavy footlocker and a long walk to a telephone.

Vera wasn't the only member of Evelyn's staff fired by Scott. A few days after the newlyweds returned from Mexico, Scott dismissed Olive Wright. Now that Evelyn was remarried, she didn't need any other companion but him, he told her, and besides, he would be taking over Olive's duties with her bills, banking, and correspondence. Although Evelyn agreed to let Olive go, she found her secretary another job with Mildred Schuchardt.

Almost immediately, Ewing urged Evelyn to turn the rest of her affairs—her stock portfolio, rental property, and bank accounts— over to him. He insisted that his experience as an investment broker qualified him to look out for her best interest better than hired professionals possibly could.

At first, Evelyn refused. John Connell of Loomis, Sales & Company had replaced J. Smith Miller of Willis & Christy as Evelyn's investment counselor, and under Connell's conservative management, her stocks and bonds had increased slowly in value to more than $220,000, yielding yearly dividends of almost $8,000. She also received a check every month for $1,400 or more in rental income from the First Wisconsin Trust Company, the firm looking after her interest in The Edgewater, the Milwaukee apartment house formerly owned by Pettit. All told, Evelyn's annual income was at minimum an effortless $15,000, an appreciable sum in 1949 dollars. Besides, Evelyn preferred to pay the hired managers so Ewing could have more time free to spend with her.

But he badgered her. At every opportunity, Scott demanded control, even announcing to guests at parties that he alone could best manage his wife's assets. Often, he shared his strategies for Evelyn's money. To the Brawners, Scott confided that he didn't trust the stock market, and he wanted Evelyn to cash in every stock and bond she owned. For the short-term, Scott planned to store the cash in a safe-deposit box. But when Evelyn was completely "liquid," they would move abroad together, he said, to South America perhaps, or Portugal, where her money would stretch much farther. "We'll make a killing," Scott told Evelyn's former Pasadena next-door neighbors. As an afterthought, he advised Bill and Gertrude to follow his advice too.

At first, Evelyn seemed pleasantly noncommittal about her husband's schemes. By now, she knew only too well that it was all her own money, and none of his, that Ewing proposed to spend. Still, she reassured the Brawners and other friends that the United States was good enough for her and that she'd never move permanently anywhere else.

But the more Evelyn resisted, the more Scott wheedled and argued with her. Finally, Evelyn relented, and by early 1950, her stock broker was receiving telephone calls and visits from Scott, who asked detailed questions about his wife's accounts. Connell thought Evelyn managed her funds quite nicely on her own, but nevertheless he accommodated Scott as much as possible.

In 1951, Scott directed Connell to sell $33,000 worth of Evelyn's blue-chip holdings, including her AT&T stock and some U.S. treasury bonds. The sale would cost Evelyn part of her yearly dividend income, Connell pointed out, but Scott insisted that the transaction be made anyway, to move Evelyn closer to an "all cash position." Soon after, when the broker refused to waive a standard management fee at Scott's demand, Connell politely suggested that Evelyn move her account elsewhere.

Without a professional counselor in place to block his efforts, Scott assumed complete control over Evelyn's stock portfolio. When Frances Melbourn, the tax adviser who worked in the office of Evelyn's attorney, questioned the substantial drop in her dividend income, Evelyn told Melbourn that she was selling all of her securities because Ewing wanted her assets liquid, a strategy that cut her annual dividends from almost $8,000 in 1949 to zero in 1955.

Soon, Scott was making trips to Milwaukee to inspect the apartment house in which his wife held the controlling interest, and he announced that he didn't like what he found. Scott charged that the First Wisconsin Trust Company wasn't watching the operation carefully enough: The trust company allowed the manager to run a separate real estate firm from The Edgewater's business office and bought coal at a price that seemed excessively high to him. Scott recommended strongly to Jim Boyle, Evelyn's attorney, that Odgen & Company manage the property from now on, a firm personally selected by Scott.

Evelyn did make the change Scott wanted, telling Boyle that she "was continuing to live with her husband and didn't want any conflict" with him. Although the checks continued to arrive every month in her name only, Odgen's officials never met Evelyn and dealt only with her husband.

Early on, Scott expressed some reservations of his own about his marriage to an unlikely listener. In 1951, he took an opened bottle of Coca-Cola to Ray Pinker, a forensic chemist in the Los Angeles Police Department's crime lab. Scott complained to Pinker that every time Evelyn served him this particular soft drink, he experienced a "certain funny feeling." Could his wife be trying to poison him? Scott asked Pinker bluntly.

Pinker analyzed the Coca-Cola Scott provided but his tests turned up no trace of any toxins. Coincidentally, Evelyn experienced a sudden, never-explained illness about the same time and she checked into St. John's Hospital in Santa Monica for a few days of observation.

Since Scott considered managing his wife's money as his full-time job, Evelyn's income paid all of their respective expenses, from upkeep of their Bel Air home to the trips they made abroad together. Evelyn provided Ewing with miscellaneous spending money too, about $4,500 from late 1949 through the middle of 1955. Yet, when Evelyn dropped a modest $25 gift in the mail to her close friend, Marguerite Watson, in August 1954, Evelyn privately asked her friend not to mention it in front of her husband.

When Carl Vernell finally caught up with Scott on the dance floor of the Huntington Hotel, Evelyn loyally intervened and invited Vernell to stop by the house and discuss his unpaid fee with her. Vernell did talk with Evelyn on two separate occasions, and although he was encouraged by her assurances that her husband was financially sound and that he might be paid after all, Vernell was a bit put off by Evelyn herself. He thought she poured a pretty stiff old-fashioned, one that Vernell thought left Evelyn a little wobbly on her feet.

After her marriage, Evelyn saw little of her brother, whose dislike of Scott had been apparent from their first meeting. Raymond Throsby considered his sister a sharp, competent businesswoman, and he couldn't understand how this smooth-talking salesman wielded such influence over her. When Scott tried to interest him in a construction project that Raymond thought sounded questionable, Raymond tried to expose Scott as a phony to Evelyn. Though she admitted Ewing was "demanding," Evelyn refused to hear Raymond out, and their close relationship cooled.

That slight breach widened considerably when Raymond floundered into a series of financial scrapes that nearly resulted in a prison term for his admitted misuse of an employer's funds. Evelyn bailed Raymond out with several loans, including a one-year $1,300 note in March 1951, but as his troubles continued, she grew reluctant to become further entangled. Raymond appealed to his sister soon after for another $6,000, but Evelyn, acting on the advice of her husband and her attorney, refused him this new loan. Raymond threatened to commit suicide and Evelyn's resolve crumbled. She lent him $3,600, slightly more than half of the amount he wanted.

When Raymond's $1,300 note came due in March 1952, Evelyn left the issue of his repayment to her attorney. Boyle wrote to Raymond, who was working in the Marshall Islands as chief safety engineer for the Eniwetok Atomic Energy Project, notifying him that the note was due. Raymond, already upset by a fatal accident that had occurred on the same day Boyle's letter arrived, vented his emotions in a venomous, bitter letter back to his sister, savagely attacking her character. Surprised and hurt, Evelyn replied immediately with a warm letter to Raymond, explaining that the demand for payment was for tax purposes only and wishing him well. Later, Evelyn forgave all of Raymond's debts to her when they met accidentally on a Westwood street corner. Brother and sister shared a warm reunion over coffee on that afternoon in 1954, and Raymond followed up their visit with a birthday present and loving note to his sister. But Scott returned Raymond's dislike, and he considered Throsby's 1941 sanatorium stay damning evidence of Raymond's mental instability. He made clear to Evelyn that she should have little to do with her brother in the future.

With few exceptions, such as Roy Whorton, Scott's fellow stock broker from St. Louis, and his wife Polly, Ewing never folded any of his own friends into his life with Evelyn. Margaret Scott had died in 1950, leaving Evelyn as Ewing's only immediate family member. Consequently, Evelyn's friends absolutely dominated the Scotts' social calendar, although by 1955, Evelyn was even seeing much less of them.

From the beginning, Evelyn's friends were dismayed at her rash marriage. They reached the same mutual, unspoken conclusion that Evelyn—in loneliness, perhaps, or a moment of romantic abandon—had married a fortune hunter, a social carpetbagger, harmless, but far beneath her social status. Her female friends admitted Ewing's charm but mistrusted it, while their husbands, all of whom were well-established professionals, were openly contemptuous of Scott's business acumen and his unorthodox schemes to spend his wife's money. For all his drawing-room polish, they found Ewing coarse and self-aggrandizing to an irritating degree. Though he boasted of his financial killings, Brawner noticed that Scott surreptitiously slipped waiters' tips into his own pocket. But his major sin was to move Evelyn so far away from them: Pasadenans believe they occupy a special niche in southern California, and they stay firmly where they know they belong—in Pasadena, with the same friends they've had all their lives. Her friends could not forget that Scott was responsible for Evelyn's move almost forty miles away from them.

*   *   *

In September 1954, Evelyn met privately with Boyle in his office to change the will she'd written two months after her marriage to Ewing. That first will, dated November 25, 1949, divided her estate between her husband and her brother; a codicil dated January 12, 1953, had only changed a few small bequests to friends. According to Boyle's standard office procedure, a copy of Evelyn's new will, dated September 10, 1954, was mailed to Evelyn at home.

On New Year's Day in 1955, Scott insisted vehemently to other party-goers that the canniest investors were now pulling their cash out of the stock market. When Bill Brawner pointed out that the market had been stable for months, Scott dismissed Brawner's observation rudely. The market's stability wasn't the real issue anyway, Scott said. Any ignoramus who read the papers could see that the country was in grave danger of an atomic attack, but no matter where the bombs hit, Scott boasted that he and Evelyn would be prepared for the worst. On his advice, Evelyn was now stashing money in different accounts in banks around the country so that they would have plenty of cash to live on after the attack. Incredulous at Scott's plan, Brawner argued that never mind the money, they'd be lucky even to survive an atomic attack, but no amount of resistance could dissuade Scott from his strategy. No one else at the party agreed with Scott, and the conversation gracefully moved on to other topics.

If they were aghast at his investment schemes, Evelyn's friends were appalled at the comments Scott frequently made about Evelyn outside her presence. He might brag: "Look at my beautiful bride," when he entered a room with Evelyn on his arm, but as early as 1953, Scott would pull aside one or two of Evelyn's closest friends at parties for whispered confidences about her failing health. Painting himself as a long-suffering husband, Ewing might bring up the long hours he said he'd spent sitting up with Evelyn the night before or how he'd had to coax her to come to this night's party. If Evelyn was out when Gertrude, Mildred, or another friend called, Scott sometimes talked with them at length, unburdening on them his fears that Evelyn was physically ill or mentally deranged, perhaps both. Yet, when asked, Evelyn always cheerfully reported an excellent bill of health, other than an occasional flare-up of diverticulitis, which, in Evelyn's case,

29

was only a minor instance of an inflamed intestine. She appeared as sharp and competent as ever.

But Evelyn never openly complained about Ewing. She realized by now that her marriage was a difficult one, and her friends wondered if the occasional hints she dropped—"Little things don't matter," she told Gladys Baum in a rare reflective moment—were Evelyn's signal of an impending divorce. Until her plans were clear, however, Evelyn's friends could only respect her privacy and ignore Ewing as much as possible.

Although Scott's growing control over Evelyn's fortune did ease the tension, the couple still fought, sometimes painfully so. At a dinner party one night at the Scotts' Bel Air home in late 1954, Brawner noticed black and blue marks on the side of Evelyn's face and a faint crescent of purple around her left eye. The bruises looked fresh to him, despite Evelyn's artfully applied makeup. For a brief moment, he pulled her aside.

"You know, Evelyn," he said, "Gertrude and I have really missed you—we don't see much of you anymore. Have you ever thought about moving back out to Pasadena?"

"If I'm going to live with my husband," Evelyn said, "it's going to have to be out here."

Brawner talked briefly with Evelyn again several months later, in the spring of 1955. "I'm ready for the storm, Bill," Evelyn told him then. "I've sold the rest of the stocks I had left."

Evelyn did sell the last of her holdings by early 1955, worth, all told, $220,929.37. To satisfy her husband's liquidity strategy, as early as 1952 Evelyn made regular trips between her banks and her safe-deposit box, where she added hundreds of dollars at a time to the cache in her bank box. In addition, with Scott's prodding, she spent another $100,000 over the spring of 1955 to open ten $10,000 bank accounts in obedient submission to his atomic-survival plan. Scott typed the letters to open each account and watched to see that Evelyn included a check with every one. The accounts, which Evelyn did open in her own name only, were divvied out to banks in eight states: California, Connecticut, Illinois, Massachusetts, Missouri, Ohio, Pennsylvania, and Texas.

That spring, too, Evelyn took her records to Jim Boyle's office for the preparation of her 1954 federal and state income-tax returns as usual. As always, Scott's annual income was listed as "zero"; Evelyn filed a separate return to avoid embarrassing him, even though a joint return would have substantially reduced her tax liabilities.

In early April 1955, Opal Mumper telephoned Evelyn but reached Ewing instead. Evelyn was out shopping, he said, and Ewing launched into his latest account of Evelyn's condition.

"Her health is terrible, just terrible," Ewing told Opal. A recent checkup showed no signs of ill health and he had urged her to try another clinic. "Evelyn hit the ceiling," Scott said mournfully, "so my hands are tied." Before their conversation ended, Ewing added, "I prefer that Evelyn doesn't know I talked to you about all this."

Opal made a point to call Evelyn the next day, only to find her friend particularly cheerful, pleased by the very same checkup so ominously referred to by her husband. "The doctor says I'm fit as a fiddle," Evelyn announced happily. In the same buoyant mood, Evelyn had her vision checked on April 27, treating herself to a new pair of glasses with a flattering, clear plastic frame. Two weeks later, Evelyn had her regular dental checkup too.

Evelyn was still in high spirits when she accompanied Ewing to dinner at the home of Jeanette MacDonald and Gene Raymond in late April. While Evelyn and Jeanette—old friends through a mutual love of music—chatted inside, Gene asked Ewing's advice on a leak in their backyard swimming pool. As they left, Evelyn promised to telephone Jeanette soon.

On May 11, 1955, Evelyn's friends gathered at the Beverly Hills Supper Club to celebrate her sixty-third birthday. Mildred Schuchardt was traveling with her nurse in Europe, and Evelyn, remembering their near-identical birthdays, sent a bouquet of flowers to Mildred's London hotel and invited Bill Schuchardt to her own celebration. Despite the festive occasion, however, Evelyn seemed tired and preoccupied as she quietly listened to Ewing again tell her friends of his plans to move them both abroad. As her guests left, Evelyn looked relieved. "No, no, I'm just a little tired," she told the Brawners, and she promised to call them the following week.

Two days later, on Sunday, May 15, Evelyn and Ewing were the dinner guests of Arthur and Gladys Baum, who hosted a small belated birthday party for Evelyn. While their husbands watched television in the den, Evelyn and Gladys talked in the living room. Evelyn enthusiastically brought up the next European trip she and Ewing were planning; perhaps, she said, they would buy a car to tour through Spain or Germany.

"Ewing thinks I shouldn't go because of my diverticulitis," Evelyn said, "but I've been feeling especially well lately." Her doctor had encouraged this trip, Evelyn said, and if her diverticulitis did flare up, Dr. Rudolph Schindler had provided her with prescriptions for two anti-inflamation drugs, Aureomycin and Sulfadiazine, copies of her X rays, and the names of some of his European colleagues. Although she didn't mention it to Gladys, in preparation of that trip, Evelyn had just purchased $800 worth of traveler's checks, to add to the $1,600 worth of traveler's checks left over from her last trip abroad.

Before the Scotts left that evening, Evelyn borrowed a travel book from Gladys. As she had done with the Brawners a few nights earlier, Evelyn promised to call later in the week.

But Evelyn never telephoned Jeanette MacDonald, Gertrude Brawner, or Gladys Baum as promised. Two days later, on an otherwise uneventful Tuesday afternoon, she waved good-bye to Mercedes-Benz salesman Ulrich Quast from her front doorstep and disappeared into the house with her husband. Evelyn, now in the all-cash position her husband insisted she take, was never heard from again.

□ 5

On Tuesday, May 17, beauty salon manager Ellen Richmond took a telephone call just after 8:30 A.M. from a man who never gave his name.

"Hello?" said the man. "Yes, I'm calling to cancel Mrs. Scott's appointment."

"For this morning?" Richmond asked in surprise. It was unlike Evelyn to cancel so unexpectedly, just an hour before the regular 9:30 A.M. Tuesday morning appointment she'd kept ever since moving to Bel Air. Evelyn was a favorite among the salon's long-standing customers, and Richmond knew how fastidious she was about her hair. Her weekly regimen was always a shampoo and a rinse, supplemented by an occasional permanent. So conscientious was she that Evelyn even bought a special product called Ultrasol from the salon to use on her own at home.

"That's right," the caller answered, "and all the future ones too. I'm canceling all her appointments for good."

Then the man hung up before Richmond could ask what on earth had happened to Evelyn.

□ **6**

Two days passed. Then, on Thursday, May 19, came Scott's first move toward systematically consolidating Evelyn's assets under his own direct control. Step one was to gain access to her cash-filled safe-deposit box, and as soon as Evelyn's bank, the Westwood branch of Security First National Bank, opened that morning, Scott headed straight downstairs to the vault. He knew that Evelyn was listed as the box's sole owner, but Scott brought a co-renter's agreement into the bank that named him as his wife's joint tenant. Scott's name was already written in, and, the clerk behind the counter noticed, so was the signature of Evelyn T. Scott.

"What do you mean, it's no good?" Scott demanded in irritation. "Don't I have the right key?"

Lois Kleinschmidt's cheeks were crimson. He did have the right one, a long steel key, tagged box number X-3365. But in the four months since she'd worked in the safe-deposit department,

Kleinschmidt had handled only routine box admittances: When authorized signatures matched the bank's records and the correct slender keys corresponded with the master key, only then did Kleinschmidt unlock the individually assigned vault doors guarding each slim bank box. Now, as she haggled with this big, blustery man, Kleinschmidt felt her co-workers in the vault eyeing her curiously. Patiently, she began another careful explanation of the department's policy.

"Mr. Scott, I'm very sorry, but I just can't let you into your wife's box. Your wife is the sole owner. We can't admit you to her box even if she did sign this co-renter's agreement before she went out of town. We have to see Mrs. Scott come in and sign it in person here in the bank." Gently, and with as much finality as she could muster, Kleinschmidt pushed the signed co-renter's agreement back across the counter toward Scott.

"And I keep telling you she can't come in." Scott was livid. "I want to talk to your superior. Now!"

Kleinschmidt saw assistant branch manager Bill Dawson standing across the room. "Just a minute, Mr. Scott," she said, "let me get Mr. Dawson. Maybe he can help you."

Dawson listened as Scott angrily denounced Kleinschmidt and the entire bank for denying his simple—and legally executed, he added—request. His wife had signed the co-renter's agreement before she left on an extended trip. Didn't the signatures match? Scott insisted, jabbing at Evelyn's handwritten name with a finger. Dawson wasn't accusing him of any funny business, was he? What in God's name, Scott demanded to know, was going on around this place anyway?

Finally, Dawson held up his hands, overwhelmed by Scott's tirade. "Do you have any identification?" he asked.

Scott handed over his California driver's license. Dawson looked it over and compared the signature on the co-renter's agreement against the bank's official record of Evelyn's handwriting: The two endorsements seemed identical, and he silently amended ownership of Evelyn's bank box from single to joint tenancy. Dawson clocked the exchange at 10:18 A.M., Thursday, May 19, and ordered Kleinschmidt to admit Scott to Evelyn's box.

Scott's next banking chore was to set up a system that allowed him to cash his wife's checks without a lot of embarrassing questions. Frugally too, Scott decided that the traveler's checks he'd found in Evelyn's top desk drawer would be put to better use in a bank account. Within the next two weeks then, Scott discreetly opened two new bank accounts.

With $500 in cash, he opened the first account at the Bank of Los Angeles' Westwood branch on May 23 in the name of Leonard E. Scott only. Over the next several days, he added almost $600 to the account, including $300 worth of Evelyn's traveler's checks.

On June 1, Scott opened the second account. But he bypassed the two Bank of America branches nearest North Bentley Avenue in Westwood and Santa Monica where he knew Evelyn already had active accounts. Instead, Scott drove almost forty-five minutes to the Bank of America's Van Nuys branch in the San Fernando Valley, where, with $400 in cash and a regulation bank form carrying Evelyn's signature, he opened a joint-tenancy checking account in the names of Evelyn T. and/or L. E. Scott. Scott ordered an endorsement stamp for the account, specifying that it should bear Evelyn's name only. His wife traveled so much, Scott congenially told a bank officer, that sometimes he had trouble investing the proceeds from rental property she owned. Evelyn's rubber-stamp endorsement, Scott continued smoothly, would make her checks much easier for him to deposit.

On June 9, Scott stopped back by the branch to deposit Evelyn's June check, her endorsement typewritten on it since the stamp wasn't ready yet. He was back again on June 29 to transfer Evelyn's personal checking account balance of $3,255 from the bank's Santa Monica branch to the newly opened joint account in Van Nuys.

Next, Scott canceled $6,000 worth of coverage on Evelyn's jewelry, including a brooch from Pettit encrusted with one hundred diamonds. In his July 2, 1955, letter to the Ingham & Coates Insurance Company of Pasadena, Scott asked that the cancellation be backdated to May 17, 1955, for a premium refund of $3.47. For the first time, Scott then insured some jewelry of his own: a diamond-studded wristwatch, a ruby ring, and a pair of heavy gold cuff links.

* * *

As he busied himself with the reorganization of Evelyn's assets, Scott ignored most uninitiated external contact. He answered the doorbell and the telephone infrequently. Evelyn's mail was read, answered only if absolutely necessary, then discarded, or, by absentminded habit, stuck in her top desk drawer. Several letters and a note from Mildred Schuchardt were forwarded to Evelyn at a Baltimore hotel, where they were marked "Return to sender, no such person registered." But Mercedes-Benz salesman Ulrich Quast was one of the few callers who finally managed to reach Scott at home.

As Quast dialed the Scotts' number, he was confident that the sale would soon be completed. But Quast got a brush-off he didn't expect from his client. "No," Scott told the salesman firmly, "I am not prepared to give you the order at this time.

"I'm very sorry to disappoint you, but Mrs. Scott has been taken ill rather suddenly and I am going to have to take her east for treatment. You should stay in contact with me, though," Scott said just before hanging up. "It might be we can make the trip sometime after all."

But two weeks later, Scott sold his 1940 Ford to a Beverly Hills auto mechanic. From now on, he would use Evelyn's car, eight years newer, as his own.

About the same time as Quast's call, Scott picked up the telephone to hear Jeanette MacDonald asking for Evelyn. She wasn't home, Scott told her amiably, but he promised to give Evelyn a message as soon as she returned. When Evelyn didn't return her call, MacDonald tried again and again to reach her friend. But the only answers she heard were empty, frustrating rings on the other end of the line.

Other friends, the ones who usually talked with Evelyn two or three times a week by telephone, had no better luck. Gladys Baum left Evelyn's thank-you note for her birthday dinner propped next to her telephone as a reminder to call Evelyn. When the note was still there three weeks later, despite almost daily attempts to reach her, Gladys finally threw it in the trash in frustration. She telephoned the Brawners, hoping that they might know where Evelyn and Ewing were.

But Gertrude and Bill Brawner were just as mystified as Gladys. Gertrude, too, had been telephoning the Scotts almost every day since

36

the dinner at the Beverly Hills Supper Club a month ago, but no one had answered her calls either. "We don't know where they are," she told Gladys. "Evelyn didn't mention anything about it to us, but maybe they're away. Try Mildred or Opal. Let us know, will you, if you hear from her."

But Mildred was traveling in Europe until June 15, and all Opal added was that she'd been calling Evelyn too. "If we don't hear from them soon, I'll call Jim Boyle," Opal said. "He's Evelyn's attorney—he might know where they are."

After May 16, it was always Scott, never Evelyn, who opened the door when Camilla Hanson arrived each week to clean the Scott home. Politely, Camilla inquired about Evelyn's absence. "My wife has very suddenly taken ill," Scott told her, "and she's gone away for treatment in the East."

The next time Camilla asked, Scott shook his head sadly and told her that Evelyn was not making any progress. Then Scott handed Camilla a red satin bedjacket, one that Camilla knew Evelyn wore every morning as she applied her makeup. "I thought maybe you could use this," he said. "I know it has a hole in it but maybe you can fix that up."

"I'm sure I can fix the hole if . . ." Camilla said in surprised hesitation—she remembered it as Evelyn's favorite bedjacket—"if. . . . You don't think she'll change her mind, do you?"

"No, no," Scott said. "She won't need it anymore."

Scott told Frank Justice, Evelyn's handyman/chauffeur a similar story. "The only thing that the doctors have decided on is that she doesn't have cancer. I'm just afraid that something may be wrong with her mentally," Scott said.

He fired Frank a few weeks later, on June 4. "I want you to think of this as severance pay," Scott said, handing him a $100 check, more than five times Frank's usual $18-a-week salary. "I'm closing up the house to be near Evelyn back east, and I just won't be needing your services anymore."

But Scott didn't close up the house and leave town, at least not immediately. He did begin to examine his options leisurely. At last, Scott had the time and money to do whatever he wanted.

"Yes, sir, how may I help you?" It was June 14, and Frank Hanniver, manager of the Cunard Steamship Company's Los Angeles office, a cruise-ship booking agent, was answering a telephone inquiry.

"I would like to make a reservation for a room on the *Coronia*'s world cruise," the caller said. "I believe the ship sails next January 15."

"Is that for a single or a double stateroom?"

"A single, please. My wife is ill and won't be making the trip. I'd like one of these four rooms, please: R30, R33, R34, or R37."

"Yes, sir, we'll certainly try," Hanniver said. "The price on those rooms is $7,250 for the full 108-day trip."

"That'll be fine."

"Your name?"

"Scott," the caller said. "L. Ewing Scott."

Two days later, Jim Vodak, the agent who'd booked Evelyn and Ewing's previous two trips, called back to check Scott's ticketing request. "It's a little late to book the particular rooms you want," he said, "but I'll see what I can do. I understand that your wife won't be going along with you this time . . . is that correct?"

"That's right. Mrs. Scott has already been around the world, and she doesn't want to go again."

"I see. Well, I'll check on your reservation."

"All right, Jim, that's fine," Scott said. "I'll look forward to hearing from you."

Mildred Schuchardt meant to call Evelyn as soon as she arrived back in Los Angeles after her six-week European tour. But the journey home had exhausted the frail arthritic, and she went straight to bed instead. At 7:45 A.M. the next morning, June 16, Mildred was awakened by a telephone call from Scott.

"Ewing?" she asked in surprise, suppressing a yawn. "I only got back late yesterday afternoon. Is everything all right with you and Evelyn?"

"No, that's why I'm calling you," Scott said irritably. "I've been up all night with Evelyn, and I'm just plain worn out. I guess you didn't have any way of knowing it, but Evelyn has been very ill mentally and physically while you were away. I'm afraid I'm going to have to put her in a sanatorium."

"A sanatorium?" Mildred, still sleepy, wasn't sure she was hearing him correctly. "Evelyn? In a sanatorium?" she repeated incredulously.

"Yes, that's right," Scott said brusquely. "You know there are only three sanatoriums in the country that can treat her kind of neurosis, and they're all in the East. I'm going to have to take her there at once."

"Where? To which one?" Mildred asked in bewilderment. She was wide awake now. "Ewing, are you sure Evelyn needs that kind of care? Can I talk to her?"

"No, you can't. At this very moment, she is standing naked in the middle of the bathroom with a whiskey bottle in her hand, using obscene language."

"*What?*"

"Did you know how many times Evelyn has been married?" Scott asked. "Did you know that she had been married before she met Pettit?"

"Why, yes, Ewing, Evelyn told me that herself."

"I'll bet you don't know that she was married six or seven times before I married her, do you?" He sounded angry. "I sure didn't know a damn thing about all that."

"Ewing, I'm sure you must have misunderstood—" Mildred was stunned. "I'm certain that Evelyn was never married seven times."

Scott stopped. "Anyway," he said, suddenly calm, "the reason that I called you, Mildred, is that Evelyn borrowed a book from Gladys and I want to see that it's returned."

"Oh, Ewing, I don't think Gladys cares about a book. I'm sure she'd be much happier if you just took Evelyn to the sanatorium instead."

"No, no, I promised Evie that I'd return it."

"I'll be happy to have our driver come over and get it and take it back to Gladys—"

"Thank you, Mildred," Scott said, cutting her off, "but I'll just take care of it myself." He hesitated. "And, Mildred . . ."

"Yes?"

"If any of Evelyn's friends call you, just tell them that I'm taking her away for her old trouble."

"*Old trouble?* What old trouble?"

"You know, the intestinal trouble, the diverticulitis."

"Well, if you think that's best, then I'll do that," Mildred said uncertainly. "But will you please, *please,* let me know where she is? Please let me know how she is."

"All right," Scott promised, and he hung up.

At 9 A.M., Mildred dialed the Scotts' number herself. For an hour, she sat in bed, remembering Ewing's private frettings to her about Evelyn's health. On those occasions, Evelyn unfailingly had appeared perfectly healthy to her, as sharp and as cheerful as ever. Drunk and naked in the bathroom? Cursing? That description certainly didn't fit the woman she'd known for nineteen years. Mildred decided to confront Evelyn once and for all with the worrisome reports she'd been hearing from Ewing. But Mildred's call rang unanswered.

About 8 P.M. the same evening, Gladys Baum also received a call from Scott.

"Hello, Gladys," Scott said. "I'm checking your address so that I can return your book to you."

"Never mind about the book," Gladys said in relief, "I'm just so happy to hear from you. I've been trying and trying to reach you. Have you been away?"

"No."

Suddenly, Gladys realized that Scott had never called her before; always, it was Evelyn who telephoned.

"Is Evelyn ill?" she asked.

"Yes, she is," Scott said. "As a matter of fact, she's been ill for about two years."

"Well, I know she's had occasional little attacks of diverticulitis in the past, but is this something new?"

"No, it's not. But I'm going to have to take her back east, because the doctors out here simply aren't getting anywhere with it. I don't think they know a damn thing, to tell you the truth. Now, I'm closing up the house and I want to get your book back to you. What's your address?"

40

"Oh, please don't bother about the book. I'll pick it up—I'll help you close up the house. I'm sure there must be something I can do to help."

"No, no, I'll take care of everything myself."

"May I speak with Evelyn?" Gladys asked. "Or visit her before you leave?"

"Oh, no, Evelyn's much too ill. Thank you, but there really isn't anything I can think of for you to do, except to give me your—"

"Well, I'd like to know where you're going—" Gladys interrupted, determined not to allow Ewing to end their conversation so quickly. "We've all been so worried. We haven't heard a word from either one of you for weeks. We'll all want to get in touch with Evelyn, wherever she is."

"Well . . ." Scott hesitated. "I don't know just where I'm going to take her yet. Baltimore or New York, I think."

"Will you promise me that you'll get in touch with me? I've been so worried—I tried and tried to call you."

"Yes, I'll let you know, Gladys. I have to go now—oh, your address?"

"Two-fifteen Madeline Avenue. Please let me know if there's anything I can do for Evelyn."

"All right, I will," Scott promised. "Good-bye."

The following morning, Gladys mailed a short note to 217 North Bentley. "Dear Evelyn," she wrote. "I was so very sorry to hear of your sudden illness from Ewing. I hope you'll let me know if there's anything—anything—I can do to help."

A week later, Gladys received a brown paper-wrapped package in the mail. It was the book she had lent to Evelyn. Gladys called the Scotts' number immediately, and this time her call was answered. "I'm sorry," said a operator's recorded voice, "but the number you have reached has been disconnected."

For two weeks Mildred waited anxiously for news about Evelyn. She telegrammed a reminder to Ewing at home in Bel Air: "Please don't forget your promise to keep me informed about Evelyn's progress. Let me know if there's anything I can do."

Two weeks later—it was mid-July now, and Mildred was terribly worried—there was still no word from Ewing. So, despite her promise to say nothing of what he'd called Evelyn's "mental troubles," Mildred called the Brawners, the Baums, and the Mumpers and repeated her conversation with Ewing. Evelyn's closest friends were entitled to know if something was truly wrong, Mildred insisted. Didn't anyone know where she was?

No one did. But inspired by Mildred's conversation with Ewing, Opal decided to drive out to Bel Air, determined to see for herself whether anyone—most particularly Evelyn—was home. She asked Maxine Davis, a friend who knew the Scotts slightly, to ride along.

Around 11 A.M. that mid-July morning, Opal and Maxine drove slowly up North Bentley Avenue in Opal's white 1954 Mercomatic. They left the car at the curb in front of number 217 and walked to the front door. "Well, at least someone is taking care of the place," Maxine said, noticing the neatly clipped side yard. "Look at the lawn—it's been freshly mowed."

Opal rang the doorbell. A minute or so after its loud buzz, she pressed it again. "Let's check in back," she said, when no one answered. "Maybe there's a gardener—I think there's a sprinkler on in back."

They walked through the side yard to the flagstone patio flanking the rear portion of the house. Suddenly, Opal grabbed for Maxine's arm. "There's a man in there," she hissed, nodding at a large bay window overlooking the yard.

"Oh!" Maxine said. "Why, that's Mr. Scott."

"I just wanted to see if you recognized him too," Opal said softly.

For a moment, Opal and Ewing stared at each other intently; Opal, motionless, looking at the man inside the house, Ewing, staring back, moving only his wrist as he twirled a pair of eyeglasses in airy circles. "Let's go back to the front door," Opal said finally. When Ewing didn't answer the doorbell this time, Opal decided it was time to call Jim Boyle.

At first, Boyle didn't know what to make of Opal's call. Fleetingly, he wondered if perhaps Opal wasn't overreacting; everyone knew, after all, that Evelyn traveled as often as she could. But as he listened, Boyle realized disconcertedly that he hadn't heard from Evelyn recently either. His last visit with her had been in April, when Evelyn stopped by his office to pick up her 1954 tax returns. Three months was an awfully long silence for Evelyn, Boyle admitted to himself; he knew Evelyn was a pragmatic, efficient woman, who always mailed her travel itinerary to him, in case some emergency should occur. And that story from Ewing to Mildred about Evelyn naked in the—it was unthinkable! In the twenty-odd years of their friendship, never had Evelyn been anything other than the quintessential lady—refined, feminine, and gracious.

So, Boyle promised Opal that he would do a little investigating of his own. First, of course, Boyle telephoned the Scott residence but he heard only the same recorded disconnection notice that was bewildering everyone else. Boyle started dropping by the house at odd hours, sometimes stopping to ring the doorbell, sometimes just driving on by. Late one evening, as he waited at the front door, Boyle thought he heard a radio or TV set on inside the house; early one morning, when Boyle tried knocking on the back door instead, he saw handwritten instructions left out for the milkman underneath a still-burning porch light. But the door was never answered.

Boyle was worried now too. It just wasn't Evelyn's style to be so strangely out of touch. He checked his files for the name of the firm that managed Evelyn's Milwaukee apartment house, and on July 22, 1955, he wrote Odgen & Company a letter in which he voiced his concern:

> I have been personal counsel for Mrs. L. Ewing Scott for many years. I
> believe your company has taken over the management of her interest in

the apartment property in Milwaukee which was formerly handled by the First Wisconsin Trust Company.

I have recently endeavored to contact Mrs. Scott but apparently she has not been at home for some time. Friends have told me that Mr. Scott indicated he might have to take her East for medical care. It occurs to me that either Mr. or Mrs. Scott might have been in touch with you, and if so, would you please advise me where she may be reached.

A few days later, Boyle's letter was forwarded to Scott, and he sent the management firm a brief reply. "Thanks for forwarding the letter from Mr. Boyle," Scott wrote. "It is a mystery to me why Mr. James Boyle did not try contacting me here at home. I shall handle the situation and thanks again for sending the letter." But Scott made no effort to contact Boyle, and the attorney's query went un-answered by anyone.

Other friends were looking for Evelyn too. One of them rang the Scotts' doorbell just after sunset on July 24, when Scott, his hat in hand, opened the door to find a man he didn't recognize standing on his front porch.

"Is Evelyn here?" the man asked.

"No, she's not," Scott said bluntly. "Who are you?"

"I'm Bill Mumper, Evelyn's stepson," the man said, thrusting a handshake forward. Like his Aunt Opal, Mumper had made this trip to Bel Air specifically to look for Evelyn. If he failed to see her, however, Mumper hoped to find Scott home long enough to ask him a few questions. "You and I have met a couple of times at parties at Evelyn's old house in Pasadena. My wife"—Mumper motioned toward his car, where Dorothy was waiting—"and I were just in the neighborhood and we thought we'd stop by and see Evelyn."

"Evelyn is ill," Scott said matter-of-factly. "She is in a sanatorium in Baltimore."

"A sanatorium? Which one?"

"You know, she's really not doing very well there," Scott said obliquely. "I'm thinking of taking her someplace else. I'm only here now because I have to decide what to do about the house, either rent it or sell it."

"Oh, I see," Mumper said, straining to keep the conversation going. He didn't think Scott was especially happy to see him. "Rent it or sell it, you said?"

"That's right." Scott put his hat on. "I'm on my way out for the evening now, Mumper," he said. "But I'll tell Evelyn you stopped by."

Roy and Polly Whorton, Scott's old friends from St. Louis, picked a late summer afternoon to stop by and visit. Although he was glad to see them, Polly sensed that Ewing seemed a little sad.

"I don't know what to think," Scott told his friends. "Evelyn is gone, and to tell you the truth, I don't even know where she is. I think maybe she's gone east and might possibly be in a sanatorium. But I just don't know for sure."

Scott met the Whortons a few weeks later for dinner, and Roy asked if he'd heard anything from Evelyn.

"Not a word," Scott said.

Scott entertained other friends at a small dinner party he hosted on July 28 at the Jonathan Club. His guests were Mr. and Mrs. Lawrence Grannis, who brought along a friend they wanted to introduce to Ewing. She was Harriet Livermore, the stunning, wealthy widow of Jesse Livermore, the infamous "Wolf of Wall Street" speculator who leaped to his death during the '29 crash. During dinner, Scott morosely told his guests that he couldn't seem to stay married very long at all. "My first marriage lasted just five years, and now," he said, "my second wife has left me too."

Scott's slight encouragement was serious business to Ulrich Quast, who still hoped to sell the Scotts the Mercedes sedan they'd test-driven on May 16. Over the summer, Quast telephoned the Scott residence periodically, but he heard only the same recorded notice of disconnection. In August, on the way home from a day-long family outing at the beach, Quast stopped briefly by the Scott home. When no one answered his knock, Quast slipped his business card under the front door and left, finally admitting to himself that this sale had trickled away.

* * *

In New York, Marguerite Watson was wondering why Evelyn hadn't written in almost three months. Marguerite was anxious to know that Evelyn had received her last two notes, lest Evelyn think her ungrateful for the most recent brown-paper-wrapped box to arrive from California. Evelyn's packages always included some unexpected luxury—once she received an entire boxful of hats—but to Marguerite's astonishment, this latest package had arrived in late May with only a virtually new silver fox stole inside. Evelyn, Marguerite thought in amazement, had been especially generous this time.

In the past, however, Evelyn's boxes had always been preceded by one of her chatty notes, and the packages unfailingly arrived addressed in Evelyn's own sprawling script. Now, for the first time, Marguerite noticed that this box was addressed in a heavy and unfamiliar hand. When her first note went unanswered, Marguerite worriedly sent a second letter and hoped that Evelyn would write a prompt reply. By early July, when her second letter also went unacknowledged, Marguerite sent her third note to Evelyn: "It's been months since I've heard from you," she wrote. "Unless I hear from you by return mail, I'm going to try to reach the Mumpers at your old address."

Dear Marge [began Scott's immediate reply],
Your letter has been received which I am answering. Evie has had a mental break down, which has been developing over a period of time, and frankly, I sometimes wonder why I was ever born. The few friends who know about the situation have been most helpful and considerate, but of course, as you can well understand, it is not advisable to broadcast the matter because whenever a cure is effected, the fewer who know, the better it will be for Evelyn. There are too many now who know about the psychiatric treatments she took a few years ago.
The problem appeared in small ways and progressed to the point where she was giving away her clothes, furs, and jewelry. I would like to get some of the things back, especially my mother's jewelry. But so far, (sic) have not had any success.
The future appears to be a long questionable road, paved with heavy expense. However, I do not allow my mind to dwell on this situation, and make a point of not discussing the problem unless necessary, as it is

too easy to reach a morbid state over something that is so close. Hence I am trying to condense the facts into as few words as possible.

I do note what you have written about the Mumpers. We have had no contact with them for some reason that is not clear to me for many months, and as a consequence, know little about them.

Hope you have recovered from the attack of bronchitis.

Sincerely, Ewing.

Marguerite was shocked and outraged at Ewing's letter, lined with his thinly hidden accusation that Evelyn's mailings to her were a sign of mental illness. She was certain that whatever Evelyn had included in those packages were items that she really didn't use. And Marguerite still had the one piece of jewelry that Evelyn had given her years ago, a scarab ring Clem Pettit bought in Egypt long before Ewing met Evelyn. As for the furs, well, there had been just one, which had arrived, Marguerite remembered, in the latest package with the unfamiliar handwriting on the label. After thirty-five years of friendship with Evelyn—and three unexplained months of silence—Marguerite was incensed by Scott's letter. That night, she wrote back to Ewing:

It is utterly impossible for me to think of Evelyn with a mental breakdown. She has always been so well-poised and such a clear thinker. But these things do happen, I know. And they are not one of our doing, which makes the situation more tragic. You do not say whether Evelyn is home with you or in a rest home. Is the situation so bad, Ewing, that she is not permitted to hear from anyone? I wish there were some way I could help, but at the moment, I am too bewildered to think.

Regarding things she has given away, you are obviously alluding to the things Evelyn has sent to me. But I cannot understand why you would object since Evelyn sent her discards to me long before she married you. . . . Ever since I have known Evelyn, she has been a beautifully groomed woman. . . . Regarding furs she gave away, the only fur piece I received you packed and addressed to me. . . . With reference to your mother's jewelry, Evelyn never mentioned it, nor did I ever see her wear any other jewelry other than what I always knew she had. Certainly I never received any.

My friendship with Evelyn goes back a great many years, and I have

47

known her to be only the finest in every respect. Your letter has just about torn me into little bits. . . . I will be very grateful if you will keep in touch with me and let me know when I can write to Evelyn. Please be assured I would follow your instructions explicitly in how and what I should say.

Very sincerely, Marge.

Marguerite wrote another letter that night, a decidedly different one, which she mailed to the office of the Los Angeles district attorney. Along with it went a photostat of Scott's letter and her firm conviction that something awful had happened to Evelyn.

Marguerite's letter arrived a few days after district attorney S. Ernest Roll had a telephone call from Jeanette MacDonald, who was suspicious over the three-month unexplained absence of her good friend Evelyn Scott. Since her call wasn't the first one Roll had received from some Hollywood luminary—it certainly wouldn't be the last—the district attorney automatically agreed to look into Evelyn's absence as a courtesy to MacDonald. "Baby-sitting movie stars again," Roll commented as he assigned MacDonald's request to investigator Nick Cimino.

Although Marguerite's letter from the opposite end of the country voiced identical concern over the very same woman, Roll, already overworked, doubted that the two reports were anything more than a remarkable coincidence. He said as much too, as he passed along Marguerite's letter to Cimino.

But then Bill Brawner, an old friend and a respected attorney, stopped by Roll's office on July 29, 1955. He brought Arthur Baum, publisher of an East Los Angeles newspaper, with him, and together, Brawner and Baum outlined what they knew about their close friend and her abrupt disappearance. Most troubling, they pointed out in an hour-long talk with Roll, was the strange, evasive behavior of her husband, who spoke of institutionalizing a woman they believed to be perfectly healthy and avoided specific questions from friends about where she could be reached. Evelyn wasn't the type of woman to disappear for three months without a word to anyone, and something must be terribly wrong, Brawner and Baum insisted. In the scandal-shy style of a Pasadenan, Brawner asked Roll for a quiet investigation into the disappearance of Evelyn Scott.

□ **8**

A quiet investigation is a discreet, unofficial poke into somebody else's business, a prudent course if matters might find a way to mend themselves. As far as the district attorney was concerned, Evelyn could reappear at any moment, happy, healthy, and with some perfectly sensible reason for her sudden absence. Only unofficially, then, did Roll consider Evelyn missing, and he put the hunt for her low on his staff's priority list, not requiring the services of his top deputy, Adolph Alexander, or, for that matter, the talents of his best prosecutor, J. Miller Leavy. In charge instead was assistant chief deputy George Kemp, who would direct the efforts of Chic Ebbets, chief of the investigations bureau; Tom Doherty, a district attorney's office staff accountant; and investigators Nick Cimino and Joe Gebhardt. A few days after Brawner's visit, with August hanging hot and dry in the motionless air, Roll assembled the team in his office.

"Okay, now, let's go through it, step by step," Roll said to the five men seated in a loose half-circle before him. A fan sent a cooling breeze out into the room, but the district attorney, tall and silver-haired, with a full mustache, took off his sports coat anyway.

"First of all," Roll went on, "Evelyn Scott is either alive or she is dead. If she's alive, I want to know about it before we stick our necks out too far on this one. If she's dead, we want to know how she died. If it was an accidental death or death by some natural cause, we want to know where her body is. No one in their right mind hides a body unless there's a pretty damn good reason. If we aren't satisfied that Evelyn Scott died naturally or accidentally," Roll said, "men, we've got a homicide investigation."

"Got a motive?" Cimino, a tall man with pitch-black hair, asked.

"She wouldn't just run off and leave her husband for somebody else, would she?"

Roll shook his head. "I don't know. Maybe. But she's sixty-three years old and I'd guess she's pretty well set in her ways. We don't have much to go on yet, but she married Scott five or six years ago and apparently he's had quite a few ideas about how to spend her money. He's telling different stories about where he says she's been for the last couple of months, and he's gone out of his way to avoid her friends."

"You don't think she might have left him?" Cimino pursued his question. "Maybe he's embarrassed and he doesn't want anyone to know about it."

The district attorney shrugged noncommittally. "Who knows? We have to consider any possibility. All Jeanette MacDonald told me was that Scott promised to give his wife her message but Mrs. Scott never called back. Nick, you and Joe talk to some of her other friends—start with Bill Brawner.

"Chic," Roll continued, "see if you can't persuade her husband to talk to you. Tom, you see what you can find out from their bank accounts—if she's alive, someone's paying for her upkeep and it's bound to show up somewhere.

"Just one more thing," Roll cautioned his men as their briefing broke up. "Don't forget—this is only an exploratory investigation. Let's be sure we keep it a very quiet one."

Bill and Gertrude Brawner, a handsome, long-established Pasadena couple, still lived next door to Evelyn's previous residence on South San Rafael. "Evelyn has an independent streak, but Ewing still seems to dominate her," Brawner told investigators Cimino and Gebhardt as his wife wrote out the names of other friends—the Schuchardts, the Mumpers, and the Baums—the detectives needed to interview. "She gives in to him in every way. My impression is that she'll do anything to avoid a clash with him."

From her wheelchair, Mildred Schuchardt repeated Ewing's exact words to the investigators: "He said, 'At this very moment, she is standing naked in the middle of the bathroom with a whiskey bottle in her hand, using obscene language.'" She shook her head with frail firmness. "Evelyn would never do something like that."

Though now an invalid, Mildred's features bore the unmistakable imprint of an exquisite young beauty. She carried herself with sterling self-assurance, despite her wheelchair, and Cimino admired her poise under distasteful circumstances. "Did you ever see Mrs. Scott overindulge in alcohol?" he prompted her delicately.

"Absolutely not," she answered without hesitation. "Why, Evelyn hardly drinks at all."

"Everyone is very fond of Evelyn," offered Gladys Baum. "We all just sort of—tolerate—Ewing. They were here for her birthday dinner, and Evelyn was her usual vivacious self."

"Did you get the impression that Mrs. Scott was upset about anything?" Gebhardt asked.

"No, she had no worries that I knew of," Gladys said, as she strained to remember each nuance of that conversation three months earlier. "Nothing out of the ordinary on her mind at all as far as I could tell."

Gebhardt interviewed Maguerite Watson by telephone; she reported that she'd found the wrapping paper from the fur stole Ewing had addressed to her and she promised to send it on to Gebhardt. "I do so hope you people out there find her soon," Marguerite added anxiously. "She's such a lovely person and always so full of life."

Jim Boyle told the detectives about his visits to the Scott home and promised to call if his as yet unanswered letter to Odgen & Company yielded any clues to Evelyn's whereabouts. Boyle was asked for a copy of Evelyn's will—the investigators hoped to find a potential monetary motive—but reluctantly citing attorney-client confidentiality, Boyle declined to make it available.

Cimino and Gebhardt checked into Scott's background too, looking for friends and business associates to question about his life before his marriage to Evelyn. But no one they interviewed recalled meeting any of Scott's friends, and even other Jonathan Club members could add only cursory details about the man who described himself to them as an investment broker. He had no police record, the investigators quickly learned, but neither did Scott have an easily identifiable employment record. A search of state and federal tax rolls didn't help much either, since no tax returns had been filed in his name for at least eight years. None of this routine information was incriminating, of course, but the detectives did think that Scott's past was turning out to be more than just a little bit difficult to trace.

As Cimino and Gebhardt angled for leads about the Scotts, Tom Doherty, a crack CPA who played to his uncanny resemblance to actor Barry Fitzgerald with a lilting bit of Irish wit, sketched an outline of Evelyn's and Ewing's respective financial backgrounds. With Brawner's tip that Evelyn had had substantial stock holdings, Doherty put in a couple of calls to local stock brokers. On the third try, a call to E. F. Hutton & Co., Doherty found what he was looking for: an account in Evelyn's name for the purpose of buying and selling stocks.

Her account was closed in February 1955, when Evelyn sold off the last of her holdings, but E. F. Hutton obligingly provided Doherty with copies of its activity anyway. Those records included the name of her bank, Security First's Westwood branch, which was listed as the bank endorsee on the final check Evelyn received.

At Security First, Doherty located $16,632.04 and a safe-deposit box in Evelyn's name. That box, the bank informed Doherty, was transferred to joint tenancy with her husband on May 19, 1955. He jotted down the date in his notes, just in case it might be important later on.

Doherty telephoned every other bank in the Wilshire-Westwood area and, not surprisingly since she was a wealthy woman, came up with three more substantial accounts in Evelyn's name: $21,670.23 at the Citizen's Bank and $13,095.44 at the Bank of America (both located in Westwood), and $14,446.54 at the California Bank in Beverly Hills. Internal auditing records showed that all four accounts had been dormant for at least three months.

Doherty turned up four accounts in Scott's name at the same time, including two joint accounts Scott had shared with his mother before her death. Those two accounts, along with a third one opened shortly after his marriage to Evelyn, were now closed. But the fourth account, opened in Scott's name only at the Bank of Los Angeles' Westwood branch, was just three months old. To his notes, Doherty added the date it was opened, May 23, 1955, plus the serial numbers of a string of traveler's checks the record showed deposited in the account.

52

A call to American Express identified Evelyn as the checks' purchaser. In September 1954, Evelyn had paid $1,500 for twenty checks in $100 and $50 denominations. Seven months later, in April 1955, Evelyn had bought another series of eight $100 checks worth $800. Five checks had been cashed almost a year ago in London, but a flurry of others had been deposited over the last three months in Scott's new bank account. Doherty requested copies of the checks returned so far.

In mid-August, two weeks after the investigation's start, the five-man team met in Roll's office again to compile the miscellanea collected so far about Evelyn and Ewing Scott. Of particular note was the substance of Ebbets' two-hour interview on August 2 with Scott, who told the investigator that Evelyn was a cancer-ridden alcoholic, offering as proof a cabinet well-stocked with the liquor Scott said was hers: bourbon, Scotch whiskey, gin, vermouth, and several vintage wines.

"When she left, Scott says she must have had about eighteen thousand dollars in cash with her," Ebbets said. "He says she kept it in two envelopes, which disappeared at the same time she did. Scott claims that she drove down to Westwood Village for some special kind of toothpaste she liked"—the detective glanced at his notes—"that was on May 16, 1955, and she just never came back."

"What was that? He said she disappeared on May 16?" Doherty said, shuffling through his papers to find the two dates he wrote in his notes. "I think we just may have something here."

Since Scott himself had pinpointed the date he said Evelyn left him as May 16, 1955, his entry into her safe-deposit box with the signed co-renter's agreement three days later, plus his deposit of Evelyn's traveler's checks into the Bank of Los Angeles account he opened on May 23, were the first telltale links between Scott and an obvious motive to engineer Evelyn's sudden absence: her money. Roll asked Donn Mire, a highly regarded independent handwriting expert, to join the investigating team. Mire's job would be the comparison of Evelyn's known signatures with the ones presented as authentic after May 16.

Scott seemed untroubled by the "official" interest in his wife; it was as if his interview with Ebbets had answered all questions about Evelyn now and forever. Unimpeded, he continued to deposit her monthly checks and traveler's checks in his accounts throughout the summer, while living comfortably in the luxurious home paid for by his wife. Although Scott largely ignored the doorbell—the telephone remained disconnected—he did go out frequently. His major preoccupation was with Harriet Livermore, the rich blond widow introduced to him by friends.

Scott wooed Harriet in the same genteel manner he'd used to court Evelyn. He escorted her to parties and invited her on a day-long drive (in Evelyn's red coupe) to Laguna Beach, a resort ninety minutes south of Los Angeles. On August 15, three months after Evelyn vanished, Ewing treated Harriet to a candle-lit dinner at an expensive inn overlooking the ocean, followed by an unhurried drive through the Santa Monica Mountains back to town.

Their route that night took them over unpaved, unlit roads, but Harriet thought Ewing navigated with confidence. For some time, each sat wrapped in the privacy of mutual silence, Ewing occasionally interrupting to point out a landmark or a canyon he thought might someday be filled with new housing developments. On Mulholland Drive, he slowed the coupe to a crawl and pointed for her benefit toward the home he said he owned in Bel Air.

By now, Harriet realized that she knew almost nothing about Ewing, not much more than that he made a charming if occasionally stuffy escort. She noticed that Ewing eluded questions about himself, but hinted broadly at his net worth. He'd sold all of his stocks and bonds in favor of a "liquid position," Ewing mentioned soon after they met, and he made frequent passing references to the property he said he owned in Milwaukee.

But Harriet remembered Ewing's breezy remark the night they met, that his first wife had divorced him and his second one simply deserted him months ago. It seemed curious, she mused to herself, that a woman would leave without a forwarding address, not to mention a little capital. That night, as they rode along in silence, Harriet decided to try a little discreet prying into the affairs of her tight-lipped companion.

"You know," she said, breaking into the night's stillness, "my family—my mother's family—comes from St. Louis . . . I wonder if perhaps we might have some mutual friends?"

Ewing coughed and cleared his throat. "I'm having so much trouble with my throat," he said, ignoring her question. "My wife is a chain-smoker, and I think I've contracted some sort of difficulty with my throat from sitting in the same room with her."

"Really?" Harriet waited a moment. "Your wife's been away for some time now, hasn't she?"

"All I know is that she sent me on an errand, and when I returned, she was gone."

"Gone? Just like that?"

"That's right. I haven't heard a word from her since. You know, she is not only a chain-smoker, but, my God, she drinks like I don't know what. I've never seen a woman who could drink like she does."

Harriet was thinking out loud, her attention still snagged on Evelyn.

"How could it be possible," she asked, "that a woman would go away unprepared like that, without notifying her friends or contacting her bank . . . or you . . . or anyone?"

"She always has a great deal of money with her, at least eighteen thousand dollars. But she's done this kind of thing before, you know. We were in a hotel in Chicago once, on our way to Europe. She stepped in the elevator first, and that was it, the last I saw of her." Ewing coughed again. "I don't think this night air is very good for my throat."

"The last you saw of her was in the elevator?" Harriet prompted him.

"That's right. I wasn't too surprised though," he continued. "I waited there in Chicago for several days, and the day we were to go on to New York, I packed up all her things, went to the airport, and she came right up to me there as if I'd only seen her an hour before."

"Didn't you ask her where she went?"

"Yes, I did, but all she said was, 'It's none of your damn business—you know I've done this before.' But you know what I think?" he asked, glancing toward Harriet and lowering his voice to a conspiratorial undertone. "I think she had a girlfriend on the side and just didn't want me to know about it."

"You mean she was a lesbian? But she was a married woman."

"I know she was. I know she was," he repeated. "But I found pictures of nude women among her things."

"If you feel so dreadfully toward your wife—as you certainly must—why don't you just get a divorce?"

"I'll never get a divorce." The unpaved roadway curved sharply, and with one last jolt, the red coupe burst into the bright lights lining a populated strip of Mulholland Drive. "No," Ewing continued, "I'm just going to wait until she is gone seven years and then she'll be declared legally dead."

□ 9

Tom Doherty studied the Scotts' bank records, poring over the photostats with his head bent almost to his desktop, so weak was his eyesight. But his persistence paid off: Through clearing house and Federal Reserve Bank records, Doherty located seven out-of-state bank accounts in Evelyn's name, each one holding a balance of $10,000. Not a cent of those funds was missing.

But Doherty noted, too, that Evelyn seemed to have unusually regular banking habits. He noticed a pattern, dating back at least three years, between her checking-account withdrawals and visits to her bank box: between March 10, 1952, and August 9, 1954, Doherty counted 65 cash withdrawals *and* 65 entries into her safe-deposit box. Forty-seven entries were made on the same day as Evelyn's withdrawals, while the remaining 18 bank-box visits all fell within a day or two of the respective withdrawals. Curious, Doherty added up Evelyn's withdrawals for that twenty-nine-month period: The total came to $57,177 *in cash*. But where was that money now?

Handwriting expert Mire was working on his comparisons of the witnessed and questioned versions of Evelyn's signature. From Boyle's office, Mire had obtained copies of Evelyn's known signature from the will she signed in her attorney's presence in September 1954. Mire didn't see the contents of the will, however; for his purposes, all he needed was the autograph Evelyn left behind. His gross—or naked-eye—examination looked promising, but Mire needed an infrared-light examination to prove his findings conclusive.

Over dinner at the Beverly Hills Club one evening in early September, Ewing described to Harriet in enticing detail the trip he was planning for the following spring, a world cruise aboard the *Coronia*.

"The *Coronia*'s a beautiful boat. I'm trying to make reservations for January. I don't suppose," he asked coyly, "that you'd be interested in coming along, would you?"

"No, I've made the trip already—really, I have no desire to go again."

"You're sure about that?"

"Quite."

Yet a week later, Harriet's mail included a packet of brochures outlining the *Coronia*'s itinerary. She threw the pamphlets away.

Ewing tried once more to tempt Harriet into traveling as his companion, this time on a Christmastime cruise to Central America.

"You know, Harriet," he told her soberly, "the holidays are lonely times for people like us. Wouldn't you like to go to Guatemala with me?"

"This is an invitation?"

"Yes, it is, but it will not be on a platonic basis."

"Oh," said Harriet. "Well, no, thank you."

In late September, Scott was notified that his booking request for the *Coronia* cruise came too late to reserve one of the four staterooms he'd requested. Scott was offered alternative accommodations on the *Coronia,* but he rejected the other bookings as too expensive. Instead, he asked another tour operator, the Thomas Cook Travel Agency, to make his travel arrangements on a West Indies cruise scheduled to leave the United States on March 11, 1956. When his reservation was confirmed, Scott paid for his $1,141.29 ticket with a check drawn on his joint account with Evelyn.

About a month after his letter to Odgen & Company, which had gone unanswered, Boyle, frustrated, tried writing to Scott at home in Bel Air:

Dear Ewing,
I have tried several times to get in touch with Evelyn or you, but have been unable to do so. When I could not reach you by phone, I made three separate trips to the house. Unfortunately, no one was home, but there were indications that you were living there. I will appreciate it if you will call me upon receipt of this letter as I would very much like to talk to you.

Cordially, Jim Boyle.

A reply written on the stationery of Chicago's Drake Hotel arrived at Boyle's office several days later.

Dear Jim [Scott wrote],
Your letter of September 2 has been received. I'm quite sure there is nothing at this time that requires your services; but should the need arise, either Evelyn will contact you direct [sic] or through me. The papers here indicate the weather has not cooled to normal. Hope you have a change soon.

Cordially, Ewing.

Insulted, Boyle responded immediately, sending copies of his letter to the Drake Hotel and to 217 North Bentley. Boyle sent a photostat of Scott's letter with his reply to the district attorney's detectives:

You have suggested that I was offering to perform services for Evelyn. This, of course, is not the case. Not having heard from her since April and having been contacted by several of her friends who say they have been unable to reach her or learn anything about her, I have been trying to reach you or Evelyn for the past six or seven weeks but without success.

My interest in Evelyn, as you should know, is because of my long friendship for her and not because I want to render legal services. If she is ill or other misfortune has struck her I would like to know about it. I expressed this concern in my previous letter and I am somewhat surprised that you have not called to let me know the details. Always before either you or she has done so. I would, therefore, very much appreciate your calling me on receipt of this letter so that I can be brought up to date.

58

The Drake Hotel returned Boyle's letter marked "No such person registered," but the copy to the house in Bel Air was never returned. This time, Scott did not reply to Boyle.

Detectives interviewed an Odgen & Company official by telephone, only to learn that Evelyn's income checks were being deposited as usual every month. That discovery led Doherty to the joint account Scott had opened on June 1, 1955, at the Bank of America's Van Nuys branch. Doherty sent an investigator out to pick up a copy of the account's records and the signature card he learned carried Evelyn's endorsement.

So far, Doherty had noticed that Scott was the only one writing checks—nearly $4,000 worth—off the account's $8,000-plus total deposits of Evelyn's rental income. He saw, too, that Scott's largest check was to the Thomas Cook Travel Agency, and Doherty passed this tip along to Gebhardt and Cimino. He sent a copy of the signature card with Evelyn's name handwritten in to Mire for a forgery examination.

Doherty found three more $10,000 out-of-state accounts in Evelyn's name. Other than a two-dollar service charge, not a penny of the combined total balances of all ten accounts—$99,998—had been touched.

After the red satin bedjacket, there were more gifts of Evelyn's personal belongings to Camilla—five lacy white handkerchiefs and a slightly worn calfskin handbag. Camilla always asked about Evelyn's progress but Scott told her that "these things take time."

Still, she cleaned Evelyn's room every week as usual, even though Scott said his wife would be away for a long series of treatments. Then one fall morning, as she dusted Evelyn's glass-topped vanity, Camilla noticed that a few of Evelyn's cosmetics seemed to be missing. She didn't think anything about it, though, until she saw that the closet door was slightly ajar too. As she closed the door gently, Camilla couldn't help but see an unfamiliar dress hanging inside, one she thought looked too small for Evelyn.

Despite the district attorney's probe, Bill Brawner, a long-faced, thoughtful man, was doing a little sleuthing of his own. Methodically, he telephoned Evelyn's friends and acquaintances around the country, culling their memories for possible clues. When was Evelyn last heard from? What did she say? Did Evelyn mention any travel plans, or—Brawner hated even to bring it up—a sanatorium stay for her health? But no one remembered hearing from Evelyn after May 16, 1955.

His own friends on the East Coast searched patient records at every mental hospital and sanatorium in New York and Baltimore on the chance that Evelyn really had been institutionalized. They found no trace of her. Brawner offered rewards for information about Evelyn's whereabouts in newspaper ads around the country, with no better luck.

Soon, he was looking for Evelyn's brother too. Brawner remembered meeting Raymond Throsby once or twice many years before, but he had no idea where he might be now, possibly still working abroad. Brawner checked telephone directories around the country for Throsby's name, with no result, then ran ads in the personal columns of major metropolitan newspapers, discreetly using the name and address of a business associate: "Raymond Throsby, pls. contact H. H. Montgomery regarding your sister."

A week after Brawner's ad appeared in the *Los Angeles Times* on October 14, a surprised Throsby telephoned Montgomery, who arranged a meeting between Throsby and Brawner on Monday, October 24. Ironically, Raymond was not only still living in Los Angeles, he was working for an insurance company located across the street from Brawner's law firm!

Brawner grilled Throsby closely about his sister and their relationship; baffled, Raymond tried to answer the attorney's questions as best he could. Finally, he told Brawner frankly that he'd had little contact with his sister in recent years.

"My relations with Evelyn were very good before her marriage, but the last time I was at the house, Scott was listening at the door. Evelyn's very keen and independent—I've never understood how Scott has gotten the best of her."

"Do you have any recall of what you might have been doing on May 16?" Brawner asked. "That was a Monday."

"May 16 of this year? I don't know—working, I expect, if it was a weekday," Raymond said with a shrug. "Maybe you'd better tell me what this is all about."

Brawner studied Throsby for a moment. In him, Brawner saw the flicker of Evelyn's own quick grin, and the cheerful nod and bob of her head. "Because," the attorney said, at last satisfied that Raymond had nothing to do with Evelyn's disappearance, "something happened to your sister about that time. No one's seen her or heard from her in five months, and your brother-in-law doesn't seem very interested in helping us find her. You're her only living blood relative, aren't you?"

Raymond, not sure he understood Brawner's point, nodded. "That's right. We're the last of the Throsbys."

"Well, Raymond," Brawner said, "I think you should consider legal steps to find Evelyn or to find out what happened to her. I'd start by taking Scott to court to make sure he doesn't squander away your sister's money until you've found her."

Raymond didn't like Scott, but he wasn't sure he believed Brawner's broad hint. Still, Throsby promised Brawner that he would talk to Roll first about the district attorney's confidential investigation before deciding whether or not to take legal action against his brother-in-law.

But Roll had little to offer Raymond. So far, the probe had found nothing more conclusive than an odd array of coincidental and contradictory circumstances. He had no firm evidence yet that something had happened to Evelyn, Roll told Throsby; still, he had no proof to show that something *hadn't* happened to her, either. With several months of digging already invested in the search, the district attorney asked Raymond to be patient. His investigators needed time to find his sister or find out what had happened to her. Throsby agreed to wait.

With the suspicion planted, however, Raymond started his own

61

search for Evelyn. He dropped by her home at odd hours, looking for anything that might seem amiss. Throsby knocked or rang the doorbell, but neither his sister nor her husband ever answered. Once Raymond thought he glimpsed Scott watching him from the shadows inside the house, and he pounded so hard against a window to attract Scott's attention that he cracked the pane of glass. If Scott saw or heard his brother-in-law, he didn't answer. After another visit, Raymond left a note pinned to the front door, asking Scott to call him about Evelyn, but his brother-in-law never did.

By mid-November, Throsby couldn't bear to wait any longer to confront Scott. About 8 A.M. on November 11, Raymond parked his car across the street from his sister's home, where Bentley Circle split off from North Bentley Avenue. He watched the house and waited. Thirty minutes later, Throsby's patience was rewarded as the Scotts' electronic garage door jolted into action. He rolled his car forward until he completely blocked their driveway.

Raymond saw Scott walking toward him, and he turned his face away, shielding himself from Scott's view until they were just inches apart. Throsby faced Scott squarely then; he thought Scott whitened as he realized he was facing his brother-in-law.

"Well, Raymond," Scott said unpleasantly, "you're the last person I expected to see here."

"Where's my sister?" Raymond asked, getting out of his car to stand face-to-face with Scott.

"I don't know where she is," Scott said testily. "She's out on a drunk somewhere. You know what a heavy drinker she is."

"You're a goddamn liar, Scott. Evelyn is no drunk."

"She is too. She's got mental problems, just like you," Scott said nastily. "You still up there in that hospital, with the rest of those crazy birds?"

"Don't try and change the subject. What did you do with her?"

"I didn't do anything with her. She left me. But I know she's been back here. We have a common rendezvous point inside the house where we leave messages for each other."

"Did Evelyn leave you a message?"

"No, but the vase has been moved. That's where we always leave our little notes for each other."

"You're lying," Raymond said threateningly. "You've told one too many stories, Scott. You haven't done a damn thing to try and find her—you didn't even report her missing."

"Why should I?" Scott said peevishly. "The district attorney knows she's missing—that's all I care about. But if she doesn't show up soon, I'm going to get a divorce."

"You lying son of a bitch," Raymond said, his voice rising angrily. "I think you did away with her."

"I've already been interrogated by the authorities—that's all I have to say about it." Scott turned and walked toward the garage.

"Well, if you won't report her missing, you bastard," Raymond shouted at Scott's back, "*I* will."

By fall, Harriet was seeing less and less of Ewing. Whatever initial enthusiasm existed for him faded with familiarity. Ewing frankly bored her, and Harriet was troubled by that nasty business about his wife. She simply couldn't picture a woman leaving without good reason. She mentioned her misgivings over lunch one October afternoon to a woman she knew to be a Pasadena social acquaintance of Evelyn's. "Harriet, don't you know?" her friend asked in mock horror. "They think he did her in! Everyone's been talking about it for months." By the time Ewing picked her up for a party two nights later, Harriet knew they were on their last date.

But Ewing, too, seemed to lose interest in Harriet. Since late summer, he had been dating Marianne Beaman, a petite brunette divorcée introduced to him in August by a mutual friend named Patricia Deadrick. Marianne, forty-six, was gracious and sweetly feminine, yet—uncharacteristically for Scott—she possessed only very modest financial assets and lived frugally on the salary she earned as a dentist's receptionist.

On their second date, Scott told Marianne about his missing wife. "She's disappeared before, but only for two or three days at a time," he said. "I still love her though, and I hope someday she'll return to me."

Still, within weeks of their meeting—Scott as suave and as smooth as ever—their dinner dates were lasting until breakfast. Over that autumn, Scott gave Marianne several "gifts," items he told her belonged to his wife that she no longer used. Those presents included three expensive leather purses, a leather hatbox, and a fingertip-length black lamb's-wool cape, all of which, Marianne noticed, were gently worn.

On November 14, 1955, Scott tried to enter Evelyn's bank box again. This time, however, branch manager Robert Robinson, aware of the official interest in Evelyn's affairs, personally refused to allow Scott access unless his wife appeared in person to approve his entry. No amount of arguing could change Robinson's mind, not even Scott's reluctant man-to-man admission that marital troubles with his wife would make it "very difficult" for him to persuade her to come in. After Scott left, Robinson notified the district attorney's office of Scott's unsuccessful attempt to gain access to Evelyn's bank box.

A week later, Scott spent an extended Thanksgiving holiday in Las Vegas and unexpectedly bumped into Roy and Polly Whorton on the steps of his hotel. Startled, Scott introduced the woman he was es-corting to his friends as his wife.

At Christmastime, Scott ordered cards from Dorothy Fox, the same card-company representative who'd sold Evelyn her holiday greetings in previous years. Scott narrowed his choices to an indecisive three designs, and Fox suggested he ask his wife's opinion. "No, Mrs. Scott's much too ill," he said. "She couldn't possibly look at them." Finally, he ordered fifty cards engraved "Evelyn and Ewing Scott"; Scott called Fox at home several days later to request an additional box of cards with no engraving at all.

Engraved cards arrived during the holidays at the homes of the Brawners, the Baums, the Boyles, the Mumpers, and the Schuchardts, all mysteriously bearing a St. Petersburg, Florida post-mark. Yet Scott didn't visit Florida at any time during that holiday season, nor did he take the cruise to Central America he had men-tioned to Harriet Livermore. Scott checked into San Diego's ritzy Kona Kai Club instead, accompanied by a woman who signed her breakfast checks as "Mrs. L. E. Scott."

By the start of 1956, Scott's life-style finally fit the patrician, opulent image he so dearly coveted. For the first time in his life, Scott, fifty-nine, alone held the purse strings to a small fortune, treasure enough to live his life out in grand style. Never mind that every penny was appropriated from Evelyn's assets: there was plenty of cash on hand, a luxurious home, and a tidy monthly income that cost no more in effort than a trip to the bank. More importantly, Scott, magnificently self-confident, believed that his evasive explanations for Evelyn's absence satisfied both her friends and the district attorney's investigators.

In January, he self-assuredly proposed marriage to Marianne, and she accepted, knowing that Ewing was still legally married to Evelyn. But since August, their lives had fallen together into an intimate, untroubled pattern of shared evenings and long weekends together. Marianne worked every day—answering the telephone and scheduling dental appointments—but two or three afternoons a week she found Ewing waiting outside in Evelyn's red coupe to take her to dinner. Some Sunday afternoons were spent together at her modest Santa Monica apartment, Ewing working with his papers spread out across the dining room table, Marianne readying dinner in the kitchen. He escorted her to parties and squired her to fashionable west side night-spots, such as the Beverly Hills Supper Club, where their dinner tabs were charged to Evelyn's account.

At a west side shop, Ewing picked out an elegant, not-too-extravagant cocktail dress, and watched approvingly as Marianne modeled it for him. He continued to be generous with his household effects, giving Marianne more lightly worn items, including leather luggage and some bathroom furnishings he said weren't being used—a scale, a heater, and a night-light. For Christmas, his modest gift to her was a beaded handbag.

Now, though the doorbell occasionally rang late at night or in the early hours of the morning, Scott lived essentially undisturbed at 217

North Bentley Avenue, making plans for his financially secure future. Nine months had passed since Evelyn vanished, and to Scott, no one seemed to be doing very much about it.

He was wrong. On the evening of February 13, 1956, Scott was detained in the lobby of the Jonathan Club by investigator Cimino. He was driven home and interrogated in a marathon interview session lasting from 10 P.M. that night until late the following afternoon.

The nocturnal interview was Roll's idea. The district attorney was under increasing pressure from Throsby and Brawner to find Evelyn or to arrest her husband. Roll hoped that the hours of rapid-fire, repetitive grilling might trip up Scott on some crucial detail: Despite his initial reluctance to investigate, Roll was certain now that Scott knew much more than he said he did about his wife's disappearance.

The district attorney's suspicions were fueled by three suggestive pieces of evidence: the results of Donn Mire's handwriting analysis, an interview with Scott's first wife, and a check that the Thomas Cook Travel Agency told investigators Scott wrote for a trip abroad.

Using infrared light, a blue-light process to enhance hidden handwriting characteristics, Mire compared the authenic samples and the questioned versions of Evelyn's signature. He concluded that the signatures on the co-renter's agreement and on the joint-account form, plus the countersignatures on Evelyn's traveler's checks cashed after May 16, were forged—traced, probably, from a genuine signature held up to a windowpane and meticulously copied.

Cimino and Gebhardt found Scott's first wife in Santa Barbara, living with her husband, a retired opera singer named Fernando Villa. Mrs. Villa, clearly unhappy at any link to her former husband, told the investigators she had been physically and mentally abused by Scott. Soon after that interview, the Villas left on an extended European vacation to avoid any further involvement with Scott.

Roll knew all too well that without the victim—Evelyn—an indictment against Scott would be tough to get. He wasn't even sure he could make a fraud charge stick: Though Scott was living off Evelyn's income, legally, community-property funds may be spent by a wife— or a husband. But with Scott's West Indies trip as his excuse—who knew, after all, if Scott planned to return to the United States, let alone Los Angeles?—Roll moved his investigators in.

Scott did not demand to have an attorney present for the questioning, even though his answers could be used against him in a court of law; he was arrogantly certain that he was his own best salesman. Just after 10 P.M., then, Scott found himself sitting stiffly in a high-backed chair that someone had carried up from the dining room to the office, facing a roomful of questioners.

Only George Kemp directly faced Scott. Cimino, his arms folded on the back of a desk chair, sat to Kemp's left, while Ebbets and Gebhardt leaned their chairs against a wall to the right. Directly behind Scott was Brawner on a comfortably worn couch; seated a few feet away was Throsby, staring intently at his brother-in-law's profile. Scott was not happy to see Throsby included in this gathering, and at first he ordered him out of the house. But Kemp suggested to Scott that Throsby remain, the better to get this little matter straightened out, he said. Scott, not even slightly placated, didn't answer and refused to look at Throsby.

Kemp was designated as the chief interrogator, and he started off slowly with a couple of nice easy questions to let the two of them get to know each other better: Kemp knew he'd have plenty of time for the hard ones later on. Where was Scott from? Kemp asked conversationally. "How'd you meet your wife? You like it here in Brentwood?"

"This is Bel Air," Scott corrected him.

The interview wore on, a gamy face-off between them as Kemp gradually speeded up the pace. He still had the endurance he'd learned years ago as a long-distance college track runner, and Kemp was prepared to grind out the same questions over and over again, until he felt satisfied that Scott was either telling the truth or covering it up. By 5 A.M., however, not a period was out of place, and Scott appeared as unruffled as his starched white shirt, save for an oozing, slightly bloody cold sore on his lower lip. Kemp knew he was going to have to be patient.

"Okay, Mr. Scott," Kemp said evenly, "will you please tell us one more time about the last time you remember seeing your wife?" He was ready to run Scott through each minute detail of his narrative again.

"The last time I saw my wife," Scott said smoothly, "was on May

16." The question had been asked and answered half a dozen times already.

"What time did you last see her?"

"Late afternoon, about four-thirty or five."

"What did you do that day?"

"We went for a test drive in an automobile." Scott picked at his lip with the edge of his thumbnail. "She wanted to buy it and have it delivered in Europe."

"What kind of car was it?"

"A Mercedes-Benz. But you boys know you can check all that out."

"Yes, Mr. Scott, we'll do that." Kemp, thin and wiry, stretched his cramped legs out in front of him and folded his arms against his chest. "Now, why don't you tell me what happened after that?"

"Well, she asked me to go back down to the village and buy her a can of special tooth powder, Effremin, I think it was, because she said she was all out. You know," Scott said, shifting in his chair to a more comfortable position and elaborating on his answer for the first time, "I chided her a little bit because we could have stopped while we were out test-driving this new car. But anyway, I got my car out and went down to the store for it, and when I got back, that was it. She was gone."

Kemp stared at Scott intently. He pulled his legs back and sat forward. Scott's story, maddeningly airtight all night, had been that Evelyn went out to run her own errand and simply never returned. For the first time, Scott slipped. Kemp tried not to show his excitement.

"You say you went out and bought her this tooth powder?" Kemp's voice was deliberately even.

"That's right." Scott seemed completely at ease. "As a matter of fact, I think I still have the same can of Effremin upstairs. I don't use it myself."

"Didn't you just tell me a little while ago," Kemp asked as coolly as he could manage, "that Mrs. Scott went out for the tooth powder herself?"

"No, no, that's not right." Scott stopped worrying his lip long enough to waggle a finger paternally at Kemp. "You must not have been listening very well. I told you from the beginning that she sent me out to get it."

"I see." Kemp let Scott's mistake pass. Let him think he won this point, he decided. Over Scott's shoulder, Kemp suddenly noted Throsby's glaring focus on his brother-in-law. Instinctively, Kemp signaled to Ebbets.

"Why don't you let Throsby show you around the house," Kemp said quietly to the investigator. "See if he notices anything out of the ordinary. Ray?" Kemp said, beckoning to Throsby.

Startled, Throsby looked at Kemp and blinked. He was nearly numbed by his intent gaze on Scott. He stood mechanically and started toward the doorway. Before he reached it, Raymond wheeled abruptly to face Scott.

"You know, I don't believe one goddamned thing you say," he said thinly, jabbing his right index finger in Scott's direction. "You're nothing but a cheap, lying son of a bitch. I don't even believe that little Mexican marriage you pulled off is any good here.

"But you know what I do believe," Throsby choked out, half a cry swelling in his voice, "I believe you murdered my sister for her money." Awkwardly, he turned and stumbled on toward the door, letting Ebbets guide him from the room.

Scott watched his brother-in-law leave without a word. "Evelyn and I were married twice," he said, once Raymond was out of earshot. "The second time in Nevada."

A few slight seams of daylight laced the edges of the shuttered windows behind Scott. It was almost dawn. Kemp picked up his questioning. "Where's your wife?" he asked bluntly.

"I don't know," Scott said, looking straight at Kemp. Scott didn't so much as blink.

"Ever tried to find her?"

"No." Scott was rubbing both eyes.

"Why didn't you call the police?"

"I keep telling you, she's done this kind of thing before," Scott said irritably, finally showing signs of strain. "She just takes off and never says a word about it to me."

"You ever planning to look for her?"

"I thought that's what you boys were supposed to do." Scott's attempt at lightness sounded grimmer this time. His fists had opened to fingertips that were kneading their way along his cheekbones in small, pinched steps. "I was going to wait a year before I started looking for her."

"A year?" Kemp was incredulous. "Didn't you think that maybe something might have happened to her? Maybe she might be in trouble and need your help?"

"No, I didn't; at least, I·didn't until you boys pointed it out to me. I'd never thought of that view before you mentioned it, but now I'm going to hire detectives and check back through her whole life to try and find out where she is."

"Did you ever tell anybody you were taking Evelyn to a sanatorium in the East?"

"No."

From the corner of his eye, Kemp caught Brawner's silent rebuttal, a slow shake of his head from side to side. "You never said you were taking her to a sanatorium?" he asked again.

"No, I didn't," Scott said. "But to tell you the truth, she was drinking heavily"—Brawner shook his head vigorously—"and I did think maybe she went off somewhere to get medical attention. I told her a number of times she should have help, but she just told me to mind my own business. When she said that, I thought she had no respect for me." Scott sounded as wounded as a snubbed suitor. "I took her at her word."

"Why do you think Mrs. Scott needs medical attention?"

"She has cancer in several areas of her body—she's had those cancerous things—tumors—removed from her face. She's been showing signs of mental aberrations, and she's an alcoholic—did I mention that?" Scott was tiring. "I drove her to the doctor's office many times, but I never got past the receptionist's desk. I even called the doctor once but he refused to talk to me."

Scott was rambling and Cimino leaned over to Kemp. "You see what he's doing to his lip?" Cimino asked softly. "It's starting to bleed."

"Yeah, I've been watching him too," Kemp said. "He's been pinching his cheeks and digging at his eyes with his knuckles too."

"I wonder what he's up to," Cimino said thoughtfully. Both men turned their attention back to Scott's monologue.

"You know," Scott was volunteering then, "we discussed a lot of places she could go for her treatment, and Mexico was one of them."

"Where in Mexico?" Kemp asked.

"I don't know."

"Did you ever look for her there?"

"No."

"Why not?"

"She has her own assets and I thought she'd gone somewhere for help. I didn't think she needed to be reported missing."

"Are you willing to take a lie detector test?" Kemp asked curtly.

"No." Scott seemed surprised at the question. "I can see right now that I'm going to have to hire an attorney too."

At midmorning, Cimino found himself alone with Scott. Raymond's house tour had turned up little of value—the unopened can of Effremin tooth powder, three dozen empty hangers in Evelyn's closet, and an 8-by-10 black-and-white portrait of his missing wife on Scott's dresser. Kemp was talking quietly with the other investigators in another room. Scott and Cimino had been in the same stuffy upstairs room for twelve hours now, and for some minutes, they said nothing to each other. Scott closed his eyes to rest. Cimino paced to stretch his stiff legs.

At the desk, Cimino picked up a thin book titled *How to Fascinate Men* he had noticed earlier. On the cover was a woman wearing an engagement ring, winking conspiratorially at the reader over a man's shoulder. The book's 103 pages were professionally, if crudely, typeset.

"You write this?" Cimino asked, even though he saw the cover named Charles Contreras, Ph.D., as author.

Scott opened his eyes and nodded wearily. His lip was flecked with dried blood and his left eye wore a faint ring of purple.

"You mind if I borrow it?"

"Go ahead," Scott said tiredly. "But I'd like it back, please, when you're finished with it." His eyes slipped shut again as Cimino started to read.

Chapter One: The Stages of Winning a Man

The most important person in your life is YOU and never for one moment forget it. Every individual on this earth is trying consciously or unconsciously to obtain the same thing and that is happiness—millions of people striving for the same goal and each one following what is hoped is the right road.

What follows in this book is written to help that important person YOU to travel the right road.

A SUCCESSFUL BUSINESS MAN WOULD NOT ATTEMPT TO SELL A PRODUCT, IRRESPECTIVE OF ITS MERITS, WITHOUT FIRST LOOKING OVER THE POTENTIAL MARKET, ANALYZING COMPETITION, PREPARING HIMSELF WITH ALL THE KNOWLEDGE POSSIBLE ON THE SUBJECT, AND THEN PRESENT HIS PRODUCT IN THE BEST POSSIBLE MANNER.

These same principles, which have been found so effectual in business, can be used with equal success by any woman desiring to attract men to herself.

It must not be thought that a purposed effort to master the art of captivating men is not feminine. It is certainly feminine to be winsome, adorable, or bewitching and there is nothing immodest for any girl to make use of these attributes when she wants a chance to live a larger, lovelier, and nobler life.

Startled, Cimino realized he was reading a guidebook for marriage-minded women hunting for wealthy husbands. In amazement, Cimino read on.

The Five Basic Principles

The first thing to know is that every man, in being won, passes through five stages . . . ATTENTION—INTEREST—DESIRE—JUDGMENT—and ACTION. A man cannot be won unless his attention has been attracted, unless the attention grows into interest, unless the interest grows into desire, and unless his desire is sustained by his judgment.

If a man is steered successfully through the first four stages, he will be ready for the fifth stage—ACTION—when he surrenders to the desire that has been created in him. . . . It will be observed that the prospective buyer has (to be) maneuvered through each of the five stages. . . . The completed sale requires all five stages.

Cimino was shocked. Secretly, he'd kind of admired Scott's unmistakable polish and even wished a little sheepishly that he'd acquired some of the same élan. But Cimino was the son of poor Italian immigrants, and he remembered waiting on tables as a kid just to get food for his family during the Depression. If Cimino substituted masculine word forms for the feminine ones used, Scott's message was explicitly clear: For all his savoir-faire, Cimino thought disgustedly, Scott was nothing more than a smooth-talking hustler, a gigolo feeding off whatever wealthy woman could be manipulated into footing his bills.

Kemp, Ebbets, Gebhardt, Throsby, and Brawner returned just then, and Cimino tucked the slim paperback volume into his coat pocket to finish later. He figured that the district attorney might be interested in reading it too: Scott couldn't have outlined his fortune-hunting instincts any better if he'd tried.

Scott lifted his head and opened his eyes as his questioners returned. He said nothing and waited expectantly for the next question he knew would come. Kemp started again. "Why do you suppose," the detective asked, "that Mrs. Scott would go off and leave all her money behind?"

"Well, she didn't leave empty-handed. After she left, I subsequently discovered she had withdrawn $15,000 from our bank account."

"*Your* bank account?" Brawner interrupted.

"All of my assets were in her name," Scott said, unfazed by Brawner's broad hint.

"What assets?" Kemp asked.

"I brought a good deal of money with me from St. Louis. I had a very successful investment business there."

"What was the name of your company?" This information was new to Kemp.

"The L. E. Scott Company."

"Where was it?"

"I don't remember the exact address, but it was in St. Louis."

"Where's that money now?"

"Well, I put it all in Evelyn's name. I gave her $34,000 to put into the property in Milwaukee."

"Can you prove that that transaction took place?"

"No, you see, I gave her the money in cash, all in twenty-dollar bills."

"*Cash?* Where would you get that kind of money?"

"From my business."

"What business?"

"My business in St. Louis."

Kemp tried another line of questioning. "Why didn't Mrs. Scott take her traveler's checks with her?"

"I don't know."

"You signed her name to them, didn't you?" Kemp was no longer trying to be pleasant.

"They were already signed. I found them in her desk drawer." Scott's answers were spartan ones now; he was clearly exhausted.

"I understand you think you're going on a little trip," Kemp said thinly.

Scott looked surprised. "That's right," he said guardedly. "I am."

"Well, I wouldn't plan on making that trip just yet. We'd like to find your wife before you go anywhere."

"Well, you'd damn well better be quick about it," Scott snapped, "because I'll take any trip I want."

About 4 P.M. that afternoon, February 14, Scott ended the interrogation by force when he heaved a telephone directory against the wall. "You people have been in here for two days, asking me the same questions over and over," he shouted angrily. "You can't prove I've done a goddamn thing. If you have anything else to say to me, you'll do it with my attorney present."

"Just remember you're in technical custody, Mr. Scott," Kemp warned him. "I'd cancel that cruise if I were you."

Since it was St. Valentine's Day, Marianne expected to see Ewing, and she did. About 8:30, four and a half hours after the district attorney's investigators left 217 North Bentley Avenue, Scott pounded on Marianne's front door.

"My God, Marianne," he said, as she stared in shock at Scott's bleeding lip and bruised face, "those birds from the DA's office just beat me up."

Scott's composure had returned by the time Donn Mire telephoned two days later to ask for a handwriting exemplar. Obligingly, Scott invited Mire out to the house that afternoon, but before Mire arrived, Scott banked Evelyn's February check at the Bank of America.

At Mire's request, Scott wrote out his own name, Evelyn's name, their home address, and what his "five-foot-one, 117-pound, white-haired, blue-eyed" wife was wearing the last time he saw her: a tan suit, small hat, and the gold wedding band he gave her. Scott wrote out the alphabet too, and the numbers between one and twenty.

Mire thanked Scott and headed back to his office. His examination of Evelyn's writing on letters, postcards, and other documents had convinced him that the co-renter's form, the joint-account signature card, and twenty-three of her twenty-eight traveler's checks bore traced signatures. For the first time, those questioned signatures could be compared with her husband's handwriting.

The infrared-light process had helped Mire pick out the outstanding characteristics of Evelyn's genuine handwriting, the unique way she wrote her capital letter *E,* and the small *e, l,* and *n* in her first name. Evelyn's capital *T* for her middle initial and the small *c, o,* and double-*t* combination in her last name were distinctly her own. Scott's writing was just as characteristic, especially his flourishing capitalized *L, E,* and *S.* Mire hunted next for any similarities between Scott's handwriting and the questioned signatures.

He spotted the parallels almost immediately. The idiosyncrasies of Scott's writing were unmistakable in the traced signatures, most obviously in the lower-case letters of *n, c,* and *o.* Scott had traced his wife's signatures, Mire was certain, and Scott, he concluded, not Evelyn, had addressed the fur stole's label to Marguerite Watson.

After the all-night interrogation, the district attorney put the Scott house under a twenty-four-hour watch. "You will let us know, won't you," Roll kidded Cimino, who was assigned to the surveillance team, "if you see Mrs. Scott going in or coming out?" Yet Cimino rarely even saw Scott, since Evelyn's evasive husband was now secluded at the Jonathan Club.

Cimino had finished Scott's book, written, the detective thought, like a marketing textbook for unsophisticated, first-year business students: "A man in business considers the best points of the products of his competitors and how to overcome them with some of his own, and then concentrates on what he has to sell. This same method is a good one to use by the woman in search of a husband."

But Scott did display remarkable insight into human nature. His approach to happiness was a total one, with exhortations on positive mental attitudes, healthy eating habits, and regular exercise. Yet, clearly, there was a dark side too, a cool twist to Scott that matter-of-factly urged his students to use anyone who might be of service to them. Scott included "homework," exercises to help his pupils hone their skills, much as he had done. Hang a bulky winter coat at a man's height, Scott counseled in one example, and use it to practice "appropriate cuddlesomeness."

General Plan of Approach

There is no reason in these lessons to take other than a realistic view of husband seeking, for in the final analysis it resolves itself into a business proposition that can have good or bad results financially.

Either the man is a satisfactory provider of money during his productive years or he fails in this essential requirement.

In a section written with Evelyn—or someone just like her in mind, Cimino figured—Scott wrote:

The woman of means can afford to waive such a requirement for there are men of character who, because of certain circumstances, are not a financial success but can contribute in other ways to make the marriage equitable. [For older women, Scott advised selecting] . . . a man nearer her age, without money but with an educational background similar to her own. This type of woman must be careful to select a man of proper character and avoid the 'ne'er-do-well' who may be a chronic drunkard.

76

Social Success

The first rule in being a success socially or in any field of endeavor is to remove all sense of inferiority and inequality from the mind.

The second rule is to be polite under all circumstances but never diffident. When meeting someone with superior accomplishments you can admire them but never consider yourself inferior because you do not have the same assets. The most cultured people in society are proud, noble personalities who have no particular accomplishment except pride and self respect.

Scott summed up his philosophy on marriage:

Every individual, as has been stated in Chapter 1, wants to obtain the same thing—happiness. We all have our own ideas how to reach this goal, but a good marriage with mutual confidences is one of the best vehicles to use to travel to a happy destination, and while these chapters have placed stress on marriage as being comparable to a business arrangement, so also is the whole subject of living a business matter.

The successful man in business uses intelligence in making decisions, for he knows that haphazard judgments and actions will surely bring chaos and ruin. Intelligence and good judgment in making a successful and happy marriage are even more important because marriage is far more important than any business.

Cimino returned the book, as promised, to Scott, but he made a copy of it first, and passed it on to the district attorney. Roll stuck it in his files on Scott.

Scott, meanwhile, was still managing Evelyn's affairs as if they were his own. He paid the December 1955 property taxes on 217 North Bentley ($1,012.86) with a check drawn on the joint account. Scott filed Evelyn's 1955 tax return right on time too, taking her records to Walter Backman, an accountant of his own choosing, not to Boyle's office, as Evelyn had done every year. Despite Backman's advice, Scott filed Evelyn's usual separate return, with his income listed as zero. On a gross income of $16,617.13, Evelyn's tax was $3,222.05; the deductions Scott listed included Evelyn's visits during the previous year to her physician, dentist, and oculist. Scott picked up the completed and unsigned tax forms in mid-February; he wrote in Evelyn's signature and circled his initials next to it.

From his Jonathan Club quarters, Scott defiantly prepared for his cruise departure on March 11, 1956, Kemp's warning notwithstanding. With checks drawn on the joint account, Scott paid $503.75 for $500 worth of traveler's checks on February 29 and paid $441.62 to the Jonathan Club in dues, room charges, and entertainment expenses. On March 3, he dropped a note to Odgen & Company, asking that Evelyn's checks—including the one for March—be held in Milwaukee for him until otherwise notified. Three days later, Scott visited the Whortons at home. He gave Roy a thick white envelope and asked him to put it away somewhere safe for him.

Just after sunset that same night, March 6, 1956, Roll joined Cimino and another investigator, who were parked a discreet distance from 217 North Bentley Avenue in an unmarked car. Thoughtfully, the district attorney spread the next day's editions of the *Los Angeles Times* and the *Examiner* out across his lap, where Evelyn's wide smile was splashed across their front pages, the very sensational scandal that her friends had tried to avoid. A "missing" person does nothing illegal by wandering out of sight for a while, Roll knew, but despite seven months of searching, he had no direct proof of foul play. If Evelyn reappeared as abruptly as she disappeared, the district attorney didn't relish explaining to this socially prominent woman why her husband—who had no prior police record—was the chief suspect in her absence. But the matter was out of Roll's hands now.

Evelyn's brother, out of patience with the pace of the DA's quiet probe, had filed a petition in Los Angeles Superior Court that morning for control of his sister's fortune. His brother-in-law, Throsby's suit alleged, was systematically looting Evelyn's estate while refusing to notify authorities of her nearly ten-month absence. Ironically, a missing person's report on Evelyn had yet to be filed.

"It's in the papers tonight, boys," Roll told Cimino, gesturing at the bold-type, banner headlines: WEALTHY MATRON MISSING NINE MONTHS, HUSBAND FAILS TO FILE REPORT, read the *Times*. "I hope to hell we're right."

Those same headlines flabbergasted and infuriated Bill Parker. Los Angeles' tough law-and-order chief of police, always mindful of his own political flank, demanded to know why no one, most of all Roll, had told *him* about the seven-month-long investigation taking place in his jurisdiction. Indignantly, Parker fired off a letter to Roll, sarcastically couched in respectful officialese:

> If, as a result of your investigation, there is, in your opinion, any possibility that a crime has been committed in the city of Los Angeles, in connection with Mrs. Scott's disappearance, it is respectfully requested that you make available to the Los Angeles Police Department all pertinent evidence in your possession.

Roll replied immediately with an explanation—so far, there was nothing more than the circumstantial suggestion that Evelyn's absence involved a criminal act—and a diplomatic offer of his department's complete cooperation. But the district attorney couldn't resist taking a potshot of his own at Parker. He asked pointedly for the police department files on Mimi Boomhower, the missing Bel Air matron Scott had once bragged he knew well: "We would like to have a report on the Boomhower matter and be advised as to . . . the last date any investigation was made. To my knowledge, this office has not been kept currently advised."

Parker refused to answer Roll's missive. "I might point out to the district attorney," he huffily told a *Herald* reporter instead, "that Mrs. Boomhower disappeared in 1949 and I was not appointed chief until August 1950." Still nettled, the long-faced, balding Parker sniffed privately to his staff that the police department certainly would have solved the Scott case by now, had it been properly notified seven months ago, and he launched a full-scale police investigation under chief deputy Thad Brown. Assigned to work with Brown were Captain Bob Lohrman and Sergeants Art Hertel and Herman Zander from homicide. The combined police and DA forces created a small army of detectives, all of whom were now "officially" interested in Evelyn's whereabouts.

The sudden furor over Evelyn embarrassed Roll, and her continued absence didn't look good for his office. The district attorney's investigation needed a fresh approach, with the clout of a top man on the case. J. Miller Leavy was his circumstantial evidence expert, but Roll knew that Leavy was preparing to prosecute Stephen Nash, a toothless homosexual arrested for the casual disembowelment of a ten-year-old boy. That barbaric murder—Nash left his victim dying in a bloody heap underneath the Santa Monica pier—would bring Leavy enough publicity, Roll reflected. He asked Adolph Alexander, an ambitious, cigar-smoking native New Yorker, to take over the investigation instead.

Alexander and the newly assigned police detectives were briefed by George Kemp on the morning of March 7. Nearing noon, Kemp summed up the evidence collected so far: "Right now, we don't have enough evidence to place Scott—or anyone else, for that matter—under arrest. All we have is a missing person and a lot of stories to check out."

Under Alexander, the investigation resumed with what was now little more than a legal formality: a missing person's police report on Evelyn, filed and signed by her brother on the afternoon of March 7. Detectives planned next to interview Scott, but since the story hit the headlines on the evening of March 6, Scott had dropped out of sight and no one knew where to find him.

Investigators weren't the only ones looking for him. Reporters and cameramen immediately staked out the house on North Bentley, each one hoping to snag Scott first for an exclusive interview. Evelyn's red Dodge was in the garage, but the newsmen saw no further hint that anyone was home.

Process servers for Throsby's attorney, W. Ernest Pitney, an associate of Brawner's, were hunting for Scott too, primed with a subpoena ordering Scott's appearance at Throsby's trusteeship hearing on March 26. And when his name popped up in the papers unexpectedly, uniformed sheriff's deputies armed with a debtor's court judgment against Scott followed newsprint gossip to the Jonathan Club, where he was rumored to be in seclusion. That year-old court action to collect $6,027.00, the bill Scott incurred in 1950 to print ten thousand copies of *How to Fascinate Men,* was filed by the Wolper Printing Company. Despite a signed contract, Scott picked up just twenty-five of the slim volumes and ignored the subsequent past-due payment notices he received. Four days before Evelyn became page-one news, Wolper's attorneys had finally managed to place a lien for the amount he owed against the Scotts' joint bank account. A startled desk clerk at the Jonathan Club told the deputies on March 8 that Scott had checked out the previous afternoon.

The first news stories put Scott among the ones who tried to keep Evelyn's disappearance quiet, "to the point," reported the *Times,* "of [his] refusal to file a missing person's report." As the week wore on, Scott's whereabouts were still as much of a mystery as Evelyn's, and the papers, thwarted in their efforts to photograph or to interview him, were forced to print sketches of Scott instead. All the more frustrating to them was the fact that Raymond Throsby wasn't available for interviews either.

Yet, if Scott eluded public scrutiny, he did look after personal matters. On the morning of March 7, Scott called Odgen & Company vice president Helen Bellman to announce a sudden change in his travel plans. At Scott's request, Bellman promised to airmail Evelyn's March check to him immediately, rather than to hold it in Milwaukee as Scott had asked only four days earlier. That evening, Scott stopped by Marianne's apartment with a box of things he asked her to store temporarily in her closet, a portable typewriter and a large carton of silver among them.

At Marianne's urging, Scott finally hired an attorney too: Charles Beardsley, the lawyer who had handled the divorce proceedings for Marianne's former husband. As senior partner of Beardsley, Hufstedler & Kimball and a past president of the state bar association, Beardsley, handsome and gregarious, was considered one of California's top civil attorneys. Seth Hufstedler, Beardsley's talented young partner three years out of Stanford's law school, would assist with Scott's case. On Beardsley's strong recommendation, Scott reluctantly canceled his West Indies cruise three days before its March 11 departure.

On Beardsley's advice again, Scott voluntarily presented himself without warning at Roll's office for questioning on Thursday, March 8, where, within minutes, he was served with his citation to appear for debtor's judgment hearing on April 4. Scott accepted his subpoena without comment and handed it over to Beardsley.

Roll and Parker sat in on this impromptu interview, but the district attorney and the chief of police carefully maintained an official distance from the inquiry. The questioning was left to their investigators: Suspicion and circumstantial suggestion aside, Roll and Parker both realized that nothing so far conclusively ruled out Evelyn's return. Adolph Alexander, next in rank, asked Sergeant Zander to question the elegantly attired Scott.

"Okay, why don't we start off at the beginning," Zander suggested. To him, Scott looked like nothing so much as a mature gentleman of means—intelligent and obliging in a situation that he and his prominent attorney found most distressing. "Suppose you tell us about the last time you saw your wife."

"It was May 16, 1955," Beardsley answered.

"What happened?" Zander was a little surprised to hear Beardsley, rather than Scott, answer.

"Mrs. Scott sent my client out to buy tooth powder. When Mr. Scott returned about thirty-five minutes later, she was gone."

Zander eyed Beardsley in puzzlement. Of course, an attorney could answer any questions directed at his client in an informal interview such as this one—a protection for Scott should the case ever go to court—but Zander had hoped to hear Scott's own replies instead. Very deliberately, he posed his next question to Scott.

"Mr. Scott," Zander emphasized, "why didn't you report your wife missing?"

"Because," answered Beardsley, just as purposefully, "she's gone off like this before."

The conference went on for another hour, with Beardsley answering virtually every question. Zander even tried questioning Beardsley, wryly wondering to himself if Scott might answer instead, but the handsome man before him remained mute. Scott's voluntary appearance thus did little to fill out the missing person's report filed a day earlier by Raymond Throsby.

After the interview, Alexander made a point to pause a moment in the office doorway of J. Miller Leavy. Leavy was a good friend, and Alexander admired him. When Alexander came up against tough cases, Leavy was often his sounding board, for Leavy possessed an innate sense of strategy for cases that seemed hopeless. "Scott is one smooth son of a bitch, all right," Alexander said now, angling himself against the doorjamb as he lit a fresh cigar. "Very slick."

Leavy, at his desk, looked up at Alexander. He pushed his heavy black eyeglasses frames back into place. "What have you got on him?"

"Not a goddamn thing. Yet." Alexander's cigar settled in a corner of his mouth. "But I find it hard to believe that Scott'd hire a top-notch attorney like Beardsley unless he knows more than he says he does about his wife's disappearance."

"No direct evidence?"

Alexander shook his head.

"Well, sooner or later, he'll make a mistake," Leavy said, "they always do. They never tell the same story twice. You give Scott enough rope and he'll hang himself."

"I sure as hell hope so." Alexander disentangled himself from Leavy's doorway and started off down the hall toward his own office. Though Leavy had said little, Alexander was encouraged: Leavy always saw possibilities.

□ **14**

Leavy's life had been full of possibilities. Handsome, self-assured, extraordinarily bright, he was the firstborn American son of an immigrant shopkeeper, one of the best of a generation to graduate during the Depression. Leavy was a born prosecutor: principled, ethical, and dedicated. At fifty-one, he enjoyed a formidable reputation.

J. Miller Leavy's biography is the stuff of which American dreams are made. His father, Nathan Leavy, was born in a London slum as his grandparents, Polish Jews, waited to resettle in the United States. Their family name then was Kudahy; an overworked immigration officer at Ellis Island mistakenly but lastingly renamed them Leavy. From New York, the Leavys moved to Pennsylvania, near Philadelphia, where Nathan, a tailor's son, met and married Jenny, the daughter of a immigrant German butcher, whose own family name had been Americanized from Mueller to Miller.

By trade, Nathan Leavy was a cigarmaker, but a more lucrative salesman's job with Goldsmith Brothers, a wholesale liquor dealer, opened up in Arizona, and the Leavys moved west. Julius Miller Leavy, named for his maternal grandfather, was born August 12, 1905, in Tucson, the second of four children.

As Arizona voted itself dry in the days before the Eighteenth Amendment instituted Prohibition as a national virtue, Nathan Leavy looked for an alternative opportunity. He found it almost six hundred miles farther west in Los Angeles, where Leavy opened one of the city's first hops-and-malt shops at 109 East Fifth, just below Main Street. His home brew was sold through mail-order sales, too, and as a boy, Miller spent his weekends boxing hops for shipment across the country, even though the pollen set his allergies afire. Repeal later transformed the shop into a bona fide liquor store.

It turned a handsome profit, flourishing as Los Angeles exploded with the furious energy of a frontier boom town. The Leavys built a home on South Gramercy Place, an elegant new boulevard peopled with other prospering burghers. Miller lived at home and attended UCLA, not the sprawling campus that blossomed later in the hills of Westwood, but the old Vermont Avenue grounds, where Leavy's friends included Ralph Bunche, who was later to serve as under secretary to the United Nations. In 1927, Leavy graduated from UCLA with a dual degree in economics and political science.

He applied to law school at Harvard, and was put high on the school's waiting list. When a place opened up, the university telegrammed Miller in Los Angeles. But Leavy never saw that telegram, or even learned of its existence until many years later: it was hidden from him by his father, who feared that Harvard's rumored anti-Semitism might affect Miller and his studies. Instead, Miller entered the University of Michigan's School of Law.

When he graduated and returned home in 1930, Miller brought Winora Runcourt, a lovely, bright, graduate nursing student from the university's teaching hospital, back with him to Los Angeles. Miller passed the California bar exam the following year, but jobs for young attorneys were scarce in 1931. Though the couple's affections were serious ones, Miller and Winora—Win, he called her—judiciously decided to wait with marriage. Winora found a nursing job at Cedars of Lebanon Hospital on Fountain Avenue, with a dormitory room nearby, while Miller lived at home with his family on South Gramercy Place.

In October 1932, Leavy managed an appointment to the district attorney's office through a well-connected family friend. But civil service exams, the usual precursors for such hirings, were rarely given in those Depression days of tight budgets, and for eleven months, Leavy worked as an appointee without a salary, first in complaints, then in preliminary hearings. Lessons he learned then proved invaluable later on; under the tutelage of an old-timer around the office named Percy Hanner, Leavy was schooled in the thorough preparation and commonsensical courtroom style that became his trademark. A bizarre white-slavery case that no one else wanted to prosecute earned Leavy his first headlines and his first paycheck in November 1933. As 1934 approached, Leavy's future suddenly looked very promising.

But ten days into the new year, Winora awakened in her dorm room with a peculiar stillness in her left leg; almost immediately, the numbness deadened her other leg too. Tests diagnosed her strange malady as an inflamed spinal cord. After months of hospitalization with little change in her condition, Miller found Winora an apartment on Fordmore Hill near his office. The practical nurse he hired looked after Winora during the day, but Miller spent his lunch hours, his after-work evenings, and his weekends with her.

In 1936, Miller was appointed to the trials division of the district attorney's office. With no improvement in her health for more than three years, Winora had come to the difficult, irrevocable decision to return home, and reluctantly, Miller put her on a train back to Standish, Michigan, in December 1936. They corresponded—Miller frequently sent Winora avocados, the leathery-skinned fruit she'd grown fond of in California—until Winora's death many years later. Her paralysis never abated.

With Winora's departure, Leavy threw himself into his work, spending hours at his desk researching and strategizing each new case. He was learning to think like a thief, a con man, or a killer, to put himself inside the skin of someone who deliberately walked outside the justice system he was sworn to represent. Before the start of every case, Leavy first asked himself some tough questions about his evidence: Had the confession, if one existed, been freely given and obtained without using force? Were the witnesses competent? Was the physical evidence unbiased? Was it enough to obtain a conviction? If his answers were yes, then Leavy constructed his case as an artist might, fitting each piece of evidence into its proper place in a life-sized mosaic of a crime.

Yet, as preoccupied as he was with his cases, Miller did pause long enough to notice a spirited, dark-haired beauty now working as a secretary in the district attorney's office. Her name was Violet Pringle, and Leavy drove her home several times after work or office functions before he came around to asking her out. By the end of 1937, however, Miller and Violet were dating steadily.

Paul Wright's 1938 trial, one of Leavy's most famous early cases, was a sensation in every afternoon's headlines. The frail, thin-lipped Lockheed executive claimed he saw his beautiful wife and his best friend locked in a lewd embrace on the Wrights' piano bench, and, burned by a "white flame" of passion, Wright shot them both. Despite the best dramatic efforts of his noted defense attorney, Jerry Giesler, who sat casually on the blood-spattered piano bench during his final arguments, the jury needed just four hours to return a manslaughter conviction for two murders that Leavy and his co-counsel Ernie Roll had convinced them were deliberate, premeditated killings.

Later that year, Miller and Violet married, and for $1,750, the Leavys bought a 67-foot lot on a wide new street in the San Fernando Valley. For $6,000 more, they built a comfortable one-story home in Burbank, about twelve miles from downtown Los Angeles. A homey brick den overlooked a backyard spacious enough to accommodate the large garden where Violet planted roses and Miller grew squash in the summertime. The Leavys, childless, lived quietly there, neither of them ever real "social buds"; they preferred occasional intimate gatherings with a few close friends to grand-scale entertaining.

When Caryl Chessman's case first came along in 1948, Leavy initially considered it unremarkable, a routine, three-week-long kidnapping-with-intent-to-commit-bodily-harm case. Instead, it would follow him through more than a decade's worth of Chessman's appeals. Chessman, nicknamed the "Red Light Bandit" for the red cellophane he used to imitate a police car's spotlight to lure his young female victims, was a parolee accused of two rapes, one against a teenager who was subsequently confined to a mental institution. Leavy won the case and a death sentence for Chessman.

But the untimely death of the court reporter during the trial thrust Chessman and his lengthy appeals into the national spotlight. Chessman charged Leavy and the presiding justice, Judge Charles Fricke, with fraud in preparation of the trial transcript from the notes of the dead court reporter. That and other strategies kept Chessman alive for twelve years, long enough to author two books and become an articulate martyr to the foes of the death penalty. But his appeals at last ran out, and Chessman did die in San Quentin's gas chamber on May 2, 1960.

After the Chessman trial came another highly publicized capital-punishment case, the melodramatic 1953 trial of pretty Barbara Graham. With co-defendants Emmett Perkins and Jack Santo, the redheaded, doe-eyed Graham was charged with the murder of a sixty-two-year-old widow named Mabel Monahan during a robbery in her Burbank home. Graham's alibi rested on the word of a man who had volunteered to testify that she was with him in a motel room on the night of the murder. Leavy's first question for Graham's benefactor was his occupation: To Graham's visible shock, the witness replied that he was an undercover officer for the Los Angeles police force. With her co-defendants, Graham was executed on June 3, 1955.

To Leavy's lasting disgust, Graham was immortalized in the 1958 film *I Want to Live,* which won Susan Hayward an Academy Award for her portrayal of Graham as a warm, innocent woman convicted by trickery. Hollywood's interpretations aside, however, Leavy's absolute faith in the integrity of his evidence was later confirmed by then San Quentin warden Harley Teets, who told Leavy that Graham had finally admitted her guilt weeks before she died.

Violet Leavy liked to attend her husband's major trials, and once, to her horror, she watched as Miller was flattened by a courtroom punch from James Merkouris, a defendant who had already distinguished himself with the obscenities he screamed during the proceedings. Merkouris, the son of a Greek Orthodox priest, was on trial for murder, accused of stalking his former wife and her second husband for two weeks, then breaking into their ceramics shop and coolly executing Despine and Robert Forbes with a .38 revolver in one hand and a .45 in the other. Leavy was not hurt by Merkouris' punch, though only the persuasion of two other attorneys holding his arms prevented Leavy from returning the favor in kind. Merkouris spent the rest of the trial strapped in a steel chair located in a specially built glass cage, which was sound proof, air-conditioned, and equipped with a telephone line to the defense counsel's table, and Leavy was satisfied that he landed his own knock-out punch when Merkouris was convicted and sentenced to death. After the verdict, Violet waited for a quiet moment alone with Miller. "You're in a class by yourself," she told him then, the greatest compliment Miller was certain he could possibly receive.

As Merkouris' case wound its way through the legal system, Leavy found himself prosecuting Merkouris in a second murder trial, and again, the prosecutor won a capital-punishment judgment for the killer in his glass cage. But Merkouris' death sentence was commuted to life imprisonment by former California Governor Edmund G. "Pat" Brown, who said he had "grave and substantial doubts" about Merkouris' sanity.

To Leavy, this "modern" psychiatric view that a criminal such as Merkouris could not stop himself from committing his crimes was just so much nonsense, and it helped to make him one of California's foremost advocates of capital punishment. Leavy was convinced that the only proper test for criminal insanity was the M'Naghten Rule, written by the English court in 1843. Simply put, the M'Naghten Rule was (and still remains) the primary standard used by most American court jurisdictions, including those in California, to test criminal insanity as a defense: Was the accused capable of distinguishing the difference between right and wrong at the time of the crime? Did the accused understand the nature and quality of his act? Did the accused know that he could be punished for his crime? If the answers to these three questions were yes, then Leavy always prosecuted with the vigor that the law demanded.

At least a dozen men and one woman went to their deaths, thanks to Leavy's potent prosecution. Finally, a friend in the state attorney general's office urged him to witness an execution, the better, argued his friend, to understand the enormous responsibility of asking a jury for a sentence of death. So, since prison authorities routinely invite the prosecutors of capital cases to executions, Leavy watched as Stephen Nash, the psychopathic killer who eventually confessed to eleven "pleasure" murders, was strapped into one of the two chairs inside the gas chamber. "I never lived like a man, but I'm going to die like a man," Leavy heard him say though the glass that separated them, and as Nash's head began to bob with the weight of gaseous unconsciousness, Leavy saw the dying man's lips move again in a soft, gasping whisper. The prison doctor, overhearing through his stethoscope, repeated Nash's words: "It's slow, but I can take it."

Nash's final victim, the one whose death had brought him to this last cyanide kiss, was ten-year-old Larry Rice, whom Nash had molested, disemboweled, and left to linger on toward death underneath the Santa Monica pier. Nash's death, as slow as it might have seemed to Nash, was, to Leavy, a far more merciful one than that of little Larry, who finally died on the operating table as horrified doctors worked for almost three hours to save his life. Leavy felt no compassion as Nash was pronounced dead; as far as Leavy was concerned, Nash died not like a man, but like a criminal.

Chessman, Graham, Merkouris, and Nash all shared the same sort of twisted cleverness that Leavy found lurking inside the men and women he faced in court day after day. Though Leavy found that criminals usually shared other traits as well—the capacity for absolute denial, the overblown ego, and the gross self-concern—the prosecutor made it his personal challenge to bring them down with an ingenuity even greater than their own. That element was what excited him about this new case Adolph Alexander kept talking about, the Scott case. It was shaping up into a considerable legal contest, one that threatened to break new ground in circumstantial-evidence law. Yet, the possibility that excited Leavy more than anything else was the chance to prove that Scott wasn't quite as smart as he thought he was.

But Leavy knew he had been passed by for this assignment, and from Lloyd Emerson of the *Examiner,* who said he had seen a memo written by one of his newspaper's executives on this very subject,

Leavy even thought he knew why: district attorney Roll's jealousy over the publicity that Leavy's cases had naturally garnered. Leavy liked Roll; there was certainly no open animosity between them. It was just a mutual, unspoken determination that each would do his job the way he thought it should be done. If Roll wanted to leave him out of this case, Leavy knew that choice was Roll's right. But nothing could prevent him from taking a keen interest from the sidelines, and that's just exactly what he decided to do.

□□□□□□□□□□□□□□□□□□□□□□□ **15**

Scott and Beardsley appeared just as unexpectedly at Roll's office on Friday afternoon, March 9, 1956, a day after Scott's first voluntary interview, and this time, Scott started off without his attorney's help. He had a few new ideas about where his wife might be, theories that supported in every way his failure to file a missing person's report. To the same audience who's listened to him the previous day, Scott brought up Evelyn's previous marriages.

"I want to say this so that you'll have a better understanding of my situation." Scott, nattily turned out in a charcoal-gray suit, white shirt, and maroon tie, exuded absolute confidence. "When we were first married, I thought I was Evelyn's third husband. It wasn't until years later that I found out I was number five or possibly number six. I wish to point out that all of her former husbands are now pushing up daisies, and"—he paused—"*all* of them were *cremated*."

His insinuation settled in the air for a long moment. No one else said a word.

"I think that she may have gone to live in the east with a son by one of those former marriages," Scott continued, "a son and a marriage that she never wanted me to know about." From his breast pocket, Scott drew out a worn photograph; as he held it, he unconsciously smoothed out its frayed edges with a manicured finger.

"A little over a year ago, I came across this photograph." He laid the picture of a tall man and a small boy not more than three years of age on the table before him. Sergeant Zander picked it up and studied it. "Judging by the style of the man's collar," Scott went on, "I'd have to say that the picture was probably taken around World War One. When I asked Evelyn about the photograph, she told me it was none of my business. She's always reticent about her past life, so I've never considered her disappearing acts unusual. Besides," Scott added, "I've always had a pretty good idea about where to look for her. She's been out all night before, you know. On all these other occasions, I'd see her car parked at this particular place over on Kelton Avenue, but she always came back after a day or two. When she didn't show up this time, I had to go over and and pick up her car with an extra set of keys and bring it back to the house myself."

Zander passed the picture to Alexander, who scrutinized it closely. The smoke from Alexander's cigar curled around the photograph's edges and wafted away. Everyone waited silently for Scott to finish his statement.

"I also think she might have gone to a sanatorium on her own," Scott said. "She told me that she had undergone psychiatric treatment years ago and we discussed a number of sanatoriums where she could be treated."

"Do you remember the names of those sanatoriums?" Zander asked, at last breaking into Scott's monologue.

"Well, I think the one we talked about the most was in Baltimore—it might have been John Hopkins Hospital, but I really don't remember which one it was. I'll have to check my records and see if I wrote it down."

"Can you tell us what you thought was wrong with your wife?"

"Yes, I can," Scott answered smoothly. "She's been showing signs of some mental aberrations. You may not know this but she has cancer and she is also an alcoholic."

"And you think she might have voluntarily checked herself into one of these places that take care of that sort of thing, is that right, Mr. Scott?"

"That's right."

"But you don't know for sure that that's what she did, do you?" Zander wanted to be clear on this point.

Scott shook his head soberly. "No, I don't."

"Did you take her to one of these places yourself?"

"No, I didn't do that," he said. "Boy, then she really would have hit the ceiling."

"Mrs. Schuchardt and Mrs. Baum tell us that you called them at home to say that you were taking Mrs. Scott back east, to put her in a hospital yourself."

"Oh, no, I never said that I was taking Evelyn away," Scott said earnestly. "I don't believe I even have their telephone numbers."

"You never called your wife's friends, never told them that you were going to put Mrs. Scott in an institution?" Zander's voice hung on the edge of disbelief.

"No."

Zander settled his wiry, compact frame back into his chair. For a long moment, he studied Scott's face. "Well, frankly, Mr. Scott," he said finally, hoping that feigned confusion might draw Scott out, "this whole thing just doesn't make sense to me. I went over and talked to your wife's doctor, Dr. Schindler on Wilshire Boulevard, a day or two ago. He tells me that he saw your wife six weeks before you say she disappeared. He treated Mrs. Scott for her intestinal troubles, diverticulitis, I think he said it was, but otherwise he said Mrs. Scott seemed to be in splendid health—no signs at all of any mental breakdown, or cancer, or drinking problem. Now, can you tell me why you think you think your wife was suffering from all these ailments?"

"Well, Evelyn told me herself that she had these cancerous growths removed from her face. But she never tells me what she is doing to have these things taken care of now. The reason I thought maybe she was going to get herself treated is because—" Scott coughed. "Say, could you open the door a little, please," he asked, pointing at the entryway to Roll's office. "That smoke"—he gestured at Alexander's cigar—"is a little hard on my throat." Scott waited until it was opened to his satisfaction before he continued.

"Anyway," Scott said, "for about a month before she disappeared, she was shipping her clothing out to some place back east—why, she even sent off a new fur. After she left me, I thought that maybe she's been sending all of these things off to one of those places where they treated problems like hers. I thought maybe she was going to get the help I keep telling her she ought to have."

Zander already knew about the silver-fox stole that Marguerite Watson had received, but he let Scott continue. "Is that right?" the detective asked Scott evenly. "How'd you find out about the fur piece?"

"Evelyn asked me to take it off the insurance list."

"I see." Zander nodded appreciatively. "She ever ask you to cancel the insurance on anything else?" he asked casually, picking up a thick file folder from the desk. He flipped through it as Scott answered.

"No, she didn't."

"You sure about that? She never asked you to cancel the coverage on her personal belongings or anything like that?"

"No."

"Did your wife have much jewelry?"

"Some."

"She leave any of it behind when she . . . left . . . so suddenly?"

"Well, yes," Scott said. "She left—oh, a gold watch I gave her—it was my mother's—and another watch I bought for her in Switzerland. There was a third piece too, one that she could wear as a pendant on a chain around her neck or as a pin."

"Anything else? Anything more—*valuable?*"

"No." Scott seemed mystified at Zander's interest in Evelyn's jewelry. "Why?"

The detective found the piece of paper he wanted. "Why'd you cancel the insurance policy on her jewelry then?" he said, glancing it over.

"I didn't cancel anything."

Zander handed the paper to Scott. Beardsley moved his chair closer to Scott and looked it over too. It was a copy of Scott's July 2, 1955, letter to the Ingham & Coates Insurance Company of Pasadena, which listed the five costly pieces of his wife's jewelry Scott asked to have removed from their coverage: a brooch with fourteen large diamonds and eighty-six smaller stones, a pair of earrings, a white-gold wristwatch, a bracelet, and a strand of cultured pearls.

"Oh yes, now I remember," Scott said. Zander thought Scott sounded a little surprised, but he saw no change in Scott's expression as he handed the letter back to the detective. "These pieces all belonged to my mother—I gave them to Evelyn after we were married."

"Is that right? What year did you tell me you married Mrs. Scott?"

"Nineteen forty-nine."

"That sure is strange then," the detective said. "Your wife first insured these pieces in 1946."

"Well, actually, I just gave her the stones"—Scott faltered slightly—"and Evelyn had them remade into pieces she already had."

"I see. Where's the jewelry now?"

"Well, I found these items in a velvet pouch about a month after she disappeared," Scott said, his composure back in place. "I put them away in a safe place and canceled the insurance since they weren't being worn. I didn't want to leave them unguarded in the house."

"Where's the jewelry now?"

"I have it put away," Scott said stubbornly. "It's safe where I have it."

"We'd like you to bring it in and show it to us." Chief Parker spoke up for the first time.

"Well, that involves a lot of effort on my part," Scott said unhappily. "What if somebody steals it?"

"We'll provide you with a couple of officers for security," offered the chief.

"No, no, that won't be necessary," Scott said quickly. He conferred in a whisper with Beardsley. "You'll have to wait a few days, until I can get some new insurance on it."

"Next week'll be fine," Parker said, satisfied.

Zander picked up the questioning. "Where'd you get thirty-three hundred dollars' worth of your own jewelry to insure?"

"It's mine," Scott said, resisting Zander's probing.

"A wristwatch with diamonds"—Zander looked over the letter again—"a ruby ring, and a pair of heavy gold cuff links?" His voice curled with skepticism.

"Those were gifts."

"I see." Zander moved on. "Where'd you get the signed co-renter's agreement to enter your wife's safe-deposit box?"

"Mrs. Scott," Beardsley said, answering quickly, "apparently thought it would be better to have joint tenancy. They agreed that he should have the card with his signature and her signature upon it in case a possible emergency arose."

"What were you looking for in there, Mr. Scott?"

"Well, I was looking for a contract in connection with a civil matter."

"That's the book you wrote, is that right?"

"I didn't write it," Scott said. "I only helped out as a friend with the financial backing."

"And you thought your contract was in your wife's safe-deposit box?"

Scott nodded.

"Did you find it?"

"No, I didn't.

"What were you looking for the next time you went to her box?"

"Well, I thought Evelyn might have returned and replaced it in the box."

"Where'd you get the signature card you used to open your joint account with Mrs. Scott?"

"Mrs. Scott signed it about the same time she signed the co-renter's agreement. For exactly the same reason," Beardsley said.

"I see. Mr. Scott," Zander continued, "I understand that you've been advising your wife on how to manage her money. Can you tell me why you wanted her to be in a cash position?'"

"No, I never told her to do that," Scott said. "She started all that business on her own—she just suddenly started to liquidate all of her holdings."

"That wasn't your idea?"

"No, it wasn't. I don't know why she did it—she has a regular monthly income every month from an apartment house in Milwaukee."

"You've both been living off that income pretty well, isn't that right?" Zander's voice was even, but Scott caught his intimation.

"I can account for every penny," Scott said defensively. "You know," he said, seizing his chance to control the conversation, "I don't know just what bracket you think we were in, but I didn't think we were financially able to afford that other car. I drove a 1940

Ford and she drove a '48 Dodge—I couldn't see that we really needed a new car."

Forcefully, Scott kept on talking. "And after she set it all up, she didn't even want to go for the demonstration ride. She went only after I told her that either she went or we would just forget the whole business. After all, we are not the type of people to have arguments. Either we would sit down and discuss a matter or else we would just let it die a natural death. That's just the way it was with us."

After two hours of talking, Scott was rambling, and his listeners had heard enough for one day. Chief Parker brought the interview to an end with a final question: Would Scott agree to a police search of the premises at 217 North Bentley Avenue? After a surprised pause— and another whispered conference with Beardsley—Scott gave his conditional approval. The search would be permitted, Beardsley said on behalf of his client, with the understanding that Scott and Beardsley both would be present and that no one other than the searchers would be allowed onto the premises.

Parker nodded his agreement to the two stipulations.

"That's fine. We'll see you out at the house about ten o'clock tomorrow morning." Although Parker said nothing more to Scott or Beardsley, he later told his men that they would be hunting for the body of Evelyn Scott.

□ **16**

By the time Beardsley and Scott pulled into the driveway of 217 North Bentley just before 10 A.M. the next morning, March 10, reporters and newsreel cameramen were already interviewing and photographing search-team members in front of the house. When Scott was spotted inside his attorney's car, the newsmen hustled around it furiously for a glimpse or a clear shot of Evelyn's furtive husband. Scott acknowledged the commotion with a thin smile and a wave, but he ignored the questions tossed at him as he headed for his front door. Scott paused only when he recognized George Putnam, a television reporter he had met once at the Jonathan Club; he greeted Putnam amiably by name and with an old-school handshake. Scott made one more stop at the mailbox for Evelyn's airmailed March check before opening the house for its inspection by authorities only.

With the zest of a born salesman, Scott, smiling and joking, started off an ensemble house tour, followed by his attorneys, Alexander, chief police deputy Brown, forensic chemist Ray Pinker, three crime-lab technicians, five homicide detectives, and a police photographer to capture the whole operation in still photographs. With unmistakable pride, Scott first showed off the downstairs' finer points: the intimate den, the dining room overlooking the Los Angeles skyline, the kitchen equipped with built-ins for large-scale entertaining. Most of the furnishings, though, especially the larger pieces, were covered by dusters.

To the newsmen out in front, homicide detective Zander gave his own room-by-room house tour, with a walkie-talkie he'd hooked up to a police car radio. Zander detailed the crime lab's work, as technicians moved steadily from room to room, sweeping each carpet or wood floor with a special high-suction vacuum for traces of clues. The slightest smear or blotch was tested with benzidine, a chemical reagent that would cause even a very *old* bloodstain, Zander pointed out, to turn an unmistakable shade of blue. Pinker was examining one such brownish stain when Zander's makeshift loudspeaker fell maddeningly silent for ten suspenseful minutes. The reporters listening outside stirred excitedly, sure some clue was frustratingly beyond their purview. But, noticeably disappointed, Zander announced Pinker's conclusion, that the spots weren't bloodstains after all, but ordinary, everyday rust stains.

The downstairs tour was just about over when Scott pointed dramatically to a tall and rather unremarkable-looking built-in bookcase in the den. With an expectant flourish, he tripped a hidden trigger, and the bookcase swung out from the wall to reveal a secret cabinet still stocked with the liquor shown to investigator Ebbets the previous August. "There it is, gentlemen," Scott announced grandly, "my wife's liquor. She's an alcoholic, you know. She buys it by the case and asks me to bring it in from the car for her."

"Why would an alcoholic leave so much liquor behind?" asked Brown, unimpressed.

"I don't know," Scott said seriously. "All I know is that she's got plenty of money with her, so I guess she's bought herself some more of the stuff by now."

Scott took his tour upstairs next, where two of the three rooms—Scott's bedroom and the room Evelyn and Ewing mutually shared as an office—were obviously still in use. In the office, investigators found some papers they hoped might help their search for Evelyn, including a $63.86 canceled check dated December 28, 1955, written to the Kona Kai Club of San Diego.

When the tour inside was finished, most of the searchers moved outside. But Brown asked Scott to drive him to the spot on Kelton Avenue where Scott had said he saw his wife's car parked on occasion, including the morning of May 17, 1955. Scott agreed and Beardsley offered to drive. Alexander stayed behind to oversee the next phase of the search.

The 600 block of Kelton Avenue, three-quarters of a mile from 217 North Bentley Avenue, wound through west Los Angeles just west of UCLA, an elegant street lined with spreading trees and stately apartment houses. Midway through the block, Scott pointed to the approximate location where he said Evelyn usually left her car. Beardsley pulled over to the curb and the three men paused there, still in Beardsley's car, for a moment.

"Once, when she was gone for several days, she told me something I hadn't known," Scott said. "That there are certain places in Westwood which have no time limit on parking. I guess she found that out when she started parking here. But anyway, I had to take a cab out here the next day after she disappeared and pick it up. I had to spend most of the day getting it all cleaned up."

"Why was her car so dirty?" Brown asked quickly.

"Well, I found matted grass on the floor, as though someone had been walking through wet grass and then wiped their shoes on the mat. It looked like the birds had been at it for a couple of days too."

"And you knew to look for it here?"

"Well, it was here on a lot of other nights," Scott said. "To tell you the truth, I think she has a girlfriend over here and she just does not want me to know about it."

"A girlfriend?" Brown asked, not sure he had heard Scott correctly.

"That's right," Scott said. "My wife has what you might call an 'unnatural affection' for other women."

The newsmen outside 217 North Bentley Avenue were impatient to dig up stories of their own, since they were not allowed to witness firsthand the search of the Scott home. A couple of reporters started off up and down the street, knocking on the doors of the Scotts' Bel Air neighbors.

"Evelyn's a regal, stately woman," said Maxine Green, who lived at 281 North Bentley, "really, a very pleasant woman. Evelyn a cancer-ridden alcoholic? That's unthinkable."

One neighbor, then another, mentioned nocturnal "noxious" odors to reporters, the ungodly aroma they remembered emanating from the Scotts' incinerator on several different times about a year ago. Those smells were reported to the local fire patrol, but no one ever learned just what was burned on those chilly spring nights. Another neighbor volunteered that the house had seemed deserted over recent months, with only gardeners seen quietly working around the property.

By coincidence, those gardeners, a father and son, were scheduled to work that Saturday, and, astonished at the horde of policemen dig-ging in the yard, they told investigators that there had been no land-scaping changes there for three or four years. They offered to help the officers with their spades, joining half a dozen investigators already fanned out across the yard armed with ten-foot-long steel probes honed to knife-edged tips.

Evelyn's elegantly landscaped yard had been divided up into quad-rants, using a massive oak tree in the center as the axis. Alexander asked all investigators to probe each fourth of the yard, so that the entire area would be scoured by many sets of eyes. Zander, his walkie-talkie loudspeaker in hand, served as a macabre master of ceremonies.

"The probing procedure is commonly used in police work to discover the presence of buried bodies," Zander elaborated coolly. "The poles are thrust into the ground as far as possible. If the rods suddenly— ease—into something soft"—Zander paused to let the image settle into the minds of the newsmen outside—"we bring 'em up *quick* and sniff the tips of 'em. You can't miss the *smell* of a dead body."

99

There, Zander's chilly narrative ended abruptly once again, and the reporters in front shouted to their colleagues down the street to come quickly, that something had been found. But moments later, Zander announced that the bones found buried in a shallow flowerbed grave were the remains of some long-dead feline.

Police sergeant Art Hertel watched the search from the wooden deck overlooking the backyard. After fifteen years on the police force, Hertel knew there were moments when instinct took over from logic. Something didn't feel right here, but so far Hertel couldn't quite put his finger on whatever that something was. He had nothing to show for his intuition so far but the blisters and sore back muscles he'd earned from his turn with the steel probes.

Hertel walked toward the service yard, a patch of cement planted with a tinny revolving clothesline. An incinerator built into a low retaining wall marked the property's northern rim, and Hertel could see beyond it to the neighboring hillside where the uncultivated terrain pitched downward into brief canyons of thick scrub. He squatted at the incinerator first and craned his neck to look inside; he saw only the sooty brush marks of a crime-lab technician who had already collected its contents for closer analysis. Hertel straightened up and leaned against the wall.

He could see several men still working in the yard, some with shovels that flashed white-hot light in the afternoon sun. As the diggers ate away at the yard's landscaped prettiness, Hertel was reminded of some digging he'd done himself a year or so earlier. That case was a wife-killing too, where, Hertel remembered suddenly in amazement, a wealthy nurseryman had smugly buried his wife's body on his next-door neighbor's property, sure that the police would never think to look for her makeshift grave there.

Inspired, Hertel turned around and hopped up on top of the wall. He dropped four or five feet down to the other side into a thick cushion of leaves, a brittle top layer hiding several inches of moist decay underneath. Squatting, Hertel started rummaging around in the alternately dry and damp foliage until his hand passed over something hard. He brushed away the leaves to look.

It was a tooth.

Electrified, Hertel dug around the tooth gingerly. It moved suddenly and Hertel lifted a partial dental plate easily from its earthy jowl. There were five yellowed teeth in all, grit clinging to them like crumbs. It looked too weathered to test for fingerprints, but Hertel delicately wrapped it in his handkerchief anyway and slipped it in his pocket. On his knees, he kept searching, brushing aside the piled leaves to see what else might be hidden there.

Twelve inches away, Hertel spotted two dozen or so white tablets, some already disintegrated into minute chalky mounds of powder. Interspersed amid the pills were clumps of a golden gooey gelatin that looked like medicinal capsules softening on a wet bathroom sink. Nearby, Hertel found an empty Effremin Tooth Powder can, a hairbrush, a piece of wampum jewelry, a black cigarette holder, numerous filters, and a tube of oily-looking stuff in a tube bearing a brand-name label that Hertel could just barely make out: "Ul-tra-sol," he read to himself. A few feet farther away, half-buried by leaves, Hertel found two pairs of eyeglasses, one pair dark-rimmed, the other a lighter color with thin black lines striped through the plastic.

With the lid of the Effremin can, Hertel scooped up as many of the tablets and white powder as he could. With a twig, he spooned some of the yellow goo into the can's bottom half. As he scraped up the samples, Hertel heard a shout. It was Scott, back from his tour of Kelton Avenue.

"When you boys get through there," Scott called out amiably from the deck to the searchers below him, "come on in the house and have some lemonade. Hey, what's he doing down there?" Scott asked Brown, noticing Hertel crouched on the other side of the retaining wall. "He's on my neighbor's property."

"Just looking around, I guess," Brown answered.

"All right," Scott said, "I don't think they'll mind." He waved unconcernedly to Hertel, who snapped off a half-salute in return.

Satisfied with one last rummage through the leaves that he had left nothing behind, Hertel hoisted himself back over the wall to the Scotts' backyard. Quietly, he took Alexander aside and showed him the plate, the glasses, and the other odds and ends that looked like the collected miscellany of a woman's nightstand drawer. It was just a policeman's hunch, he told Alexander, but, after all, they were searching for the body of a sixty-three-year-old woman who might have worn dentures and glasses.

One by one, the other searchers were secretly told of Hertel's find. But since no one knew yet if the items really belonged to Evelyn, they were admonished not to pass along news of the discovery to anyone, particularly a reporter. Hertel kept the denture and the eyeglasses in his possession. As he suspected, Pinker confirmed later that the items were too weathered to reveal even latent fingerprints. But Hertel turned over the tablets and capsules to Pinker for lab analysis.

Before the search ended about 3 P.M., Hertel casually asked Scott for the names of his wife's dentist and optometrist. "I haven't the faintest idea who they are," Scott told him. Alexander had a pretty good idea who would know, however, and late that afternoon, Bill Brawner was reached at home. Brawner, who confirmed that Evelyn did in fact smoke cigarettes, knew the names of Evelyn's dentist and oculist: respectively, Dr. Reginald Coldwell and Dr. Albert Chatton.

At Alexander's suggestion, Hertel drove the denture out to Dr. Coldwell's Pasadena residence that night. "Yes," the dentist said, turning the plate over and over in his hands as he examined it, "I'm certain it's Mrs. Scott's. But why don't you bring it into my office on Monday and let me check my records just to be sure?"

So, on Monday morning, March 12, Hertel drove back to Pasadena, where Dr. Coldwell and Frederick Ungerer, his appliance technician, examined the denture against Evelyn's patient records. The five synthetic teeth crafted so faithfully by Ungerer—the first and second bicuspids, the first molar on the upper right, the second bicuspid and the first molar on the upper left—fit precisely into the gaps of Evelyn's smile, authentic down to an acrylic repair Ungerer had made on the denture in 1952.

"We call it an upper removable," Dr. Coldwell said. "She was wearing it on her most recent visit to me."

"Did Mrs. Scott ever complain about the way it fit?" Hertel asked. "Would she have had any reason to throw this denture away?"

"No, I don't think so. The bridge is still in wearable condition," Dr. Coldwell replied. "I know I cleaned it on the last visit she made to me and I think she would have mentioned any problems to me. Now, it's been almost a year since she's been here, so I don't know how it would fit her today."

Hertel's intuition bristled. "Do you have the date on Mrs. Scott's visit?"

"Yes, sure," said the dentist, looking at Evelyn's records again. "May 13, 1955. By the way," Dr. Coldwell added, "I saw her husband once here as a patient too."

Hertel nodded. He figured that Scott must have known the name of his wife's dentist. He turned to Ungerer. "Is there any chance that this denture isn't the one you made for Mrs. Scott?"

The technician took the bridge from Hertel and looked at it again. "I've never met Mrs. Scott," he said with a soft German inflection. "But I made this"—he gestured with the denture at Hertel—"with my own hands. You see, every craftsman has individual little things he does—the way the clasps are made, the way the gold design is made, and so on. I can absolutely identify this denture as my own work."

Later that week, Hertel stopped by Dr. Chatton's office in Westwood, where Evelyn had ordered two pairs of eyeglasses from another oculist's prescription. As he waited, Dr. Chatton tested the lenses and checked the two pairs of frames Hertel had found against Evelyn's records.

"The prescription and the frames correspond exactly with the glasses Mrs. Scott was using the last time I saw her," Dr. Chatton soon told him. "She was farsighted, so I recommended that she wear her glasses for reading or any close work."

"When was she here last?" Hertel asked.

"She ordered a new frame—this one, the Silver Striped Angelic," Dr. Chatton said, picking up the lighter of the two frames Hertel had brought to show him. "This frame used to be clear plastic, you know, but it could fade from sitting out in the weather the way you say you found it. She also ordered new lenses for the other pair—that's the Black Top Flight frame—at the same time. That was on April 27, 1955. She picked up both pairs two days later, on April 29."

"Can you positively identify these glasses as the ones you made for her?"

"First of all, the prescription is an accurate and correct match. But also," Dr. Chatton said, pointing at the edge of a lens in the Angelic frame, "I did here what we call 'hand edging' to shape her lenses to fit the frame she wanted. I can identify these glasses as Mrs. Scott's because I can always tell what my own work looks like."

"Did you ever do any work for her husband?"

Dr. Chatton shook his head. "No. But I do remember once he asked about a special kind of eyeglass case he wanted. I didn't have it, but I made a note about it on my desk and the next time one or both of them came in, I said I was unable to find the style that Mr. Scott wanted. But that's about the only contact I had with him."

Alexander shared this intriguing new evidence with Leavy. "We've got her denture and her eyeglasses," he announced triumphantly, cradling them for Leavy's view in his upturned hands. "They've just been positively identified."

"That's just great, Alex," Leavy said. "But you know as well as I do that two pairs of glasses and five false teeth won't count in court as part of Evelyn Scott's *body*. You've still got to prove both elements of the corpus delicti—first, that she's dead, and second, dead at the hands of her husband."

Alexander nodded. "Right. But I'm not going to show this stuff to Scott until I get him on the witness stand. How's he going to explain how these things wound up in the next-door neighbor's yard? That his wife went out there and tossed her teeth and her glasses over the backyard fence just before she ran off?"

Leavy smiled. "Look, Alex, that evidence isn't strong enough alone to prove murder. You're going to need something else to convince a jury that she's dead if you don't find her body. Scott couldn't have known her stuff was out there—all he'd had to do was drop it in the nearest dumpster and no one'd ever known the difference." Leavy's phone rang and he reached across his desk for it. "Well, hang on to your evidence, Alex," Leavy said. "Only an act of God could have kept that stuff out there after all this time. That's bound to count for something with a jury."

The tube of Ultrasol was traced to the beauty salon at Bullock's, a Westwood department store, where manager Ellen Richmond told detective Zander that Evelyn bought the product regularly to use at home. Although she had been a steady client there for years, Evelyn hadn't made an appointment in months, Richmond said, and checked her records for the exact date of Evelyn's last scheduled visit: May 17, 1955. That morning, Richmond told Zander, Evelyn's standing Tuesday morning appointment was abruptly canceled by a man who never gave his name. She never made another appointment.

Zander followed up on the canceled check written to the Kona Kai with a visit to the Shelter Island club, located near San Diego. Kay Pawluk in the general manager's office obligingly pulled Scott's registration card from her files, which listed visits in October and December 1955. Scott had made both visits with his wife, Pawluk told an astonished Zander, and she showed the detective a breakfast check with the distinctly feminine signature of "Mrs. L. E. Scott." But Pawluk couldn't remember what the woman had looked liked, and the only other information she could provide to Zander was the couple's home address: 217 North Bentley Avenue.

As soon as he got back to Los Angeles, Zander told Brown about the signature of "Mrs. L. E. Scott." Brown had another lead already from a Beverly Hills Supper Club waiter, who had tipped off investigators that Scott dined there frequently with a dark-haired woman, charging their meals to his wife's account. Brown decided to put in a call to Scott's attorney.

From the interviews with Scott had come other leads that, no matter how remote the connection to Evelyn might seem, Alexander knew must be checked. The death records of Evelyn's previous two husbands, Pettit and Mumper, were searched for the slightest hint of impropriety, based on Scott's thinly veiled innuendo. But each man's death certificate had been correctly certified by a physician, and telephone calls to those doctors left investigators satisfied that both men

105

died of natural, if regrettably premature, causes. The photograph of Evelyn's "son" by a previous marriage was identified by Raymond Throsby as himself, photographed as a boy with an uncle. And Millard Seville, a driver for the Yellow Cab Company, recalled picking up a man who looked like Scott at 217 North Bentley Avenue on May 17, 1955, and dropping him off three-quarters of a mile away in the 600 block of Kelton. But Seville didn't remember where his passenger went next, or if a red car had been parked along the street.

Investigators located the 1940 Ford sedan Scott sold two weeks after Evelyn disappeared. Crime-lab technicians tested Scott's car and Evelyn's Dodge coupe with benzidine reagents, but they found no hint of blood.

Tom Doherty, meanwhile, was still trying to trace the cash that Evelyn withdrew from her bank accounts through his analysis of her personal expenditures and her deposits in other accounts. Finally, Doherty reported to Alexander that the only place he thought the missing $57,177 could be was in Evelyn's safe-deposit box, based on his study of her unmistakably regular pattern of cash withdrawals and vault entries. After a conference with Alexander, the district attorney decided it was time to see what Scott had been really after in Evelyn's bank box.

On March 14, 1956, and under orders from Roll, Scott opened his wife's safe-deposit box for an audience of his attorneys, Alexander, Pinker, and several other investigators. At first glance, it held a disappointing assortment of routine miscelleanea: one red folder, a canvas sack imprinted with "Federal Reserve of Philadelphia, No. 4," five paper clips, and eight loose rubber bands. One of the folder's six compartments contained a gold cigarette holder with the initials of Clem Pettit engraved upon it.

But inside the canvas bag were two large mailing envelopes tightly sealed with transparent tape. One envelope, with the typewritten label "Sample From First Claim," contained a brownish sandlike substance. The second envelope, similarly marked "Sample From Second Claim," held the purest, whitest sand that Alexander had ever seen. Evelyn's bank box, transferred to joint tenancy three days after her husband said she disappeared, held no cash at all, just the paper clips and rubber bands used by banks to keep loose bills together.

When the pebbly contents of the envelopes were unsealed, Alexander looked at Scott for an explanation of how the sandy stuff made its way into her box. "I have never seen it before," Scott announced solemnly. "I have no explanation whatsoever for it." So, a couple of bank envelopes were filled with samples and turned over to Pinker that afternoon for examination.

But Pinker was already absorbed in his analysis of the substances found by Hertel. With a call to the Horton & Converse Drug Company, he obtained samples of drugs that approximately matched the appearance and composition of the tablets and gelatin. With instruments capable of identifying any crystalline substance in the world, samples of the known and unknown drugs were placed on a lead slide, rotated at a fixed speed, and bombarded with a monochromatic X-ray beam, a process that essentially recorded each one's compositional "fingerprints."

Pinker subjected the known substances to additional "weathering" tests, too, re-creating with water and infrared light the alternating wet and dry spells that might have reasonably occurred while those unknown substances lay under their leafy canopy. Pinker identified at last two separate medicines, Aureomycin and Sulfadiazine, the anti-inflammation drugs that Evelyn's doctor quickly confirmed had been prescribed for her diverticulitis.

Pinker's attention turned next to the ashes swept from the firebox of the Scotts' incinerator, and he spread those cinders out on a paper-covered table for a naked-eye examination. As he broke the biggest ashes apart with an oversized metal spatula, Pinker counted 20 hosiery fasteners for girdles, the metallic remnants of a delicately crafted, distinctly feminine belt buckle, thin tatters of a lightweight black fabric, and several minute fragments of bone.

□ **18**

On March 15, Beardsley identified Scott's "mystery woman" companion as Marianne Beaman, and he insisted that there was nothing clandestine about the couple's public appearances together. Two police officers tried to question Marianne that afternoon at the dental office where she worked, but, startled, Marianne refused to answer any questions. A few hours later, however, as Beardsley and Hufstedler listened, Marianne agreed to an interview with chief deputy Brown.

"How did you meet Mr. Scott?" Brown asked first.

Despite her apparent nervousness, Marianne, dressed simply in a neatly tailored suit, seemed controlled and well poised. "I was introduced to Mr. Scott by a mutual friend, Patricia Deadrick, at a party on August 21, 1955." Without prompting, Marianne added, "He telephoned me about a week later and invited me to dinner. I've seen him about once a week ever since."

"Did you know that Mr. Scott was married?"

"Yes." A slight color flushed Marianne's cheeks, but her voice remained even. "The second time we had dinner, Mr. Scott told me that his wife was missing."

"Go on."

"Mr. Scott said that he loved his wife very much and missed her terribly, and that he hoped she'd return soon to him. He told me that Mrs. Scott was a very secretive sort of person and that she drank excessively. He said she had gone off like this before for a couple of days at a time.

"But he didn't seem bitter," Marianne added after a slight reflective pause, "even though she left him like that. He just felt that she was mentally ill and he wanted her to have the kind of psychiatric treatment he felt she needed."

"What else did he tell you about his wife?"

"Well, he thought she tried to poison him several times by putting something—arsenic, I think he said it was—in his coffee."

"Did he tell you when Mrs. Scott did that?"

"I think it was 1951 or 1952. I'm sorry," she said, shaking her head and breathing deeply to retain her poise, "I just don't remember."

"That's fine." Brown noted, appreciating Marianne's willingness to supply details, unlike Scott, who was habitually vague. He changed the subject. "Did Mr. Scott ever tell you how he earns a living?"

"He said he was a retired securities and investments broker."

"Did he tell you where he worked? Or when he retired?"

"No. I didn't ask."

"Where does Mr. Scott think his wife is now?"

"He says she might have gone somewhere on the East Coast or maybe on a cruise to Europe. Ewing—Mr. Scott," she corrected herself, "told me that his wife liked to travel."

"Did he mention any specific places she might be?"

"No."

Brown studied Marianne. "It's Mrs. Beaman, isn't it?" he asked neutrally. "You're divorced, is that correct?"

"That's right."

"Where's your ex-husband now?"

"He died about four years ago, of a heart attack."

"I see." Brown nodded thoughtfully to himself. "Have you ever visited 217 North Bentley Avenue?"

"Only once, a few days ago. Mr. Beardsley was with me."

"Has Mr. Scott given you any gifts?"

Marianne looked at Beardsley. "Well, Mr. Scott is sort of an intelligent spender, I guess I'd have to say," she answered a little reluctantly. "He did give me a handbag, a small beaded one, for Christmas last year, but I don't think he's really the type to make an extravagant display of money."

"Anything else?"

"No."

"Mrs. Beaman, have you ever used Mrs. Scott's name?" Brown asked abruptly.

"Mrs. Beaman's relations with Mr. Scott have nothing to do with Mrs. Scott," Beardsley interrupted. "I don't think that question is relevant."

"Did you take any out-of-town trips with Mr. Scott?"

"That's not relevant either," Beardsley said.

"Has Mr. Scott proposed marriage to you?"

"Oh, we don't have any romantic attachment at all," Marianne said hurriedly, the flush highlighting her cheeks again. "We're only—warm friends—that's all."

Brown persisted. "But has Mr. Scott ever mentioned marriage to you?"

Before Beardsley could stop her, Marianne looked down at her lap tightly. "No," she said softly, "he hasn't."

As their interview ended very late that afternoon, Marianne agreed to an official search of her Santa Monica apartment. Two officers accompanied her home that night, and, as she watched with Beardsley, they looked through her closets and cupboards for jewelry, clothing, or anything else that might have belonged to Evelyn. They found only Ewing's typewriter, some silverware, and a small overnight case that Marianne said she was told once belonged to Ewing's mother.

Pinker's study of the ashes from the Scotts' incinerator was finished. Temperatures in the firebox had not been hot enough to melt the bone fragments, which, Pinker concluded after closer scrutiny, were the remains of a lamp-chop dinner.

He started work next on the identification of the grainy samples taken from Evelyn's bank box. Pinker's chemical tests showed that the specimen labeled "Sample From Claim Number One" was nothing more than common plaster sand, the basic building block of home-construction materials such as mortar, stucco, or concrete. The second sample was white silica sand, used to manufacture glass and ceramics products, or found in cigarette urns and children's play boxes.

From his memory of the Scott home, Pinker recalled that a whitish material had been dumped near the retaining wall of the Scotts' garage. Some large particles and a fine dust of the stuff, he remembered, had coated the surfaces of the leaves of surrounding shrubbery; water and wind had not yet had time to wash it away. In the garage itself, Pinker remembered a half sack of another sandy-looking substance.

So, with Scott's permission, Pinker stopped back by the house on March 15 to collect samples of both substances, which he used in microscopic tests and sieving comparisons with the materials found in Evelyn's safety-deposit box. The substances proved a perfect match to the materials taken from in and around the garage at 217 North Bentley Avenue. A further check in the office turned up a supply of envelopes seemingly identical to those found filled with sand in Evelyn's bank box.

* * *

March 16 was to be another long day of interrogation for Scott, and he arrived at Parker's office with Beardsley and Hufstedler, dressed as always in a three-piece suit. At least outwardly, Scott seemed calm, but the tightness to his smile burst almost as soon as the session got underway at midmorning. Scott's temper flashed at a photographer who asked him to move closer to his questioners for a picture. "This whole thing is getting to be a production," Scott snapped, "and I'm getting damn tired of it." Nevertheless, he complied.

Alexander decided to interrogate Scott himself this time, and he was determined to elicit from him the kind of personal vignettes that Scott avoided to bring his hazy past into focus. Alexander asked first about Scott's midwestern childhood. "Where in St. Louis did you grow up?" he asked.

"I don't remember the exact address, but there were a number of other houses on the street." Unhurriedly, Scott sipped a cup of coffee. His temper had disappeared as instantly as it appeared. "I do remember there were a lot of trees—I don't know what kind they were, maple, maybe—we lived on that street in a two-story house and I do know that it was in the best section of town."

"Do you remember the name of the school you went to?"

"No, I don't. All I know is that I went to a private school until my father got into a little financial trouble and then I switched to a public school."

"What sort of work did your father do?"

"He was in the oil business."

"Doing what?" Alexander pressed him.

"He was in business for himself."

"What kind of trouble did he get into?"

Scott dismissed the question with an impatient wave. "Oh, just the kind of thing that any man in business might get into from time to time."

"Did you go to college?"

Scott nodded. "Washington University. But you may not have heard of it. It's a small college."

"When were you there?" Alexander made a note to himself to ask a detective to check the school's records.

"Nineteen eighteen, or thereabouts."

"That's when you graduated?"

"Oh no, I never graduated," Scott said quickly. "I just attended some lectures without credit and I don't think that the school kept track of it."

"What did you do then?"

"I went to work."

"Where?"

"At an import-export company, Bulter Brothers in Chicago."

"Whom did you work for there?"

"I don't know what the man's name is now, but anyway, I think they went out of business some time ago."

"How long did you stay there?"

"Well, to tell you the truth, I stayed there until I wasn't moving fast enough," Scott said confidently, "then I went to work for the Standard Oil Company as an auditor. When I left that job, I went into the investment business, which is what I've done ever since. Now, what else do you want to know?"

"What training did you have to go into this kind of business?"

"It's always been my feeling that you have to get out there and slug it out before you really learn anything about business," Scott said, "and I had to learn a *damn* hard way."

"So you had no formal training in the securities business?"

"Well, I think my business experience is worth 90 percent of what someone else learns in business school," Scott said. "Don't you?"

"What investment company did you work for?" Alexander asked, ignoring Scott's question.

"Halsey, Stuart. Then I was the branch manager for the A. C. Allen Company after that."

"Can you give me the names of some of the people you worked with?"

"No, I can't—that's quite a ways back for me. I really don't remember just who I worked with, to tell you the truth, and I'm not sure that they'd remember me. But anyway, after a while, I opened up my own company, the L. E. Scott Company, I think I called it, and I was very successful. After that, I guess I just got tired of St. Louis and I moved out to Los Angeles." Scott turned to the court reporter sitting near him and extended his coffee cup. "Would you please get me just a halfa cuppa more?"

Alexander reached over for the cup and handed it to another officer in the room instead. "Get Mr. Scott some coffee, please," he said. He looked back at his notes to regain his place in the questioning.

"Did you go to work out here?"

"Well, yes, of course," Scott said. "I didn't think anybody else was going to take care of me. I went into the real estate business for a while, and then I opened up an insecticide factory."

"I thought you were in the investment business."

"Well, yes, I was," Scott answered smoothly. "Those businesses were investments."

"What was the name of the insecticide company?" Alexander pushed him for details.

"The Seaboard Chemical Company."

"Where was it located?"

"I had two offices, one on Ford Street—I'm not too sure now just where it was—and one in Northridge out in the San Fernando Valley."

"What was the address of the office in Northridge?"

"Well, I can't remember exactly where it was."

"You still own Seaboard?"

"No, I sold it a number of years ago to a Jewish lawyer fellow I used to go to school with."

"What's his name?"

"I don't remember."

"Did you ever serve in the military?"

"No, but during the war, I worked in Washington for the Pentagon."

"Doing what?"

"Well, I really can't tell you very much about it—my job was classified by the government. But it had to do with supplies for the British and Russian armies."

"What was the name of the man you worked for?"

"I don't remember."

An hour-and-a-half break for lunch did little to help Scott's memory, even though Alexander's questions honed in now on Scott's activities in the ten months since his wife's disappearance. "Mr. Scott, if you were expecting your wife to return, why did you close out her checking account?"

"I didn't close out anything."

"Her account at the Bank of America in Santa Monica?"

"Oh," Scott said. "Well, you see, that account originally contained about $24,000. She took out $20,000 to open up a couple of these $10,000 accounts I told you she was setting up all over the country. Say," Scott interrupted himself and pointed to an open window, "do you think you could close that just a little bit?" He waited until the window was shut before he continued.

"Anyway, after she left, I found a check already made out by her for the purpose of closing out the rest of the account, so I went ahead and did it for her."

"I see. She just left that check all made out for you to find?"

"That's right. It was in her desk drawer."

"Can you explain to me why you wanted your wife in an 'all-cash,' a liquid, position?"

"No, that wasn't my idea—I told you, Evelyn started selling off her stocks and setting up these bank accounts on her own."

"That's not what we've been told by some of your wife's friends, Mr. Scott. For example, Mr."—Alexander checked his notes for the right name—"Brawner distinctly remembers discussing with you your strategy to liquidate your wife's holdings."

"I think Mr. Brawner told you something that's just not true."

"He said you wanted to take the money and use it to live abroad."

"I never said that."

"Never?"

"No."

"The Mercedes-Benz salesman told us the same thing—he said you brought up living in Spain for a year or so."

"Oh no," Scott said, shaking his head, "I don't think Spain came up in our conversation at all."

Alexander couldn't push past Scott's flat denials. He tried another tact. "You're still taking care of your wife's accounts, aren't you?"

"Well, I've been opening her mail and answering her letters, if that's the type of stuff you mean."

114

"Anything else? How about her income taxes?"

"I filed a return in her name—you can check that out if you don't believe me—but I think you'll find it's all in order."

"Why didn't you have Boyle's office make it out? That's where your wife had it done every year."

"I wanted to try someone else to do it this year. I don't think there's anything wrong with that, is there?"

"How much did you put down for your own income?"

"Wait just a minute, please," Beardsley interrupted. "Mr. Scott has a civil hearing coming up, and I won't allow him to tip his hand about his personal financial matters in any way."

Alexander changed the subject. "Did your wife wear glasses?" he asked, his voice deliberately even. Alexander didn't want to alert Scott to the nature of the principal evidence so far collected against him.

"Yes, she did."

"Do you know where her glasses are now?"

"I imagine she took them with her."

"Did Mrs. Scott wear dentures?"

"I don't know, to tell you the truth. I never looked."

"We found some women's clothing that was burned in your incinerator. Can you tell us how it got there?"

"Well, after my wife left, I found two or three of her dresses and some of her undergarments that were all soiled," Scott said, "so I burned them. They smelled like I don't know what—I don't think the incinerator's been cleaned out since, so I suppose that's what it was."

It was nearing 4 P.M. and the interview was just about over. Parker asked the last question of the day: "Mr. Scott," said the chief, "do you have any objection to taking a lie detector test?"

"No," Beardsley answered for his client. "Mr. Scott will be available whenever you'd like to give him one *after* the civil case has been decided."

Even without a lie detector test, however, Alexander was convinced that Scott was responsible for Evelyn's disappearance. Months of investigation had shown only that Evelyn, at sixty-three, was a stable woman, not at all the type to vanish for almost a year on a whim. Only Scott portrayed her as a cancer-ridden drunk, and he had done nothing even to pretend that he was trying to find her. Scott slipped through questions about himself, his marriage, or his wife with his unabashed "I don't know," more like a sly fox than a grieving mate. Alexander had reached the only logical conclusion he could: that Evelyn's extended absence was involuntary and that her long silence meant that Evelyn could no longer speak out on her own behalf. He had to come up with the right strategy to snare Scott. On the way back to his office, he stopped by to see Leavy.

"I swear to God," he said as he dropped himself in a chair next to Miller's desk, "I've been listening to Scott talk in circles since ten-thirty this morning. All he says is, 'I don't remember' over and over again. He can't tell us where he worked, for whom he worked, or what years he was there." Alexander, tired, shook his head. "He doesn't remember a goddamn thing."

Leavy grinned in sympathy. "Damn convenient—that selective memory of his."

"Yeah." Alexander smiled wearily. "We know we can get Scott on fraud. The hard part is going to be proving that he murdered his wife."

"I don't know about that." Leavy leaned back in his chair. "Scott is what I call a classic fortune hunter—he doesn't have a pot to piss in or the window to throw it out of. Evelyn was easy prey and he lived off her, pure and simple. If you ask me, Scott knew damn well she was never going to show up again or else he wouldn't have been going around forging her name. I think I'd ask Ernie Roll and the grand jury for a murder indictment anyway."

"Why? You hiding Evelyn Scott's body somewhere?"

"No, but you don't need it—rule of convenience, Alex. You can present secondary evidence if the primary evidence isn't available. As the victim of fraud, Evelyn's the best evidence, and you can argue that only her murder is preventing her from testifying against her husband on forgery and grand theft."

Alexander stared at Leavy. "You know," he said slowly, "that might work. Roll just might go for it."

116

*   *   *

On March 22, the police department brought out its steel probes again to explore the brushy Santa Monica Mountains extending for miles around the Scott home. They hunted in isolated canyon areas where Evelyn might have wandered off alone, or, after interviews with Harriet Livermore and Ulrich Quast revealed that Scott appeared to know the area well, where her body might have been buried. Detectives checked the records of a nearby veteran's cemetery for a listing of the gravesites open at the time of Evelyn's disappearance, but a police spokesman denied that those sites, too, were probed.

Beardsley announced that a private investigator was on his way to Herndon, Virginia, a small eastern city outside Washington, D. C., where Evelyn might be in seclusion. That tip came from Scott, from an address on an envelope Scott said he'd found among his wife's personal belongings. But the attorney refused to divulge any more details "because Mrs. Scott may read this and leave town before our investigator gets there."

The search for Evelyn was grim, serious business, but, inevitably perhaps, it invited a bit of macabre humor. Poolside at a Las Vegas hotel, sunbathers giggled as some anonymous voice solemnly paged the silver-haired stock broker: "L. Ewing Scott, please call your wife." And local pundits, noting that the San Diego freeway, not half a mile from 217 North Bentley, was under construction when Evelyn vanished, wagged that squeals heard while driving along this new roadway might not be the scream of tires after all.

As the hunt for Evelyn intensified, Scott's own troubles were mounting. The Internal Revenue Service notified him that it was officially "looking into" the source of the $34,000 in cash that Scott told detectives he gave his wife for a share of her Milwaukee apartment house. Evelyn's latest income check was returned to him marked "unacceptable for deposit without the personal endorsement of the payee." Scott and his attorneys were being followed by strange men in unmarked cars that left Scott sleeping in Hufstedler's guest bedroom one night as a precaution. And, although he had countered with a suit of his own, Scott had only the start of his brother-in-law's trusteeship hearing to look forward to on March 26.

117

On March 25, Scott asked Marianne to have dinner with him; he asked if she'd still marry him when all of his troubles were over. "I'll still marry you," Marianne answered.

□ **19**

Although her brother had initiated these court proceedings, Evelyn's mysterious, handsome husband was clearly expected to be the star witness. The Superior Court chambers were packed, and among the most interested watchers were Adolph Alexander and several other investigators, all of whom were eagerly anticipating Scott's first under-oath accounting of his activities since May 16, 1955.

Yet, Scott conspicuously was absent as the fight over Evelyn's fortune started. The hearing quickly escalated from a family scuffle between her brother and her husband to a three-way battle now entangling Evelyn's attorney, who stepped in reluctantly to oppose both petitions. Boyle claimed that Throsby would be as unsuitable a trustee as Scott, and he urged the appointment of a neutral third party instead. Throsby ignored Boyle's intervention and refused to give up his bid to oversee his sister's bank accounts, the house she'd bought at 217 North Bentley, and her other monetary interests. So did Scott, at least through his attorney.

Scott's legal stance was a precarious one, a delicate positioning between two key points. He needed to establish that Evelyn was missing to retain control over her estate, yet Scott had to disassociate himself from any possible role in her disappearance. Notarized papers then, signed by Scott and filed by Beardsley, stated that "Evelyn T. Scott was last seen on May 16, 1955 and ever since that time has been and now is missing and her whereabouts are unknown," and that he "hopes and believes" his wife is still alive and will return to him. In the interim, the papers argued further, Scott or his representative, the Farmers & Merchants Bank, should be authorized to "occupy, use, preserve and maintain the interest of Mrs. Scott in all her properties."

Scott failed to appear for the second day of the hearing, and W. Ernest Pitney, Throsby's attorney, complained to Judge Mildred L. Lillie that his process servers had been unable to find Scott and serve him with a summons. "He is a material witness," Pitney argued, "and he should be produced."

"Are you going to make him available?" Judge Lillie asked Beardsley.

"If I consider his presence necessary," the lawyer replied, stung. But despite a warning to Beardsley that the court would be mightily reluctant to appoint a "trustee who has refused to come into court and be examined as to his qualifications," Scott failed to appear for the hearing's third day.

Even in absentia, however, Scott was still the center of attention. Evelyn's friends—Jim Boyle, Gladys Baum, Opal Mumper, and her nephew, Bill Mumper, among them—testified about their attempts to reach her after the "mental breakdown" Scott claimed Evelyn had suffered. Expert witnesses traced Scott's paper trail of ledger sheets, deposit tickets, credit memos, canceled checks, and other records, all of which documented and supported Throsby's charge that Scott was looting his sister's fortune through forgery.

Beardsley, meanwhile, took a dim view of the investigators seated in the courtroom day after day, waiting for Scott's testimony. "Why is it that Chief Parker has a roomful of police officers ostensibly trying to help us find the missing Mrs. Scott," the attorney asked rhetorically, "and why does district attorney Roll have his men and a stenographer here, when they haven't even found Mrs. Boomhower [the Bel Air woman who suddenly vanished one afternoon]? "Mrs. Boomhower had no husband to chase around like they've chased around Mr. Scott," Beardsley said, answering his own question.

Scott failed to show up for the hearing's fourth session, and, as Boyle had anticipated, the spotlight abruptly shifted away from him and onto Raymond and his unfortunate financial transgressions. Beardsley's cross-examination of Throsby was relentless as Raymond, intimidated and confused, admitted under oath that he was able to avoid a prison term for misusing a former employer's funds only because his sister repaid his theft.

Most devastating to Raymond's trusteeship bid, however, was the vitriolic letter Throsby wrote to Evelyn when his loan was called due. Beardsley read that letter into the record, lingering over Raymond's own words:

> Evelyn,
>
> I received this letter from your attorney Boyle recently. I presume you got a copy and it made you very happy about the whole thing. Presently I am out of the state and working. Trudy [Throsby's wife] is in Los Angeles looking after things for me and I might add that if you had half the fortitude and loyalty that she, Trudy, has, you would not be . . . [Beardsley emphasized the written words of Evelyn's only brother] *selfish* and *without character* and *senile*. When you married Munster [a reference to Norris Mumper, Evelyn's fourth husband], you said to me, 'Raymond, you can't keep the Throsby's down.' You were *drunk* at the time as you were when he died, only then you were *stinking drunk*. Remember? When I am a little bit more rational, I will answer this letter and you too. . . .

"Is that the letter you sent to your sister?" Beardsley asked.

Miserably, Throsby admitted that he wrote the letter and said that his statements were lies, only an emotional reaction to a fatal accident that had occurred the same day he received Boyle's demand for payment. "I am ashamed," Raymond said in a low voice, "very sorry and humble."

Throsby redeemed himself somewhat as a witness when he told about his two encounters with Scott, on November 11, 1955, in front of the Scott home, and again during the all-night questioning of Scott on February 13, 1956: "I asked him if he murdered my sister," Raymond said. "I got no direct answer from him."

By Friday, March 30, Scott had yet to appear. But as Pitney called Marianne Beaman to the witness stand, Judge Lillie unexpectedly brought the hearing to a close. Ruling against both Throsby and Scott, the jurist appointed the Citizen's National Trust & Savings Bank as a neutral third-party trustee, nominated by Pitney in the proceeding's closing moments. Attorney Hallam Mathews was named as Citizen's representative.

As a condition of the trusteeship, Judge Lillie asked the bank to decide if Scott had misspent any of Evelyn's separately held funds, a determination that could affect the Wolper Printing Company's

120

$6,023.40 attachment against the Scotts' joint bank account. "The court has no information about how Mr. Scott is currently supporting himself," the judge observed pointedly. "If he has misused his wife's separate funds, he will be required to repay her estate."

Immediately, Beardsley announced that Scott would appeal the decision, based on Beardsley's interpretation of legal precedent that said the husband or his nominee should be named caretaker of a missing wife's estate.

Since the start of the hearing five days earlier, Beardsley, Hufstedler, and their third partner, Helen Kimball, had been followed by the same unfamiliar cars that were tailing Scott. Although their pursuers made no effort to be inconspicuous—one good-humoredly turned down Hufstedler's friendly offer of a drink after following the attorney the three blocks to where his car was parked—they never identified themselves either.

By Friday night, however, Beardsley had had enough of this cat-and-mouse pursuit, and he decided to put a little variation in his stalkers' own game plan. Just before he left for a dinner appointment that evening, Beardsley looked for the cars he figured would be waiting for him in front of his San Marino home. When he spotted them, the attorney telephoned the local chief of police before backing his car out of his own driveway.

With three cars all in a neat, obvious line behind him, Beardsley drove unhurriedly along San Marino's peaceful residential streets, a pleasantly rich neighborhood much like the one in Pasadena selected by Evelyn and Clem Pettit. Suddenly, he made an abrupt turn into a gate-enclosed cul-de-sac behind the San Marino police station, where uniformed, armed officers were waiting. The three cars followed Beardsley into the lot; with the full length of his car, Beardsley blocked the only exit. "Hey, get out of the way," yelled one of the drivers, "I'm coming through."

"I'm not getting out of the way," Beardsley retorted, "and you're not coming through." As his pursuers were escorted inside the station to the office of the San Marino police chief, Beardsley went on to his dinner engagement.

On Saturday morning, Beardsley learned that his stalkers were members of the Los Angeles Police Department's Intelligence Squad, and he publicly demanded an explanation from Chief Parker. "He's talking about something of which I have no personal knowledge," Parker said. "I have nothing to say until I do some more checking." Parker didn't mentioned the subject again, but the pursuers never bothered Beardsley, his partners, or Scott again.

Scott's next court date was the Wolper Printing Company's debtor's judgment hearing on April 4. Mindful of Judge Lillie's stipulation to Evelyn's trustee, Wolper now refused to accept the funds it had attached from the joint account until legally convinced that the money rightfully belonged to Scott and not to his missing wife. Trent Andersen, Wolper's attorney, planned to question Scott extensively about his own separate assets.

That court appearance was a humiliating experience for Scott, with cameramen swarming around him as he headed toward the examination room. "I'm getting fed up with this," Scott shouted angrily at no one in particular as he slapped his hat up in front of his face. "Beat it, goddamn it."

"Take it easy," Beardsley said, taking Scott by the arm to lead him quickly through the crowd. To the photographers, he tossed off a conciliatory smile. "If I were as good-looking as he is, I sure wouldn't cover my face." But Scott, still fuming as he sat at the counsel table, kept his hat at his fingertips and hid behind it every time he saw a camera pointed in his direction.

Police, DA investigators, and Hallam Mathews, as the representative of Evelyn's newly named trustee, waited eagerly in the hearing room in anticipation of Scott's testimony, but they were cheated once again. Scott remained silent throughout the hearing as Beardsley tried to negotiate a settlement by turning over ownership of the 9,975 remaining copies of *How to Fascinate Men* to Wolper for resale. Andersen turned down Beardsley's compromise, pointing out that the copyright was held in the name of one Charles Contreras, at least nominally the book's author, who would have to approve such a deal. Since Scott now denied his authorship, Beardsley, defeated in his efforts, motioned successfully for a continuance until May 7.

As Scott left the examination room, he was handed two envelopes

122

by Sergeant Zander. The first one held a letter from Chief Parker informing Scott that leaving "the Los Angeles area contrary to this request will be considered flight to avoid prosecution." The other envelope held a grand jury summons for April 24. But the criminal charges Scott would face were forgery and grand theft, not murder, to Alexander's great disappointment. Despite Alexander's vigorous argument, Roll had refused to push for a murder indictment. Instead, the district attorney had promised that the grand jurors would hear *all* of the evidence and a second phase of the proceedings on "other" charges would be called then if warranted by supporting evidence.

Beardsley, a civil attorney, talked the subpoena over with Scott, and he suggested that Scott hire Frank Belcher, a criminal attorney, to handle those proceedings. Although he promised to continue representing Scott in his civil litigation, Beardsley quietly notified Parker and Roll that he would be turning Scott over to Belcher as soon as arrangements could be made.

Parker's warning aside, Scott immediately dropped out of sight again. Rumors placed him in San Francisco, where chief deputy Brown happened to be vacationing for a few days, and then in Reno. Hufstedler denied that gossip on his client's behalf and insisted he could produce Scott instantly "if it was important enough."

Then, six days after Scott's court appearance, Chief Parker finally dropped the first public hint that authorities were after more than a just a fraud conviction. Parker's revelation in an April 10 newspaper interview with Don Shannon, the *Los Angeles Times'* Washington, D.C. bureau chief, came as the chief was attending a conference in the capital. "This hasn't been published yet," the chief announced, delivering a knock-out blow to the prized, still-secret evidence Adolph Alexander had so scrupulously saved, "but we found her plate and her reading glasses behind a wall near the incinerator at the Scott house. I find it difficult to believe that a society woman would leave her home without her dental plate. This looks like a murder we'll have to try without a body."

On Sunday afternoon, two days before the start of his grand jury hearing, Scott stopped in at a west Los Angeles used-car lot. He asked Tom Nobles, a salesman for the Walker Motor Company, about buying a car—immediately—for cash. Nobles explained that no sales were made on Sundays, but he gave Scott his card anyway and suggested that Scott call him later in the week. Scott telephoned Nobles at home that night and made an appointment for 7:30 A.M. the next morning, Monday, April 23, half an hour before the lot opened for business.

Nobles arrived five minutes early to find Scott already waiting for him. As they walked around the lot, Nobles pointing out the features of different models, Scott explained to the salesman that he needed a "high-speed" car, one that could travel at 80 miles an hour or more. He had an urgent job, Scott went on, and since he expected to be away for five or six weeks, he had to have a car that was in top mechanical form.

By 9 A.M., Scott was ready to put fifty dollars in cash down on a 1953 four-door green Ford sedan, license number JLJ359. The brake lining, the gasoline lines, and the ventilators were to be checked thoroughly by a mechanic, Scott stipulated, before he would pay the rest of the $950 purchase cost. Then, with a yardstick, Scott measured the car's trunk and wrote its dimensions down in a small black notebook he tucked into his coat pocket. Before he took delivery of his new car, however, Scott had a date to keep with his attorneys and half a dozen investigators.

From papers found in his personal files during the house search, detectives had learned that Scott regularly used two aliases, Robert McDonald, the surname of his mother's family, and H. Hunt. Further checking turned up no criminal records for either alias, but detectives did find a safety-deposit box listed in the name of a Robert McDonald, opened August 1, 1955, at the First National Bank branch in Beverly Hills. Mire studied McDonald's handwriting on the bank's documents and pronounced it a perfect match to Scott's own handwriting. Through his attorneys, Scott acknowledged that the safe-deposit box did, in fact, belong to him and, at Roll's request, he agreed to open it on that Monday afternoon, April 23, 1956, for investigators, who were still hoping to find a clue to his wife's whereabouts or some of the $50,000-plus in cash that they didn't find in Evelyn's own bank box.

This appearance was Scott's first since he had been served with his grand jury subpoena, and he appeared for the late afternoon appointment looking tanned and relaxed. He had not visited the box since late February, official records showed, eight days after he was so exhaustively questioned by the district attorney's investigators. It was only his fifth visit since the box had been rented to him. Inside were five wristwatches, a handwritten (and unrelated) letter to Scott, and a scrap of paper with a few meaningless notations on it. Scott was asked if he had other bank boxes—under his own or an assumed name—but Beardsley refused to allow his client to answer.

With his official business concluded, Scott stopped back by the car lot. Satisfied with the condition of the green Ford, Scott paid off the $900 balance due with crisp one-hundred-dollar bills and signed the registration papers without hesitation as R. E. Scott. Since Scott had told Nobles that he had no local home address, Nobles inserted his own on the documents. Scott objected to a state-required sales sticker that was to be taped onto the Ford's windshield until Nobles told him that it was required by law. Scott acquiesced without further argument but he asked that the sticker be applied "lightly." Nobles complied.

When the salesman got home that night, he saw a picture of the man he knew as R. E. Scott staring out at him from page one of his evening newspaper. In astonishment, Nobles telephoned a friend who just happened to work as a detective for the Los Angeles Police Department.

Alexander, assisted by a young deputy named Arthur Alarcon, called twenty-two witnesses to testify in the four-day-long closed-door grand jury proceedings, some of whom had already testified a month earlier at the estate proceedings. One of the first was Evelyn's attorney, who Alexander hoped would reveal the contents of Evelyn's will. But, as much as Boyle wanted to aid the investigation, he reluctantly refused to make the document available as a right of attorney-client privilege.

Alexander had subpoenaed Marianne too, and on the morning of her testimony, Ewing stopped by Marianne's apartment to pick her up. With soothing reassurance, he told her he had something for her, and from a coat pocket, Ewing took out a soft cloth pouch and handed it to Marianne. Inside were the jewels Evelyn had treasured, love gifts from Clem Pettit: a sterling silver chain set with diamonds, earrings set with aquamarine gemstones, a brooch dusted with a hundred diamonds, a gold bracelet set across its width with pearls and semiprecious stones, two ropes of pearls, one with earrings to match. The jewelry, plus a fiberglass makeup kit, were now Ewing's gifts to her. He drove Marianne to the grand jury hearing in Evelyn's car.

Marianne was questioned by Art Alarcon, a twenty-nine-year-old graduate of the University of Southern California's School of Law. He had a quiet, intellectual style that could be mistaken for shyness, and it seemed to reach Marianne; she tried to answer as many of his questions as she felt she could. But when the harder, more personal questions came, Marianne read her answers from a sheet of paper provided by Beardsley that called the matter in question "not relevant, material, or germane."

This answer was the one Marianne gave when Alarcon asked if Scott had ever discussed marriage with her. But after conferring with Beardsley during the lunch recess, Marianne asked the court for permission to "clarify" her answer. "I might have mentioned it to parties that after Mr. Scott's affairs were straightened out," she said, "that we might get together."

She added a slight elaboration: "I feel that I have had nothing to do with Mrs. Scott's disappearance, and that my relations with Mr. Scott have nothing to do with Mrs. Scott's disappearance, because I didn't know him at that time."

As Marianne testified, Scott listened quietly at the counsel table. When his own turn came a day later on April 25, Scott, through Beardsley, declined to take the stand. His refusal to testify, Beardsley

126

told the court, was based on constitutional grounds that would remain in effect at least until Frank Belcher, Scott's new criminal attorney, returned from a Mexico City vacation to represent Scott in any criminal action that might be taken.

Then, as Scott watched without expression, only his wrist twisting as he twirled his eyeglasses in midair, Tom Nobles was called to the stand as the day's final witness for his testimony about the "high-speed" automobile that Scott had purchased just two days earlier for his quick trip out of town. "He said it was an emergency trip," Nobles said, "and he was very fussy about the mechanical condition of the car."

The courtroom emptied rapidly after the salesman's testimony, and Alarcon spotted *Times* reporter Gene Blake outside in the hallway. "Have they pinched him yet?" Alarcon asked.

Surprised, Blake shook his head no. But as the newsman watched a few seconds later, Scott was arrested and handcuffed by police sergeants Zander and Hertel just outside the grand jury chambers on suspicion of forgery and grand theft. Scott's secret car purchase was all the evidence law-enforcement officials needed to convince themselves that the impassive businessman might be planning another disappearing act: his own.

□ **21**

Zander and Hertel were to take Scott to the west-side police station for booking and fingerprinting, but first they stopped at Truman's, a west Los Angeles restaurant, for a leisurely dinner with Scott. In time, the conversation turned to the court case.

"You know, if Throsby's ever appointed trustee," Zander said, coolly testing Scott's self-control, "I suppose he'll move into the house up on Bentley."

"He'll *never* move in that—he'll never live in *my* house," Scott said,

127

visibly shaken. "You boys have been doing a lot of investigating about me, but when you see my wife's will, you'll see that I couldn't possibly be behind all this." Uncharacteristically agitated, Scott couldn't seem to stop himself. "You'll change your course all right. You'd be wise to dig a little deeper into that so-called brother of hers—he's behind this whole thing."

"Is that right?" Zander said. "Well, if you don't mind, Mr. Scott," he said, signaling for their check, "we have a nice quiet spot in mind where we can talk all these things over." As they left the restaurant, however, Zander made a small detour to a nearby store where he bought a handful of the cheapest and smelliest cigars he could find.

It was twilight by now, and as Hertel drove the unmarked police car along Mulholland Drive, the three men inside could see lights starting to glow in the city below them. Zander had seen other suspects who thought they were just as slick as Scott thought he was, all of them with that same exaggerated self-confidence and ego. His fifteen years on the force had taught Zander to give these types a chance to show just how damn much smarter they are than everyone else, and Scott, a meticulous man who didn't drink or smoke, was about to get his opportunity.

Hertel pulled up at a county fire station on a secluded section of Mulholland, just east of Beverly Glen Boulevard, where the roadway was no longer paved. "I hear you've been up on Mulholland Drive quite a bit," Zander said, making casual conversation as they walked inside to an airless upstairs room that off-duty firemen used as a bedroom.

"I think you've heard something incorrectly," Scott said, looking around doubtfully at the spartan furnishings, a couple of straight-backed chairs, and several iron-framed beds. "I've only been up in this area once or twice."

Hertel closed the door. "Have a seat," Zander said to Scott, selecting one of the chairs for himself as Hertel sat down in the other one. Stiffly, Scott seated himself on one of the thin bed matresses. "My God," he said, "I don't know how anybody could sleep on one of these things." But Scott adjusted himself in a position of relative comfort and faced the two detectives. Zander lit a cigar and handed it to Hertel. He lit a second one for himself. "Smoke?" he said, offering one to Scott, who declined it disdainfully.

Zander puffed on his cigar and stared at Scott. Tonight, Zander thought, might be the only chance we ever get alone with this guy, and we'd better make the most of it. "Mr. Scott," he said, blowing a cloud of smoke over Scott's head, "we've done some checking on some of the statements you've made during your various conversations with investigators, and frankly, we haven't been able to satisfy ourselves on several points so far." The end of his cigar glowed as Zander inhaled. "Can you, for example, tell me why you thought it was necessary to take out a safety-deposit box under an assumed name?"

Scott readjusted himself on the bed, out of the pathway of Zander's cigar smoke. "I find that privacy is very necessary for me," he said, "in order that I can carry on my business."

"I see." Zander sent another stream of cigar smoke in Scott's general direction. "Just what kind of business are you in?"

"I am in engaged in the merging of various corporations."

"Go on."

"Well, I study the history of these companies, and I try to select certain smaller organizations I think I can merge into a larger corporation."

Zander looked at Scott expectantly. The ashes from Hertel's cigar fell near Scott's shoes but only Scott appeared to notice. Neither detective said a word.

Finally, Scott elaborated on his answer just to break the silence. "In the course of what I do, I have to find out certain things about these companies that they may not want me to know, which is why I need to use a false name from time to time."

"What kind of information is it that you collect?" Hertel asked. He snubbed out his cigar on the cement floor and lit another one.

"Different things from different sources," Scott said, rearranging himself again.

"Can you be more specific, please?"

"No, I really can't," Scott said, coughing as he fanned the smoke away from his face. "This type of stuff is highly competitive, and if word gets out that I'm interested in such a transaction, my competitors immediately take steps to make it impossible for me to complete the transactions."

"Who are your competitors?"

"I can't tell you that. They might make it even harder for me to do my business if you start asking them a lot of questions."

Zander was on his second cigar now too. "I assume you make a profit on these transactions—you actually put up any of the money yourself?"

Scott moved down the bed several feet farther away from the detectives. "No, I don't actually invest myself."

"Do you buy anything or sell anything during the course of this transaction?"

"Look," Scott said irritably, "it's best explained like this. I just *mesh* "—Scott folded his long, manicured fingers together into a single two-handed fist—"these various organizations together."

Zander pretended to examine his cigar, rolling it between his fingers for a moment before he replaced it in his mouth. "I guess I'm not as smart as you are, Mr. Scott, because I still don't understand just what it is you claim to do. You don't invest, buy, sell, or pay for anything in these transactions—how the hell do you make money?"

"Well, if I explained to you how this really operates," Scott said with a long rasping cough, "you'd quit your job tomorrow and go out and do the same thing. You'd be making just as much money as I do."

"Making as much money as you do?" Zander pulled his cigar out of his mouth in mock surprise. "Well, as far as I can tell, your *wife* paid for every goddamn thing you've got."

"That's not true," Scott said testily. "I put a lot of capital into both of those properties."

"Oh, is that right?" Zander said. "Your name doesn't appear on the title papers to the house or the apartment building."

"That's because I put all of my assets in my wife's name."

Zander puffed. "Why?"

"I told you, because of the business I'm in." Scott moved restlessly on the iron-framed bed. "I didn't want to be in a position where if I got sued by anybody, they could take away all my assets."

"All this money you made," Hertel interjected, "how come you never filed your tax returns? You just—forget—to take care of that little piece of business for the last ten years?"

"I won't discuss my tax returns with you at this time."

Zander and Hertel were on their third cigars apiece now; the tight little room's air was ribboned with hazy bands of smoke. Zander and Hertel had been questioning Scott for half an hour, and it was almost 10:30 P.M.

"I understand you think you're a financial expert, Mr. Scott," Hertel continued. "Do you have any other clients besides your wife?"

"Yes, I do."

"Who?"

"That's none of your damn business," Scott snapped.

Fifteen miles away at the main police station, a frantic Beardsley was threatening to file a kidnapping complaint against Zander and Hertel. By 7:15 that evening, the lawyer had arranged Scott's bail through Judge Herbert V. Walker, but no one seemed to know where Scott was now. Beardsley convinced the judge to put in a personal call to Brown, who promised to try and locate Scott. Although Brown knew where Zander and Hertel had taken Scott, he wanted to give his investigators as much time as possible.

As Beardsley waited, he announced to the roomful of reporters waiting with him that he had information that Evelyn might be living in a small Mexican town, and from the police station, he placed a long distance call to the Del Rio Hotel in Sonora, Mexico. When the manager gave a physical description of a woman he knew as "Mrs. King" to Beardsley, the attorney, beaming with confidence, promised to send Hufstedler down immediately to interview "Mrs. King" personally.

"You," Zander was saying now, pulling on his fifth cigar, "told us that you think your wife is a lesbian, a drunk, and that she is mentally unbalanced. If all that's true, obviously it would have some real bearing upon her disappearance. The only trouble is, Mr. Scott, that so far, we've been unable to corroborate a single word you've said with the word of people who've known her for twenty or thirty years. Now, possibly I misunderstood you—can you tell me what your interpretation of the word 'lesbian' is?"

"Well, I don't know what you take it to mean, but I understand it to be the situation when two women have an unnatural affection for each other." Scott was concentrating on the questions and trying to ignore the cigar smoke.

131

"And what makes you think this was the case with Mrs. Scott?"

"There are several instances of it," Scott said. "When we first met, Evelyn had a secretary, or at least she said she was her secretary, but that seemed very, very strange to me because Evelyn had no more need for a secretary than the man in the moon. Yet she had this woman living with her and she spent a great deal of time in her company. As a matter of fact, shortly after we were married, I saw to it that she got rid of her."

Scott brushed the smoky air away from his face. "Another indication to me was her relationship with a woman with whom she has been associated for many years. This woman lives back in New York and she still writes to her practically every week—I think that is extremely strange and certainly constitutes an unusual relationship."

"Anything else?" Zander started on his next cigar. So did Hertel. The air was so thick that the detectives were coughing now too.

"Yes, there was this other incident in Chicago. We were staying at the Drake Hotel and she became very friendly with the woman who answered the telephone when you called downstairs for room service. I don't remember what her name was, but anyway, they would walk together quite often, and as a matter of fact she gave this woman some gifts and even went to her home one night for dinner. And at dinner, she spent a considerable amount of time talking to the head waiter—he was a Greek—I don't know that there was necessarily anything wrong with it but it just seems very unusual to me."

Hertel picked up the questioning. "You know, none of your wife's friends and acquaintances ever remember seeing Mrs. Scott take more than one or two drinks at the most. How come you're the only one who think she's an alcoholic?"

"Well, naturally they would tell you that because they're all a bunch of drunkards themselves."

"What indicated to you that your wife was mentally ill?"

"We had some artificial flowers that had been given to her and she said, 'I wish you'd get rid of these things, Ewing, they're starting to wilt.'" Scott cleared his throat. "I knew right then that something was wrong and that she was going to require some kind of treatment for this condition."

"That's the only thing that led you to believe that your wife was crazy?"

"No, there was another incident when I came down to the kitchen one morning. She said, 'Did you ever notice between ten minutes to eight and five minutes to eight there are only four minutes?'"

"So what? What significance did you think that incident had?" Hertel asked. "You don't think that maybe she was joking?"

"No, she wasn't joking!" Scott nearly shouted. "Don't you think that is extremely strange behavior? It certainly seems damn unusual to me." He added, almost defensively: "I was very worried about her then."

"You were so worried," Zander interrupted, his own voice getting louder and louder, "You were so worried that when she disappeared for a day, for two days, for a week, for a month, for almost a whole goddamn year, you did *nothing,* not one damn thing, to try and find her? You didn't even *mention* it to anyone."

"I'm telling the truth!" Scott shouted at Zander. "I had an interest in those properties, that it was my money, my money—"

"Nothing you say is true," Zander shouted. "Not a goddamn word you say is true."

Suddenly the door opened. "Hey, are you Zander?" asked a man in a fireman's uniform. "There's a telephone call for you downstairs—it's Thad Brown and he says it's important."

Zander looked at Scott, who was breathing in the cool, clean air from the wide-open door with an ugly, victorious smile. Zander's opportunity—his war of nerves and cigar smoke—was lost.

□ **22**

At 11:36 P.M., Zander and Hertel finally pulled up to the west Los Angeles police station. Hertel talked to waiting reporters as Scott, his face hidden behind his hat, was led inside by Zander for booking.

"We were waiting for a witness," Hertel told the newsmen, "who we thought might be able to identify Scott," but Hertel refused to say whether that "mystery" witness was ever found.

As he was fingerprinted, Scott concentrated on keeping his hat positioned over his features, silently resenting the photographers casually snapping pictures of this humiliating ordeal. So intent was Scott's fixation on his hat that his fingerprints turned out to be unreadable, and he had to submit to the whole mortifying experience again. This time, however, the fingerprinting was conducted in a basement room out of camera range. Then Scott was turned over to Beardsley and George Kliman, an agent for the Glasser Brothers Pioneer Bail Bondsmen. Although Alexander had requested a minimum bond of $50,000, Judge Walker had set Scott's bail at at $5,000. Scott posted the $5,000—the $500 cash premium was paid by Beardsley—and was released.

On Friday, April 27, Scott arrived punctually at 9 A.M. for the grand jury's fourth session. As was becoming his custom, Scott walked the length of the corridor between the elevator to the hearing room with his hat over his face to avoid the cameramen jostling around him for a clear shot. But he didn't realize that one newsreel photographer, NBC's Gene Barnes, was waiting for him near the hearing-room door, and Scott dropped his hat away from his face as he rounded the corner toward it. When he spotted Barnes, up went the hat again, and Scott breezed by the cameraman with a low, victorious chuckle. But Barnes got his picture, and arguably a better one, too, when Scott walked straight into the hearing room's doorjamb with an embarrassingly loud thud.

Scott remained in the grand jury chamber for only a few minutes, just long enough to decline again to speak before the panel. This time, his refusal was based upon a little-used section of the Penal Code stating that a person under investigation is not considered a competent witness unless he volunteers to testify. For this civil proceeding, Scott was represented by Beardsley; Hufstedler was in Sonora Mexico, interviewing "Mrs. King," and Belcher was still on vacation.

But Scott, or rather his attorney, did find time to volunteer to reporters that an unflattering news story in the morning papers, which recounted Scott's botched experiment with his chemical hair restorer, was false. According to the *Los Angeles Times*, none of the five bald men who had used Scott's concoction had yet to receive the cash reward Scott promised. Beardsley's vociferous denials aside, however, the Coy Watson Photo Studio confirmed that the "before" and "after" pictures Scott had ordered were waiting to be picked up. And the studio, which had Scott's business card listing his address at the Jonathan Club in their records, was still hoping to be paid for its work.

Scott returned to court late that afternoon for the grand jury's verdict, and the news he heard wasn't good. He was indicted on thirteen charges of fraud—four counts of grand theft and nine counts of forgery. The grand-theft charges were based on four transactions he made: the transfer, on June 29, 1955, of $3,255 from Evelyn's checking account to the joint account he had opened, and his use of those joint-account funds (all of the deposits were Evelyn's separately held funds) to pay $1,141.29 for his canceled West Indies cruise, $503.75 for the traveler's checks he purchased for the trip, and $441.62 in dues to the Jonathan Club. The nine forgery counts centered on Evelyn's questioned signatures on nine documents: the two bank records Scott presented to open the joint account and to enter his wife's safety-deposit box, and seven of the traveler's checks purchased by Evelyn that bore traced countersignatures.

After the indictment, Alexander again requested that bond be set at $50,000. From the testimony already heard, Alexander pointed out, it could be "inferred" that Evelyn "has been done away with," but nevertheless Judge Walker set Scott's bail at $25,000. Scott was ordered to appear on Tuesday, May 3, for arraignment and for the start of Roll's promised "second phase" of the grand jury's hearing, which Alexander hoped now would lead to Scott's indictment for murder. He was taken from the courtroom in handcuffs to the Los Angeles County Jail and booked.

Within two hours, Scott was again free. In an arrangement negotiated by his attorneys, Scott was released into the custody of bail bond agent George Kliman. Kliman was to keep Scott under personal surveillance until the next morning, when Scott was due to turn over cash collateral to the bail-bond firm. Kliman did stay close to Scott:

135

He ate dinner with Scott and Marianne at a west side restaurant, and rode along as Scott dropped off Marianne at her Santa Monica apartment. Scott and Kliman drove directly to 217 North Bentley Avenue, where they spent the night in separate bedrooms.

In the morning, Kliman was under instructions to leave Scott alone in the house for fifteen minutes, and he did, locked alone in the garage by Scott. They left the house together then, in plenty of time to make Scott's 9 A.M. appointment at the Glasser Brothers' downtown office. With credit for the $5,000 already posted, Beardsley watched as Scott counted out another $17,500 in hundred-dollar bills—17 piles of ten bills each and one pile of five bills—to pay most of the balance due. When a clerk asked Scott to fill out a property statement for the bonding firm's records, Scott replied, "I have no property." Later that day Beardsley paid the balance of the bond, plus the $2,000 premium with his personal check.

Scott's large supply of ready cash—apparently stashed somewhere inside the house on North Bentley Avenue—was a subject of intense interest to both the police department and U. S. tax agents, who strongly suspected that his bankroll was the missing $50,000 or more belonging to Scott's absent wife. An investigator was already checking with safe manufacturers to see if a strongbox had been installed recently at the Scott home. Hallam Mathews, as trustee of Evelyn's estate, was similarly interested in the source of Scott's funds, and he subpoenaed him for an accounting of Evelyn's bank balances. At the same time, Mathews was petitioning in court to have Scott evicted from the house on North Bentley Avenue as soon as possible.

That weekend, Scott promised an exclusive story to TV newsman George Putnam, if—and only if—the interview was conducted in the privacy of Putman's own home. Over his wife's vehement objections, Putnam agreed to Scott's precondition; to appease his wife, however, the newsman laboriously removed all mementos, photographs, and personal trinkets that would identify the den as a room in the Putnams' home. The final touch of camouflage were white sheets tacked across the walls.

Despite the anonymous wall behind him, Scott's solid, conservative manner was considerably enhanced by the television camera as he chatted amiably for a moment with the equally handsome Putnam; the two men could have been just as easily absorbed in private conversation over brandies at the Jonathan Club. But then Scott launched into the exclusive story promised to Putnam, a graphic accounting of his all-night interrogation with the district attorney's investigators, a brawl, Scott charged, with ten men against one. He was beaten with a telephone book, and pinned down—Scott clamped his arms tightly to his sides to demonstrate vividly his helpless position to Putnam—while other detectives punched, slapped, and insulted him. By the time his ordeal was over, Scott said, drawing his story to a magnificent close, his face was bruised, his lip bloodied, and his eye blackened.

On Tuesday night, May 1, Marianne watched that interview on television at her Santa Monica apartment. When it ended, she took a taxi to Chip's, a restaurant several blocks from her apartment where she had promised to meet Ewing for dinner. Their dinner that night was pleasant and, Marianne thought later, unremarkable.

Afterward, the couple walked outside in the lingering warmth of a southern California evening in late spring, and instinctively, Marianne turned toward the restaurant's parking lot where she assumed the red coupe would be parked. But Ewing guided her away from the car lot, and told her soothingly that he would be walking her home instead. At her doorstep, he kissed Marianne good-bye and promised to telephone her after the next day's court appearance.

Marianne, however, was not the only one who had seen Scott's television interview, and as the second phase of the grand jury proceedings opened the next day, the district attorney personally responded with obvious restraint to Scott's allegations.

"[Scott's] charge [of brutality] is false, untrue, and has no basis in fact whatsoever," the district attorney told reporters clustered outside the grand jury hearing room. "It is a figment of Scott's imagination. He is a desperate man grasping for straws and his statement is in direct line with his pattern of lies consistently told [to] law-enforcement authorities since the investigation of the disappearance of Mrs. Scott and her funds began."

Roll went on. "No force or violence has ever been used on or against Mr. Scott, and he knows it. Mr. Scott has been given the opportunity to tell all of his story under oath to the grand jury but he has refused to do so. He will again be given the same opportunity before the grand jury."

Roll kept that promise. Scott was called to the witness stand and offered an opportunity to tell the grand jury under oath about his beating by the district attorney's men, but Scott refused. In fact, he spoke not more than two words during his court appearance: When asked if his name was Leonard Ewing Scott, the silver-haired defendant replied firmly, "It is." Although Scott was accompanied for the first time by Frank Belcher, his criminal attorney, he used the same Penal Code section on voluntary testimony he brought up during the hearing's first phase to decline his chance to speak.

So far, Roll had scrupulously avoided using the word *murder* publicly, but characteristically, the city's chief of police was more blunt. Parker felt strongly that this case closely paralleled another one, that of a San Diego man named E. Drew Clark, who some thirty-three years earlier was convicted of murder even though no trace of his victim was ever found. "At least the court found some evidence pointing to [Clark's] innocence," Parker noted. "So far, in my opinion, there has been an absence of *any* evidence establishing the innocence of Scott."

Marianne waited for Ewing's call that night, May 2, but it never came. She was a bit concerned, but she comforted herself with the thought that he would probably telephone in the morning instead. He didn't call.

Thursday, May 3, chief deputy Brown was the last witness to testify before the grand jury, and he reviewed for the panel "certain discrepancies" in the statements Scott made during his many interview sessions with law-enforcement officials. For example, even though Scott told detectives that he didn't know who his wife's oculist was, Scott had talked to Dr. Chatton about a special style of eyeglass case and listed him as a medical deduction on Evelyn's 1955 tax return. Scott told Brown about his wife's horrible physical and mental condition even though her doctor, who saw Evelyn just six weeks before she vanished, told of her high spirits and robust health. Dr. Schindler, Brown added, also remembered seeing Scott in his waiting room several times and said that Scott had never tried to contact him about Evelyn's condition. And, despite Scott's comments to the contrary, Evelyn's friends of many years told authorities that Evelyn was a lady of unimpeachable habits.

But the state wasn't yet ready to press the murder charge. He asked for a three-week recess to seek court orders against the two reluctant witnesses whose testimony Alexander felt he needed to complete his case: Marianne Beaman and Jim Boyle. Marianne, court papers alleged, had "knowledge of or information concerning crimes of grand theft, forgery, and any other felonies" that Scott may have committed in connection with his wife's disappearance. And, although Boyle had cooperated as much as possible with investigators, the attorney had denied the state's request for Evelyn's previous and current wills unless ordered by the court to do so. Alexander wanted to see those documents turned over to authorities.

So, Marianne—facing those contempt-of-court charges—was especially anxious for Ewing's reassurance, and she tried not to notice that he still hadn't called by week's end. When more than five days had passed without word from him, Marianne told Beardsley about her concern. "He didn't call," she said. "I haven't seen him and I'm terribly worried about him."

On Saturday afternoon, Sergeant Zander called with the first word—news that Marianne found frightening—she'd heard of Ewing since Tuesday night. For four days, the detective told her, Evelyn's red coupe had been sitting on a Santa Monica street not far from Marianne's apartment and the restaurant where she met him for dinner. Even though the police had received several complaints about it, a patrol car hadn't gone out to look at it until that morning, when someone finally mentioned a bullet hole in the windshield to the police.

The investigating officers from the Santa Monica Police Department saw no blood, no gun, and no sign of a struggle. One slug had pierced the windshield on the driver's side, while another bullet had left a two-and-a-half-inch scar in the door metal frame above it. Part of a .45-caliber shell lay on the running board underneath the edge of the door, and the car keys were tucked underneath the floor mat. Despite the odd position of the bullet scars, a crime-lab expert concluded the shots were fired from outside the car. The coupe was impounded and the police ran a routine Department of Motor Vehicles check on it. When the owner showed up as Evelyn T. Scott of 217 North Bentley Avenue, Parker, then Roll, were notified immediately.

Yet, as troubling an insinuation as the abandoned car was, the initial official reaction to it was one of bored disinterest. Scott, after all, had been dropping out of sight routinely since the probe became public news, and local law-enforcement officials chaffed at what they considered to be Scott's melodramatic maneuverings. "We're not particularly interested in looking for him," announced Alexander, who suggested that the shot-up coupe was nothing more than an elaborate hoax. "We would like to find his wife, though."

Still, since Scott had not been seen by authorities after his appearance in court on Wednesday, Zander and Hertel started looking for him. They called at 217 North Bentley Avenue, but Scott didn't answer the door and his new green Ford sedan wasn't in the garage. Neighbors said they hadn't seen Scott around at home in days, and Scott wasn't registered at the Jonathan Club or at any of the major local hotels. The detectives called Beardsley at home, but the attorney said that he didn't expect to see Scott until Monday morning for the resumption of the Wolper case. And Marianne could only tell Zander that she was hoping to hear from Ewing soon.

But Scott failed to meet Beardsley in his office on Monday, May 7, as he had promised, and the lawyer went on to the debtor's hearing alone. "If he is voluntarily away from here, he is in contempt,"

Beardsley told the court. "But if he is unable to be here," the attorney suggested ominously, "if he is not alive or is the victim of foul play, that's another thing." After the hearing ended in a postponement until Tuesday, May 15, Beardsley called Brown to ask if Scott was in official custody again. Brown denied that Scott was being held by police.

Beardsley made the same telephone call to Brown two days later, after Scott ignored a May 9 court order to appear in Hallam Mathew's law office for a deposition about Evelyn's holdings. Tensely, Beardsley waited for half an hour for his client, along with a sheriff's deputy holding yet another subpoena for Scott, which demanded that certain financial records pertaining to Evelyn's assets be turned over for use in the Wolper Printing Company's case against him. "I'm not sure he read the subpoena [for his scheduled appearance in Mathew's office]," Beardsley said tautly, "or that we discussed the date. He had an earlier date, which I assumed he would keep and he did not keep it." But Brown denied again that Scott was in official custody.

To his attorneys, Scott, seemingly confident that he would win the fraud case, had no reason to run away. Beardsley knew that Scott risked losing the $22,500 he posted for his bond, not to mention the probability of a bench warrant issued for his arrest. "I am just afraid," Beardsley said, grimly anticipating the worst, "that he has been knocked off."

But Frank Belcher seemed confident that Scott's absence was only a temporary one. "Mr. Scott has been under investigation for a long time," Belcher said self-assuredly, just a day before Scott's May 15 arraignment, "and it's reasonable to assume he anticipated the indictment. If he was planning to flee, he would have done so by now."

Chief Parker also expected to see Scott reappear in court on May 15, and he speculated that Scott would turn up with some half-baked alibi of having been held prisoner by kidnappers. Yet, the chief did give reluctant credibility to Beardsley's suggestion that foul play might have befallen Scott. The large sum of cash Scott had produced to post his bond, Parker admitted, might have encouraged "some of the gentry of the criminal element surrounding us . . . [to] try to explore his financial potential."

Roll, however, didn't share Parker's "criminal element" theory. "I don't have any idea where he is," the district attorney commented nonchalantly. "I last saw him at the grand jury hearing. But this," Roll said, referring to the bullet-scarred car, "may be another one of those 'fantastic' things Mr. Scott likes to do, like putting two envelopes of sand in a safety-deposit box. . . . It looks like another one of his hoaxes."

When Scott didn't appear for his arraignment, the district attorney pointedly read in court the Penal Code rules on aiding a fugitive:

> "Every person who, after a felony has been committed, harbors, conceals, or aids a principal in such felony, with the intent that said principal may avoid or escape from arrest, trial, conviction, or punishment, having knowledge that such principal has committed such felony or has been charged with such felony or convicted thereof, is an accessory to such felony."

Roll denied he was referring to any particular individuals—such as Scott's attorneys—just to anyone to whom "the shoe fit." He added outside of court: "By this disappearing act [Scott] has apparently avoided taking the stand and testifying under oath in one of our civil courts. It is interesting to note that no missing person's report has been filed with the Los Angeles Police Department."

Belcher's retort to Roll was quick, linking Evelyn's disappearance to her husband's, and the overall "failure" of investigators so far to find out the truth about whatever had really happened to Evelyn.

"I cannot accept the theory that Mr. Scott's absence is voluntary," Belcher said, "there is just too much evidence to the contrary. I hope the authorities will reexamine the entire case. . . . If the answer is found to the disappearance of either of these people, it may well explain the absence of the other."

Nevertheless, as Beardsley had anticipated, Scott's bond was forfeited and a bench warrant with a "no bail" clause was issued for his arrest. A massive manhunt, drawing upon all available police, sheriff, and FBI resources, was launched immediately, twelve days after the last known sighting of Evelyn's elusive husband.

The geography of southern California offered any number of possible routes that Scott conceivably might have taken: The state's transpacific, transcontinental, and international borders are all easily crossed from Los Angeles. Two members of the Sheriff's Fugitive Detail, Sergeant Harlan Trail and Officer Ward Halinen, issued an all-points bulletin to banks, hotels, merchants, and law-enforcement agencies, including INTERPOL, around the country and to the United States' international neighbors, Mexico and Canada, describing Scott in exacting detail:

> He is conservative and fastidious in dress, usually wears a hat, and uses plastic rimmed glasses for reading [the bulletin read]. He will appear to be much younger if his nearly white hair is dyed. He stays in better hotels. Scott does not drink or smoke but does take an excessive amount of cream in his coffee. His attitude toward waiters, parking lot attendants, or others similarly employed, is demanding, and only rarely does he tip. Scott is well-travelled, and has contemplated trips to the West Indies and Central America in recent months. He has remarked to friends on occasion that "one can travel through Montreal, Canada, and on to Europe without a passport." Scott is to be held and Los Angeles will extradite.

Airline, train, bus, and ship passenger lists were searched for some indication of the direction Scott might have taken. Private garages were queried in case Scott's green Ford had been placed into storage. Beardsley denied the claim of a policeman who said he saw Scott in the office building where the attorney's office was located, while Hufstedler, just back from a disappointing, unrewarding interview with the woman in Mexico who really was "Mrs. King," not Evelyn Scott, denied rumors that he had helped Scott flee to the country south of the American border.

The police were flooded with dozens of sightings of Evelyn's handsome husband, and detectives were sent to check out promising reports in Reno, Yosemite National Park, Lake Tahoe—even a sighting in a remote northern California fishing resort—all with no further sign of Scott. Scott was "spotted" in a west side post office line, one well-meaning caller insisted to a police detective, as another officer took a similar report from a citizen who had just "positively identified" Scott as a patient in an east side sanatorium. A handful of el-

143

derly women all claimed to be the missing Mrs. Scott, and each one was dutifully questioned by investigators. None was, in fact, Evelyn.

On May 16, Evelyn's grim one-year anniversary, did not pass unnoticed by law-enforcement officials. Pointing to Evelyn's missing funds, Chief Parker now dismissed any suggestion that Scott might be the victim of foul play. "He's taken it on the lam," Parker charged, "and he's well supplied with hundred-dollar bills stolen from his slaughtered wife."

Scott's twelve-day head start put investigators at a distinct disadvantage. The only clues so far seemed to be practical jokes: one, a toy tin badge stamped with Scott's name on it, was found by a five-year-old boy in the ladies' ready-to-wear lingerie section of a downtown department store. The other was a shiny new luggage tag with Scott's name on it, the same sort of tinny-typed label punched out by arcade machines for a dime, which was found on the lawn of a Long Beach hotel. Although no Scott was listed in the hotel's registry, by coincidence, a Robert McDonald was. But this Robert McDonald turned out to be an Oklahoman in town to attend a family funeral. Not until the early morning hours of Monday, May 21, did investigators get their first real clue.

On an otherwise routine Sunday evening in Bishop, a small mountain town on the eastern rim of California's Sierra Nevada range, the proprietors of the Valley Motel saw a photograph in their May 20 newspaper that looked disturbingly familiar. Lucy Donahue checked the car license number listed in her newspaper with one she'd routinely jotted down for a Robert Scott of San Diego, who'd stayed at the motel two weeks earlier: When Number JLJ359, for a green four-door Ford, matched the number she'd noted in her records, she asked her husband, Harold, to telephone John Preku, the local chief of police, at home.

Within several hours, Preku had pieced together Scott's four-day stopover in Bishop, and he teletyped the information immediately to authorities in Los Angeles. Just hours after he left the chambers of the Los Angeles grand jury on May 2, Scott rolled his car off a thin

144

mountain road sixteen miles south of Bishop. As a tow truck hauled his car to the Ford garage in town, Scott, slightly shaken up, told the tow-truck driver that he must have fallen asleep at the wheel.

The repairs to the steering column and the body work on the front end would take three or four days, Ford mechanic Jim Clark told an impatient Scott. Scott asked Clark to hurry the work as much as possible, since he had an appointment in Los Angeles for which he was already three days late. Clark noticed a pistol in a shoulder holster lying in the trunk as he worked on Scott's car.

When the repairs were completed Saturday morning, May 5, Scott paid the $273 repair bill with three one-hundred-dollar bills and waited long enough to have his car cleaned and polished to his satisfaction. He checked out of the Valley Motel and loaded the trunk with exactly as many suitcases as the compartment would hold. Lucy Donahue saw that the Ford's back end was so crammed full of bags and boxes that Scott's last few additions, a steel briefcase and two heavy topcoats, wouldn't fit inside it. She watched as Scott slipped the briefcase underneath the two coats on the back seat. Photographs and an examination of Robert Scott's registration card by Donn Mire confirmed his identity as the fugitive investor from Los Angeles.

The news sorely disappointed Beardsley, who, like Hufstedler, had grown somewhat fond of his distinguished-looking, articulate client. As Scott's sojourn in Bishop unfolded, the two lawyers were appearing on Scott's behalf to block the dispersion of Evelyn's assets until Scott's appeal was settled. Ironically, the court ruled in Scott's favor, but Beardsley only had a few brief words for the reporters who brought him the news of Scott's sighting.

"Every man has a breaking point," Beardsley said. "I attach no significance whatsoever to the fact that he was seen in Bishop."

Belcher was more direct. "Assuming this information is correct," he said, "it certainly disposes of any foul-play theory that I was worried about. I don't have any idea where he was going—it's a complete mystery to me."

Alexander was among the first notified of Scott's trail to the northeast, and he moved quickly to try to close off Scott's routes of escape. He bore no grudge against Parker for what amounted to sabotage of

145

his prized evidence against Scott. But more than anything else, Alexander wanted to get Scott in a court room—under oath. All points immediately east and north of Bishop through Nevada and Canada were alerted to watch for Scott, and another 3,500 bulletins with a description and photograph of Scott were rushed to immigration officers along the U.S.–Canadian border. Those bulletins carried an addendum not previously listed:

> [Scott] is being widely sought not only on the [forgery/grand theft] charges but also because the district attorney, grand jury, and courts now have certain facts under consideration which might very likely lead to an early indictment for murder.

Tonopah, Nevada, 115 miles northeast of Bishop, garnered brief headlines as a possible hideout for Scott, with news reports that he had visited the desert city in April. But Nevada authorities searched the sparsely settled desert town in vain.

As the grand jury probe resumed on May 29, Chief Parker called Scott "the most wanted man in the country." Referring to Scott's cache of cash, Parker suggested that the fugitive was probably now being hunted by "the criminal army" as well as law-enforcement officers.

Under court order, Boyle produced copies of Evelyn's income tax returns for the years 1949 to 1954, with a stipulation that they would be used only to help authorities determine how much money Scott may have appropriated from Evelyn's accounts. Boyle argued successfully again, however, that to turn over Evelyn's wills would be a violation of attorney-client ethics.

And, also under court order, Marianne, dressed demurely in a dove-gray dress, at last answered Alarcon's intimate questions about her trips to San Diego with Scott. Among her admissions was that she was in fact the woman who had signed the Kona Kai's room-service checks as "Mrs. L. E. Scott" in December 1955.

After a few days of testimony, the grand jury postponed its examination until Scott was found or until August 28, 1956, two weeks after the expiration of the ninety-day grace period for forfeiture of Scott's $25,000 bond.

Another basement-to-attic search of the Scott residence was made on June 16. Alexander told his investigators this time that they were looking not just for clues to Evelyn's whereabouts but any leads to her husband as well. Crime-lab technicians pulled up several sections of loose flagstone and worked over the entire yard again with a mine detector and an X-ray fluoroscope. Inside the house, detectives found mail addressed to Evelyn, some valueless stock certificates, piles of travel brochures for destinations all over the world, and, in the basement, an elaborate, professional-looking wiretapping apparatus. Although they searched the entire house, investigators located none of Evelyn's financial records. All Scott had left behind were his tuxedo, top hat, and, Alexander noted grimly, the 8-by-10 photograph of Evelyn on his bedroom dresser.

Over the summer months that followed, Alexander called periodic meetings for the police, DA, sheriff, and FBI investigators who were trying to track down Scott, and together, they reviewed any bits of new information about Evelyn's fugitive husband. Sergeant Zander reported a couple of interesting, although largely speculative, leads that he had turned up, including Scott's tenuous connection to Mimi Boomhower, the woman who vanished abruptly one afternoon from her Bel Air mansion, but Scott's relationship with her couldn't be established beyond a casual social friendship.

More interesting, however, was an interview Zander conducted with the heir to a tuna-cannery fortune in San Diego, who claimed that his mother had dated Scott many years before his marriage to Evelyn. Their relationship ended stormily, however, said the son, with his mother's furious accusation that Scott was trying to poison her for her money. With the woman already deceased of natural causes, Zander had no choice but to drop that intriguing tidbit unanswered.

And Zander talked to Vera Landry, Evelyn's maid at the time of her marriage to Scott, who provided the explanation for the wiretapping apparatus in the Scotts' basement. Although she said she'd never actually seen the device, Vera repeated Scott's never-fulfilled orders to her to watch Evelyn's mail and listen in to her telephone calls.

By late summer, however, Alexander was forced to put the search for Scott lower on his list of priorities. Ernie Roll was suddenly taken ill, and Alexander was asked to assume his duties temporarily. Leavy, knowing that Alexander had a burning desire to try Scott, reassured his friend that Scott was bound to show up again, just as soon as he ran out of money and tried to put the make on his next unlucky target.

On September 27, 1956, Alexander and his investigators got news of the first sighting of Scott since his May soujourn in Bishop. Canadian immigration officials notified California authorities that Scott's car was among those automobiles listed in a routine check of overstayed vehicles. An R. E. Scott, driving a green Ford, license No. JLJ359, had crossed into Canada on the Ontario border at Port Huron, Michigan, on a thirty-day visitor's permit. Scott's border crossing on May 14 came a day before the warrant for his arrest was issued, a day before the search for him had even started.

□ **24**

While the hunt for Scott continued, Alexander assigned Art Alarcon and another young deputy named Lewis Watnick the task of researching "no body" murder cases and suggested that they start their work with a visit to Leavy. From Leavy's own research into circumstantial evidence cases, Leavy knew the cases that had set the legal precedents for "no body" murder convictions, based on proof sufficient to preclude every reasonable theory of the defendant's innocence.

In *People* v. *Alviso* for example, the earliest circumstantial evidence murder case on record in California, José Alviso was convicted of shooting to death John Ruhland and burning his body beyond recognition in 1880. A man with Alviso at the time described Ruhland's murder and the burning of his body to a woman friend. The court wrote:

It is very seldom that a conviction occurs without positive proof of [the death of the alleged victim], either by eyewitnesses of the homicide, or the subsequent discovery of the body; and while the general rule is clearly laid down, yet the authorities concede that there may be exceptions . . . instances of the human body being disposed of by fire, or boiled in potash, or dissolved in acids, rendering it impossible that it should ever be produced. . . . It is clear that in such cases the *corpus delicti* may be proved circumstantially or inferentially.

A similar question was faced by the court in 1925, in *People* v. *Clark,* the San Diego case that Chief Parker had compared with the Scott case. Although the body of the victim, George Schick, was never found, the defendant, E. Drew Clark, was later seen with some of Schick's possessions, including the victim's car and several items of jewelry. A witness also testified that Clark had confessed to committing Schick's murder. Clark appealed his conviction and contended that the prosecution was required to produce proof of the victim's death by producing his body. On this question of direct evidence of the corpus delicti, the court stated:

To require direct proof of the killing or the production of the body of the alleged victim in all cases of homicide would be manifestly unreasonable, and lead to absurdity and injustice; and it is believed that it is now clearly established by the authorities that the fact of death as well as the guilt of the defendant may be legally inferred from such strong and unequivocal circumstances as produce conviction to a moral certainty. . . . The strict rule contended for by [the] defendant would operate completely to shield a criminal from punishment for the most atrocious crime, and afford him absolute immunity if he were cunning enough to consume or destroy the body of his victim by fire or some chemical agency, or completely hide it away or otherwise destroy its identity, although the proof of his guilt might be of the most clear and convincing kind, and remove all possible doubt in the premises. . . .

Where, as here, the entire circumstances point with one accord to the death of the person alleged to have been murdered, the finding of fragments of a human body or of metallic articles which are positively identified as part of the body of the alleged victim, or as articles worn by him, will be sufficient, if believed by the jury, to establish the fact of death, when this is the best evidence that can be obtained under the circumstances. No universal and unvariable rule can be laid down in regard to the proof of *corpus delicti*. Each case depends upon its own peculiar circumstances. The body of the crime may be proved by the best evidence which is capable of being adduced, if it is sufficient for the purpose. Such an amount of accompanying or relative facts, whether direct or circumstantial, must be produced as establish the fact beyond every other reasonable hypothesis.

Most recent was the case of *People* v. *Cullen*. Raymond Cullen appealed his conviction for the murder of his wife and her stepfather on the grounds that the corpus delicti of murder could not be shown by circumstantial evidence alone. Cullen, a sixty-three-year-old exconvict, told a number of conflicting stories about the whereabouts of his victims, but was later quoted by a witness as saying he paid $125 to a truck driver to remove the bodies. His conviction was affirmed with a 1951 decision in which the court, citing previous cases, wrote:

> It is not necessary in order to support the conviction that the bodies actually be found. In *People* v. *Wilkins*, it was said that to require direct proof of the corpus delicti would be most unreasonable; that the worst crimes are naturally committed at chosen times, in darkness and secrecy; that human tribunal must act upon such indications as the circumstances admit; that more often than not the attendant and surrounding facts remove all mystery and supply that degree of certainty men are daily accustomed to regard as sufficient in the most important concerns of life.

Yet, Leavy warned the deputies, in each of these and other similar "no body" cases, something more telling than purely circumstantial evidence existed—physical evidence of death, an eyewitness account of the murder, or a confession to another party. Alarcon and Watnick would need something more, Leavy pointed out: a precedent holding that circumstantial evidence alone was sufficient to prove death by criminal means.

The deputies found the authority they needed in recent foreign cases upheld under the laws of England; *The King* v. *Horry* (1952) and *Regina* v. *Onufrejczyk* (1955). Both cases were considered landmark rulings: Although the opinions in each case did not declare any new principles in the laws with respect to murder, they did apply settled principles of circumstantial evidence to unprecedented facts.

In *The King* v. *Horry,* a New Zealand case, the defendant, Horry, was charged with the murder of his new wife, Eileen, for her small fortune. Horry sent letters to Eileen's parents claiming that their daughter had been traveling on a ship that had sunk, a ship, they later learned, that had never existed. Although no direct evidence of her murder was found, the court stated that "other facts so incriminating and so incapable of any reasonable explanation [were] incompatible with any hypothesis other than murder."

In the second case, *Regina* v. *Onufrejczyk,* the defendant, Onufrejczyk, was convicted of murdering his business partner, and he appealed on indirect evidence. The appellate court stated:

> This court is of opinion that there was evidence upon which the jury could infer that [the victim] was dead, and, if he was dead, the circumstances of the case point to the fact that his death was not a natural death. Then, if that established, as it does, the corpus delicti, the evidence was such that the jury were entitled to find that appellant murdered his partner.

On his own, Alarcon researched international extradition laws, now that Scott was known to have crossed the Canadian border. By chance, he discovered a quirk in an 1889 U.S.–Canadian treaty, which held that if Scott was extradited to the United States *only* on grand theft and forgery charges, then he would have to be returned to Canada before he could be tried on any other charge, including murder. So, a week after the discovery of Scott's borderjump, the grand jury's investigation suddenly resumed: Alexander wanted to be prepared with a murder indictment against Scott should law enforcement catch up with the fugitive. On October 16, 1956, a secret indictment on one count of murder was added to the thirteen forgery and grand-theft charges already listed against Scott.

Three days later, U.S. attorney Laughlin E. Waters issued a federal complaint charging Scott with "flight to avoid prosecution," a formality that cleared the way for the use of U.S. government resources in the now international manhunt for Scott. In return, the district attorney's office promised that Los Angeles would fight for Scott's extradition and bear the cost of his return to California.

151

* * *

The murder indictment was returned at least in part on the basis of the reports gleaned from Canadian law-enforcement officials of Scott's free-wheeling odyssey across Canada, which thoroughly quashed any lingering doubts that he might be the captive of some nefarious criminal element. After entering the country on May 14, 1956, Scott drove directly to Barrie, the Ontario county seat located on the west end of Lake Simcoe. He spent May 16–31 at the Queen Elizabeth Hotel in Oakville, a city south of Barrie along Lake Ontario.

Scott stayed another six weeks ten miles outside of Barrie, registered as Leonard Spencer at the Crown Motel, where he asked for and received businessman's reduced rates. Scott's days there were solitary ones: He told anyone who asked that he was an accountant finishing a massive financial document for a major U.S. firm and he was not to be disturbed. Scott did mention to several other guests, however, that he was studying Spanish in his room for an upcoming European trip. He seemed to spend much of his time washing and polishing his car.

Most evenings, Scott could be seen walking along the shore of Lake Simcoe, easily identifiable at a distance by the briefcase he carried with him everywhere. Although Scott appeared to have an adequate supply of Canadian currency that he carried in a money clip, he lived frugally, mostly on hot dogs and orange juice he bought from a street-corner vendor. When he did splurge and venture into the hotel's restaurant, Scott never tipped.

In late summer, Scott dallied briefly with a middle-aged schoolteacher who was working weekends as a waitress at a café he patronized. He treated her to dinner once or twice, picked her up from work several times late at night, and promised her a "shared life of luxury" with him if she would only come away with him. Instinctively, she turned Scott down; he was, she thought, "too smooth, too moody, and too mysterious about his past."

Before Scott left Barrie—unaccompanied—he traded in his Ford for another car with Canadian license plates. He left word at the Crown Motel that he was heading for Montreal. Instead, Scott passed the rest of the summer as Lester E. Stewart in Midland and Penetanguishene, resort towns on Ontario's Georgian Bay. In Midland, he struck up a friendship with Bob Cameron, the local chief of police,

152

who never associated this most erudite conversationalist with the "Wanted" poster hanging in his precinct's own office. When Scott left Midland, he traded in his car again.

He went on to Penetanguishene, where he lived for a month at the Brule Hotel in a room overlooking a tributary of Georgian Bay. Scott paid his board promptly in hundred-dollar Canadian notes and told the hotel manager that he was staying in his room so much because he had a major accounting project to complete. When Scott drove away from Penetanguishene, it was in yet another car.

But there Scott's trail faded, as summer yielded to fall. Throughout the autumn, winter, and early spring, investigators in Los Angeles learned nothing more of his Canadian travels. The city's newspapers now only occasionally speculated about the respective whereabouts of Ewing and Evelyn Scott. Ernie Roll died of cancer that fall, and William McKesson was soon named as his successor. Alexander, surprised and bitterly disappointed that he was not even considered as the permanent replacement for Roll, left the district attorney's office for private practice. McKesson, who had little enthusiasm for this bit of unfinished business from his predecessor's regime, put the investigation on hold indefinitely and assigned Art Alarcon to other cases. Even Chief Parker seemed to let the case drop.

Scott's whereabouts might have remained as much of a mystery as those of his wife's for years. Yet Scott, ever confident in his own abilities, couldn't resist the temptation presented by the U.S.–Canadian border, and on April 9, 1957, he crossed back into the United States. Ostensibly, his foray was to buy himself a new car at the cheapest price possible and drive it back to safety in Canada. But, really, it was Scott's own ego that demanded one more too-tempting chance to show his pursuers how very smart he was.

As the Floyd Rice Sales & Service Showroom in downtown Detroit opened on the morning of April 9, salesman Dick Leslie noticed an elegantly groomed, white-haired gentleman loitering out in front, admiring the new 1957 Ford Fairlane 500 parked in the window. The man noticed Leslie watching him and moved on, but an hour later, he was back and introduced himself to the salesman as Lewis Stuart.

Stuart seemed to know quite a bit about cars, Leslie thought, as he

153

answered the kind of detailed questions about the Fairlane's frame construction that only a true enthusiast would think to ask. Without too much hesitation, however, Stuart settled on the four-door model, with an eight-cylinder automatic transmission, an upgraded radio powered to pick up distant stations at night, power steering, and a locking gasoline cap. Stuart asked Leslie to install a special ignition switch underneath the dashboard so that even with the proper key in the ignition, no one else would be able to start the car. Stuart noted each item and its cost in a small black notebook.

Stuart was just as meticulous about the looks of the car. He even went out to the service garage to ask a painter how each color might match if the car ever became involved in an accident. Finally, Stuart chose a solid doeskin tan.

As they talked about the car, Stuart told the salesman that he needed it for a trip to the eastern United States. His wife was divorcing him, Stuart went on, and he had to get his money out of the bank accounts he had there before she could get a court order to freeze his assets. Her detectives were chasing him, and Stuart said his wife already had all of his other money and personal possessions tied up.

After three hours, Leslie finally quoted Stuart a price, $2,575, which included all the little extra items that he had requested. Stuart stood up and announced that he was going to check the prices at other dealerships around town. Leslie, annoyed at the prospect of losing a morning's effort, suggested that Stuart check back to see if he could meet whatever lower price he could find.

Two days later, Stuart called, quoting a price substantially lower than the one quoted by Leslie. The salesman suggested that Stuart take the other deal because he couldn't possibly match it. An hour later, Stuart telephoned him again, outraged. That other dealer couldn't deliver exactly what he'd been promised, and since he didn't like to do business that way, Stuart said he had decided to buy his car from Leslie after all.

For the down payment, Stuart gave Leslie a single hundred-dollar bill. Since he didn't have a driver's license, Stuart asked Leslie for a "small favor." Would Leslie mind driving him from Detroit to Toledo—the other salesman had promised to do it—where he could apply for a license without a birth certificate? Stuart also asked Leslie for an out-of-state address to use to escape paying Michigan's sales tax: Leslie gave him the address of an aunt who lived in Oak Park, Illinois.

It took two two-hour round trips to Toledo before Scott finally got his temporary driver's license. For the Ohio address he needed for the permit, Stuart stopped a moving van and asked the driver for the name and address of the best hotel in town, the Park Lane. On the way back to Detroit, Stuart asked the car salesman to take him to a bank where he could change his hundred-dollar bills into smaller currency that couldn't be traced by his wife's detectives. Unless the serial numbers were known, Leslie assured him, the money couldn't be traced.

With his new Ohio temporary operator's permit in hand on Monday, April 15, Stuart refused to accept delivery of his new Ford until it was rewaxed and repolished to his specifications. Finally, he paid Leslie the balance of the money owed with 25 hundred-dollar bills, and signed the registration papers as Lewis Stuart, currently residing in Oak Park, Illinois.

With 132 miles on his new car that Monday night, he headed north again to Canada. His final challenge was the Detroit-Windsor Tunnel, a strip of highway underneath the Detroit River linking Canada and the United States, and a routine customs check point. He started through the tunnel about dusk.

□ **25**

When he looked inside the brand-new beige Ford, Everett Bale saw a face he knew he'd seen before; the distinctive features were somehow chiseled into his memory. Seventeen years as an immigration officer had taught Bale to trust his gut, and he had a hunch about where he might have seen this face before. Bale needed time to check his instinct, however, and he chose the car's Michigan in-transit stickers, which permitted a new automobile to be driven for thirty days without registration tags, as his excuse to stall the man.

"May I see your driver's license, sir?" Bale asked pleasantly. "Do you own this car?"

"Yes, I do," Scott answered, giving Bale his day-old temporary driver's permit. "I just purchased it a couple of days ago."

"What's your occupation, Mr."—Bale looked at the license—"Stuart?"

"I'm retired now, but I used to be in the construction business. I live off my investments now."

"Where are you going?"

"To Huntsville, Ontario. I'm looking for a cottage for my wife and children."

"Do you have any other identification, sir?" Bale asked.

Stuart handed the officer a social security card in the name of Lewis Stuart. Bale noticed that the card was less than six months old. "I'm sorry, but that's all I have with me," Stuart said apologetically.

"Your identification all seems to be new," Bale said, looking the card over.

"Yes, I've been in England. I think everything I have expired while I was gone," Stuart said, adding good-humoredly, "everything, that is, except me."

"I see." Bale smiled professionally at Stuart's joke.

"Is anything wrong?" Stuart asked anxiously. "I'll take the car right back to Detroit if there is."

"Well, Mr. Stuart," Bale said evenly, "I wouldn't be too concerned if I were you—I think everything's in order here. We just have a little paperwork we have to fill out on every new car that crosses the border. Why don't you just step inside with me for a moment—we'll get everything all straightened out."

"All right," Stuart said, reluctantly yielding to him, "just let me get my glasses out of the trunk."

Inside the permit office, Bale handed Stuart a routine form to fill out, while he checked his hunch. He thought he might find Stuart's face on one of the "Wanted" posters hanging in another room. As Bale started out of the room, Stuart followed him nervously. "You know," Stuart said worriedly, "I'll be happy to take the car back to Detroit if you think there's anything out of order."

"No, please, Mr. Stuart, just take a seat. I'll be back in a moment." Bale waited until Stuart sat down again. Outside the room, Bale asked another officer to keep an eye on Stuart. "Just make sure he stays put," Bale said.

Bale found the all-points bulletin with Stuart's picture on it; the description matched him perfectly, down to the plastic horn-rimmed glasses. He telephoned the Windsor Police Department and returned to the room where Stuart was waiting for him with the completed form.

For a long moment, Bale studied the form Stuart handed him as the man before him fidgeted. He looked up to see a patrol car pulling up outside the checkpoint office through a window over Stuart's shoulder. "I'm sorry, but I can't seem to make out your writing here," Bale said. "Is your name Stuart—or Scott?"

Alarmed, Stuart reached for the form in the officer's hands. Bale held it out of his reach. "Why, my name's Stuart, isn't that what I have written there?"

"Yes, sir, that's what you wrote," Bale answered. "But the name's Scott, isn't it? Leonard Ewing Scott."

Stuart said nothing and slumped back in his chair as the police officers entered the room. Eighteen hours later, on April 16, 1957, Stuart finally admitted to U.S. FBI agents his true identity as the fugitive from Los Angeles and he agreed to be returned to the United States.

□ **26**

In Los Angeles, district attorney McKesson called Art Alarcon at home that Tuesday evening, April 16, 1957. Since Alexander's departure, no one else had been assigned to the Scott case. With Scott's capture, McKesson knew he needed to name a senior prosecutor to take Alexander's place and to work with Alarcon. But police chief Parker had asked to help McKesson make that assignment, however, and until their decision was made, Alarcon was the only logical choice to send to Michigan to escort the fugitive back to California. "Scott was caught last night trying to cross the Canadian border," McKesson told him, "so get your bags packed. You're going to be on the first plane out to Sacramento in the morning."

McKesson's staff worked feverishly all night long to ready the extradition papers that Alarcon would first carry north to California's state capitol for Governor Goodwin "Goody" Knight's signature. As Alarcon headed east a day later to Michigan, where Governor G. Mennen Williams would be offered the documents, the prosecutor hoped to whisk Scott right back to California without a prolonged extradition; if Scott fought his return to California, Alarcon knew that an arduous battle of red tape could drag on for months.

Although Scott had been charged with murder—not a bailable offense under California law—a day after his capture, a federal judge ruled that Scott was entitled to "reasonable bond." Assistant U.S. attorney George Woods, pointing out that Scott had already jumped a bond of $25,000, requested that his bail be set at $100,000.

"That bond is too high," objected Gabriel Cohn, the lawyer Scott had hired to represent him by choosing Cohn's name from a telephone directory.

"Can Mr. Scott make fifty thousand?" asked Judge Theodore Levin.

"No," Cohn said, "that's too high too."

"Well, the bond will be one hundred thousand," Judge Levin ruled.

Since Scott couldn't make bail, he was ordered held in Detroit's Wayne County Jail on the federal charge of unlawful flight to avoid prosecution. But Judge Levin did free $1,500 of the $10,400 in cash found by federal agents in a money belt next to Scott's skin, despite a telegrammed appeal from a Citizen's Bank trustee claiming any of Scott's assets or personal belongings as the property of his missing wife's estate. The money was to be used only to help defray the legal costs of Scott's defense, however. "If I am going to err," Judge Levin commented, "I want to err on the side of protecting a defendant's constitutional rights."

158

*   *   *

Alarcon arrived in Detroit Wednesday afternoon, April 17. His first stop was the Federal Building, where he would meet with assistant U.S. attorney Woods about the government's flight charge against Scott. Alarcon tiredly hoped that their conference would be a brief one; he wanted his first full night's rest since leaving Los Angeles, not to mention a long hot shower and a clean set of clothes. A guard at the entrance gave him directions to Woods' office upstairs. "You won't miss it," the guard said, but Alarcon was too exhausted to ask him what he meant.

Once upstairs, however, Alarcon quickly understood. A huge crowd spilled out of Wood's office and into the hallway; the prosecutor could see the hot white glow of floodlights inside the room. In amazement, Alarcon stepped around the cables snaking through the corridor and edged his way around the crowd's fringe to see what could possibly be attracting such mass interest. What he saw shocked him, for behind the deep polish of the assistant U.S. attorney's mahogany desk sat Evelyn's runaway husband, conducting a press conference with the self-assurance of a seasoned politician running for reelection.

If Scott noticed the arrival of the prosecutor from Los Angeles, he didn't acknowledge it. Scott was concentrating on telling *his* story *his* way, a harrowing narration of nameless assailants who tried to run him off lonely mountain roads at night, the same ones, he hinted broadly, who left his wife's shot-up car on a Santa Monica city street. He was a helpless victim, caught in the cross fire of bizarre circumstances, and Scott—no longer the camera-shy, humiliated husband—wanted everyone in the room to understand his position. Adamantly refusing to detail his eleven-month Canadian odyssey, Scott kept his audience's attention riveted on his last few hours in California and the "dramatic events" he said left him no choice but to flee for his life.

The press conference had been going on for some time before Alarcon's arrival. It started off with a statement Scott read aloud from his handwritten notes: "It is my belief," began the former fugitive, neatly dressed in a pressed blue serge suit, "that my wife is alive. I fervently believe she would come forward if it is at all possible, unless she is [being] held against her will by those who stand to profit by such

159

actions or else she may be suffering from amnesia. . . . To accuse a person of *murder*," Scott said, weighting the word with sober import as he looked toward the newsreel cameras, "especially when there is *nothing* to substantiate the charge, is a very serious matter, as my accusers will soon learn."

He planned to sue, he said, "certain individuals in authority in Los Angeles as well as other persons for defaming my character and causing me mental anguish by making unfounded and unprovable statements relating to my actions and the disappearance of my wife."

Then, removing his plastic horn-rimmed reading glasses, Scott opened the session up to questions. The more probing queries, however, the questions that honed in on Scott's own deeds or words, were deferred with an obsequious smile to his attorney.

Scott's chronicle started with the prearranged business trip he said he was taking last May, when he drove Evelyn's car to a secret location where his green 1953 Ford was already parked. He began transferring his luggage to his own car, but "someone" stole the coupe with one of his suitcases still in the trunk. Despite the theft—which Scott said he saw no point in reporting to the police—he continued on his trip.

Just outside Bishop, California, "two or three men" in an unmarked car ran him off the road. "I have my ideas about who they were," Scott insinuated darkly. From the doorway, Alarcon, still not quite comprehending the scene he beheld, shook his head in astonishment.

Scott stayed three nights at the Valley Motel in Bishop while his car was being repaired. "Then I started back for Los Angeles," he said, "but on the way, I concluded I wouldn't have much of a chance there. If I had known about the bullets"—Scott paused theatrically— "I wouldn't have even started back."

So, instead, Scott headed inland, taking northern roads to reach the Canadian border where, he emphasized heavily, he crossed the border under his own name.

"R. E. Scott?" interrupted a reporter from the *Detroit Free Press.*

"That's right," Scott replied calmly. "It's a family name but I rarely use it myself. My full name is *Robert Leonard Ewing Scott.*

"Why did you travel under a pseudonym then?" the newsman persisted.

Scott looked at his attorney, who shook his head. "Well, I had a very definite reason," he said, "but I guess I can't say what it is right now."

Scott raised his voice just once. If he was guiltless in his wife's disappearance, he was asked, why was he being so mysterious in his explanations? Coyly, Scott asked first if any ladies were present in the room. Assured that none were within earshot, Scott shouted out his answer: "I'm not trying to hide a goddamn thing! Believe me, I'm going to crucify the sons of bitches around here. There's no proof—*there is absolutely no proof*—that I have done *anything*."

"How do you feel about the murder charge?" Scott was questioned.

"It's an *asinine, ridiculous* bunch of *tripe*. I can't inherit a thing from my wife. As far as I know, she made her last will in 1949 before we were even married. Her brother was the chief beneficiary, and I know of no changes since."

Scott clearly didn't like his brother-in-law much, and he pressed his point further. "You really should be checking into that brother of hers—he's the one who's responsible for all of my troubles. He stands to profit most from her disappearance. Not I. Besides, the value of my wife's estate is only slightly over two hundred thousand—nothing near the three-quarters of a million dollar figure I keep hearing mentioned."

Alarcon had enough of Scott's press conference, and in amused disgust, he made his way out of the room. As he left, the prosecutor heard Scott's appeal to his wife following him down the hallway: "I would like for Evelyn to return and clear this thing up," Scott said, his voice cracking just slightly. "If it's something she doesn't want to explain, I won't ask her to explain any more than I have asked her to explain in the past."

Raymond Throsby and W. Ernest Pitney, his attorney, held their own press conference in Los Angeles two days later. Scott, they claimed, not Throsby, was Evelyn's principal beneficiary.

"Mr. Boyle told us on one occasion," Pitney said, "that—and I quote—'I can't tell you what the contents of her will are, but I can tell you that Scott is the chief beneficiary and Throsby is a token beneficiary only.'"

"My sister was worth $750,000 before she married Scott," added Raymond. "I imagine that she is worth a lot less now."

Throsby scoffed at Scott's charge that he was the one who had engineered Evelyn's disappearance. "I expected a lot of stuff like that to come out—he's shooting in the dark and struggling to come up with an answer for what he's done. I have a firm conviction that Scott murdered my sister and I'll tell Scott that to his face anytime. I am convinced that she has been murdered."

For his part, Boyle denied ever disclosing the contents of Evelyn's will to anyone. He pointed out, in fact, that unless new evidence was found to confirm Evelyn's death—a murder-one verdict against her husband notwithstanding, the probate court might not accept a criminal court's verdict as proof of death and decide that the seven-year presumption-of-death rule would hold Evelyn's will in limbo until May 1962 at the earliest.

Conversely, Boyle went on, the probate court might also accept the discovery of Evelyn's glasses and denture as proof of her death even should her husband not be convicted of her murder.

Chief Parker, however, was convinced that Scott killed Evelyn. "That was my conclusion when we completed our investigation, and that is still my conclusion," Parker said. "What has happened since Mr. Scott's disappearance? There is absolutely no evidence to come to our attention that Mrs. Scott is other than dead."

By failing to appear for his arraignment, Parker pointed out, "Mr. Scott has given prosecutors the ability to use a California rule of law that flight can be used as evidence of guilt."

On Saturday, April 20, Cohn and two officers of the Royal Canadian Mounted Police searched Scott's small Toronto apartment, an immaculate three-room flat on fashionable Avenue Road. They found several small appliances, a record player, a typewriter, and Scott's luggage, but no more of the $100,000 cash cache Scott was rumored to have carried away from Los Angeles than the $10,400 found at his arrest. His possessions were confiscated and returned to the United States.

On the recommendation of his legal adviser, Governor Williams did grant Scott an extradition hearing. Despite Cohn's impassioned appeal

162

that Los Angeles authorities "have so inflamed the minds of the people that it would be impossible for Mr. Scott to get a fair, impartial, and unbiased trial in California," Williams signed the extradition warrant Alarcon presented to him on April 25.

A day later, however, on a request from Cohn for a writ of habeas corpus asking release from unlawful restraint, Judge Miles Culehan rejected those same papers as flawed, and returned them to the California prosecutor for corrections. Although the judge said he objected to the warrant itself, which listed all fourteen counts against Scott but was accompanied by papers that supported only one count of forgery, Culehan, a highly partisan Republican, was known to enjoy his every opporunity to embarrass Governor Williams.

"Do you mean that we have all this hurrah to extradite a man for forging a hundred-dollar check?" Judge Culehan demanded of Alarcon in front of a courtroom largely filled by mature matrons eagerly eyeing Scott. "I'm not going to order a man returned to another state unless the papers are correct."

But when the papers were amended to the jurist's satisfaction on May 2, Judge Culehan decided that Scott, arrested on a federal charge, should be tried on the government's case before he could be turned over to the state.

"You know," the judge reminisced to Alarcon as he made his ruling, "when I was a young prosecutor, I went to Florida to extradite someone, and the judge on the case asked me if I'd ever been to Flordia before. I said, 'No, your Honor, I haven't been,' and he put the matter over for two weeks and told me to enjoy Florida. Now, have you ever been to Michigan before?"

"Your Honor," Alarcon said as delicately as he could, "I only have one shirt and one suit with me."

"Well, that's a shame. But I'm just going to put all this business over until next week. Enjoy Michigan."

After three weeks of "enjoying Michigan," Alarcon could see that the extradition proceedings threatened to drag on for months. Cohn was promising to take Scott's fight all the way to the Michigan Supreme Court if necessary, a hurdle Alarcon knew would take weeks, maybe months, to clear. The prosecutor decided to try to speed things up with a little strong-arm persuasion he though might induce Scott to drop his extradition fight. With this strategy in mind, he called Los Angeles for approval, which was quickly given. At the same time, Alarcon heard a bit of office gossip that thrilled him. "It looks like this is going to be a big case," he was told. "Parker's been over here asking for Leavy and the word is McKesson's agreed." For Alarcon, this chance was no small opportunity; he had honed his own lawyering skills by listening in the back of the courtrooms as Leavy argued cases, the better to learn the rhythm and style of a winning presentation. Now Leavy was his co-counsel, and Alarcon was delighted.

With the backing of the home office, Alarcon chanced his gambit. As the morning session started on May 11, Alarcon requested a few minutes' delay and asked Cohn to step outside to the corridoor with him.

"All right," Alarcon said to Scott's attorney, "let me tell you what I'm about to do in there. When we go back inside that courtroom, I'm going to stand up and say to the judge that we concede and that we will not pursue your client's extradition at this time.

"However, I will also tell the court that we wish the state to turn Scott back over to the federal government and we will ask them to proceed with the unlawful flight charge—and you know as well as I do that there's no defense at all for that charge. Scott will be convicted, and at his age, the chances are he'll die in a federal prision."

Deliberately, the prosecutor fixed his gaze on Cohn. "Scott thinks he can beat our case—okay by me. But the smartest thing you can do right now is to go back in the courtroom and advise your client to waive extradition. His federal case will be dismissed and he can take his chances with us."

Cohn stared back at Alarcon. Finally, the attorney nodded in agreement. "Okay," Cohn said. "Give me half an hour alone with him."

Alarcon stood up. "Fine. I'll go have some coffee. But in thirty minutes, I'm going to ask Judge Culehan to dismiss the proceedings and turn Scott over to the federal government."

Cohn huddled with Scott in a conference room for almost half an hour. But he returned to the courtroom as promised in thirty minutes to announce that Scott's extradition fight was over. Scott had agreed to return to Los Angeles as soon as arrangements could be made.

164

* * *

The $7,900 balance of the funds found in Scott's possession (of the original $10,400 in Scott's money belt, $1,500 released by Judge Levin, plus another $1,000, had gone to pay Cohn) and the keys to his new Ford Fairlane were returned to Scott before he left Michigan, and he quickly turned them over to Cohn. Cohn promised to hold the cash and car keys for Frank Girard, the highly regarded Los Angeles attorney Scott had asked to represent him in his murder trial. Girard had conditionally accepted Scott's case, pending their agreement over legal fees. In his last conference with Cohn, Scott admitted he had misgivings about his return to California: "I don't feel I have a friend to my name out there," he told the lawyer. "But I guess the facts will come out at the proper time."

Two years and two days after Evelyn's disappearance, Scott waited in the rain at the Detroit Airport for the plane that would take him back to Los Angeles, where he would stand trial for her murder. He invested a couple of coins in $59,000 worth of flight insurance that named Cohn as his beneficiary, and thanked the Detroit press corps for their "fine treatment. I'll bet you're glad to get rid of me," he joked. "This is the last time you'll ever see me."

Scott's prospects in Los Angeles didn't look bright. Like bad debts coming due, he faced not just his murder trial but the rest of his unfinished legal business, that had mounted in his absence. Citizen's National Trust & Savings Bank was suing for nearly $18,000 in illegal transactions it alleged Scott made with Evelyn's funds that, Citizen's charged, the Bank of America allowed to occur unchecked. The outstanding debtor's judgment against him for his book was steadily accruing interest. And, by sheer coincidence, Scott's capture came just hours before his appeal for trusteeship of his wife's estate was finally settled before the District Court of Appeal in Los Angeles. Although Seth Hufstedler appeared on Scott's behalf, the court sharply rebuked the former fugitive by refusing even to consider his appeal:

"Appellant has willfully and purposely evaded the process of the Superior Court," the decision read. "[He] has contumaciously defied its orders. Such contempt bars him from receiving the consideration of this court."

165

But most portentous for Scott would be a man waiting for him at the other end of his journey whom he had never met: J. Miller Leavy. As promising a counselor as Alarcon was at twenty-nine, Leavy, some twenty-three years Alarcon's senior, brought skill, experience, and absolute confidence to the prosecution team. If Alarcon's youthful style was a quiet finesse with the delicacy of a slender rapier, Leavy's seasoned, celebrated manner was a double-edged sword, capable of shearing succinctly through to the heart of the matter at hand: convincing twelve people not trained as jurists that Evelyn Scott was calculatingly murdered by her husband.

□ **27**

Scott's plane touched down two hours late to southern California's seasonally gray spring skies. Still, hundreds of spectators lined the flight-deck balcony of Los Angeles International Airport, many of them mature women hoping for a glimpse of the elegantly attired charmer. "Hey, Scott!" someone yelled, and the handsome, former fugitive glanced up just long enough to see Raymond Throsby—grinning malevolently—taking his picture. "To hell with you!" Scott snapped.

Attorney Frank Girard was at the airport to meet Scott, and after a hurried conference, he agreed to be with Scott at the Hall of Justice for the booking procedure. Scott was hustled into a waiting sheriff's car where newsman George Putnam had managed to be Scott's fellow passenger. Like two old reminiscing school chums, they chatted amiably as they headed toward the county jail. Scott liked Putnam based on their long-ago meeting at the Jonathan Club, and he trusted him as a kind of kindred spirit who could understand and sympathize with his terrible predicament. "I am just anxious now to get into court," Scott told Putnam. "You know I have nothing to hide."

In time, their conversation turned to the attorney who would handle his defense, and Scott said he was considering hiring Frank Girard. The only detail still to be negotiated was Girard's fee, which, Scott said worriedly to Putnam, might be much more than he was able to pay. Putnam suggested—and personally recommended—an alternative choice in P. Basil "Paunty" Lambros, a bright young lawyer five years out of Los Angeles' Southwestern Law School.

In fact, Lambros, an ambitious, thirty-three-old attorney, was already waiting at the county jail when the car carrying Scott and Putnam arrived. Lambros offered to conduct Scott's defense in return for a share of the rights to Scott's story as his only payment. Scott—now freed from paying the up-front fee Girard required—agreed, and by the time Girard reached the jail, Scott was already huddled with his new attorney.

Scott's arrangement with Lambros was later spelled out in a June 26, 1957, agreement that was signed by Lambros and witnessed by Frank Massad, whom Lambros had hired as an investigator for the defense. In return for his services, Lambros contracted to receive 50 percent of whatever monies Scott realized from the sale of the rights to his life story and his legal case for the production of a film, television movie, stage play, or book. In return, Lambros agreed to retain and pay as many associate counsels as Scott felt were necessary, and to serve as the only official source of publicity about the case.

Scott would be the guest of Los Angeles County until his fate was determined by the court. From his personal possessions—$127 in a money clip, a pair of cuff links, a wristwatch, a pocket watch, a ring, a tie clip, keys, two ballpoint pens, a wallet, and two combs—Scott was allowed to keep $5.35 and one of the combs. He was booked on one count of murder, four counts of grand theft, and nine counts of forgery, on May 18, and his arraignment was scheduled for May 21.

Scott spent his first day home in California accustoming himself to his new austere surroundings in the Los Angeles County Jail and granting audiences to the press. To the carefully combed defendant, who still wore a white dress shirt and a tie underneath his prison denims, no single piece of evidence absolutely linked him to Evelyn's disappearance. He answered his accusers through news interviews with great confidence and optimism, arguing that if he really had killed his wife—and there was absolutely no *proof* that he had, Scott insisted—he damn well wouldn't have gone about it in such an amateurish manner.

"Mr. Mire never accused me of forging Mrs. Scott's signature," Scott announced cheerily to a UPI wire service reporter. "He only said that her signature was traced—but he didn't say it was by me. Do you really think I would have fooled around forging my wife's signature for only a couple of thousand dollars, when there is so much money sitting around in various accounts around the country in Mrs. Scott's name? I did not do it—and there is no proof I did."

With obvious impatience, Scott dismissed the damaging discovery of his wife's eyeglasses and denture. "If I had done what Parker and Roll said I did," he asked, "would I really be such a goddamned fool as to leave those things just lying around?"

Scott used the late district attorney as both excuse and exoneration for his flight. "I was a victim," he charged, "a victim of a feud between Roll and Parker. I was the one getting kicked back and forth."

But, buoyed by the news of Roll's death, Scott said, he headed to Detroit to buy a new car, since, he claimed, his other one had been run off the road by nameless assailants. He was only "breaking in" his new car with a return to Toronto to pick up his belongings before returning to face his accusers in Los Angeles when he was apprehended. "I thought I would be able to come back here, now that I wouldn't be the football in any feud. Now I think," Scott predicted optimistically, "that justice is beginning to rise in Los Angeles again."

Scott voiced his concern about his missing wife, too. "I hope she's still alive," he said, "because I haven't got anyone else in the world." As an afterthought, he added that Lambros was offering a five-thousand-dollar reward for information leading to Evelyn's whereabouts.

Leavy looked forward to Scott's arraignment. For two years, Scott had ducked questioning under oath (other than very limited cross-examination during his extradition), though he had freely aired his theories and intimations in the pages of the city's newspapers or in television interviews such as his "exclusive" conversation with George Putnam. But Scott had publicly promised that "everything would come out at the proper time," and Leavy couldn't wait to get Scott into court and provide him with his chance.

On May 21, however, Lambros requested a month-long continuance before entering Scott's plea, so that both attorney and defendant would have time to study the 760-page grand jury transcript that had led to Scott's murder indictment. "I've got to get the rest of my practice in order," Lambros told Superior Court Judge Louis H. Burke, "and make some office adjustments so I can handle Mr. Scott's defense."

Leavy objected. "I don't think you need four weeks. I have other cases to handle too, you know."

Judge Burke settled matters with a compromise continuance of three weeks.

"Very well," Leavy said privately to Lambros as the session ended, "I hope if any defense motions are filed, it will not be a request for additional time."

"It is Mr. Scott's intention not to delay," Lambros shot back. "We will work with the court and the district attorney's office to bring the matter to a conclusion as quickly as possible."

From the counsel table, his client had a sotto voce retort of his own. "I have absolutely no use at all for that little kike," Scott said, as he watched Leavy exit the courtroom.

Lambros and Scott lingered a moment for a brief conference. The first movie-studio offer to film Scott's life story had just arrived via telegram, Lambros informed his client; he was sure it would be followed by others.

Unlike Girard, who had planned to motion for a change in venue to avoid any adverse effects of pretrial publicity, Lambros, a tall, aristocratically handsome man given to stylishly cut pearl-gray suits, had no similar intentions. Public opinion seemed to be with Scott in his terrible predicament, and Lambros decided that moving Scott's trial to another county was a foolish strategy. Over the next three weeks then, Lambros concentrated on carefully reading the grand jury transcript.

Scott also read the transcript—twice. He wrote Lambros a fifty-page legal-size memo, spelling out a neat, formal narrative of his five-and-a-half-year-long marriage to Evelyn. Point by point, Scott—articulately and firmly—categorically refuted the testimony against him, with plausible, reasonable answers. Scott's account was fat, too, with all the quirky details of memory that made his rendering all the more convincing. His narrative was only rarely kind to Evelyn, and his picture of her constantly shifted to support his self-portrait as a long-suffering, grossly misunderstood, terribly victimized husband. For example, though illness kept Evelyn bedridden for days at a time, Scott claimed, she was still strong enough to dream up and supervise the financial maneuverings that were later wrongly attributed to him. His chronicle started with his marriage to Evelyn:

> In July, 1949, the then Mrs. Norris Mumper, now Mrs. Scott, and myself took a trip to Mexico . . . return[ing] to Los Angeles somewhere around the first of August, to the best of my recollection. . . . In a short time she told me that a number of her friends had the impression that we had been married in Mexico. I tried to pass this off rather lightly but was not very successful, so, the last of August, we took a trip to Tijuana, where we were married in the customary legal procedure. Mrs. Mumper, who then became Mrs. Scott, importuned me not to advise anyone of this particular marriage or the date, as she had given a date on which we were supposed to have been married in Mexico City. . . . The Mexican marriage . . . apparently did not satisfy Mrs. Scott. The last of September we took a trip to Carson City, Nevada, where we were married [again].

Almost immediately,

> Evelyn announced that she wanted to move away from Pasadena. We looked at many houses in the West Los Angeles area and, because Mrs. Scott stated that she desired to have a two-story residence, I purchased the home at 217 North Bentley Avenue sometime during November, 1949, and, to the best of my recollection, the escrow was closed either the last of November of that year or the first of December. I recall distinctly that we had moved into the house in sufficient time to have it prepared for Christmas of 1949.

Since he was facing possible legal action at the time from two unnamed former business partners on an unspecified land development deal, "it was at my instructions alone that [the deed of] the property was entered in her name," Scott wrote. "Mrs. Scott at this

170

point was exceedingly agreeable and during Christmas Day was kind enough to make my mother very comfortable at the Bentley Avenue home."

Their first year together passed pleasantly and uneventfully, in the usual manner of two married people, until just after the death of his mother in October of 1950, when Evelyn vehemently opposed his plans to develop a housing tract in Orange County.

> Some time during the early part of 1951, Mrs. Scott advised me that she owned an undivided interest in an apartment income property in Milwaukee . . . she desired me to purchase a part of her interest in the building and, from statements of hers, gave me the impression that if I continued with the tract I would not have sufficient money to buy her interest. . . . I agreed to purchase one-half of her equity for the sum of $35,000 in cash. . . . I have never received a deed for my interest in this property as of this date.

Soon after their transaction was completed, Scott remembered, he became suddenly and violently ill. "Mrs. Scott was not ill so I concluded it was something that I had personally eaten that had disagreed with me and, inasmuch as I had recovered by the next day, I did not give any further consideration to the matter."

But again, in the late spring of 1951, Scott became similarly ill again, and he said he confided to the athletic director of the Jonathan Club his suspicions that he had received a "doped drink of Coca-Cola" served to him by his wife. He was just as sick a third time a few months later. Scott concluded that Evelyn was trying to poison him because "my money was in the house and also [in] the Edgewater property in Milwaukee [and] there was very little I could do about the matter."

Scott flatly denied any role in managing his wife's money. He gave occasional advice—if asked—or relayed Evelyn's instructions as a middleman messenger. He used his dealings with Evelyn's investment counselor as a specific illustration.

At John Connell's suggestion, continued Scott's narrative, Evelyn started converting her securities into cash. When she was charged a 5 percent fee for the cash being held in a separate fund,

Mrs. Scott took immediate exception to this charge and requested me . . . to talk to Mr. Connell. . . . I stated to Mr. Connell that I had been in the security business and I expressed some opinions which in no way involved any securities held by Mrs. Scott or any of her business with Mr. Connell. . . . I considered it strictly Mrs. Scott's affair . . . although I was not in accord with placing funds in banks . . . without deriving any interest or any income of any kind.

The disagreement over the 5 percent fee was resolved by Evelyn, who decided on her own to close her Loomis, Sales & Company account.

During a trip to New York and Europe later in 1951, Scott stopped in Milwaukee to inspect The Edgewater apartment house, his right, he said, as a part owner.

I had never seen this property and desired to make a quick analysis. Upon my arrival, I went to the building unannounced. . . . I met an employee there who told me that the property was not maintained in a manner that justified the rentals being paid by the tenants and, from an inspection made with him, I saw that the corridors, the boiler room and the roof were in a bad state of repair. [Later, The Edgewater was turned over to Odgen & Company, and the building's management was] under my direction, as all records will substantiate.

During that stay in the Midwest, Evelyn disappeared as the Scotts waited for an elevator in their Chicago hotel.

I immediately had her paged in the lobby, looked every place I thought she could possibly have gone, checked certain bars . . . but could not find Mrs. Scott anywhere. I finally returned to the room, waited all night without her putting in an appearance.

In the morning, Scott had their luggage taken to the airport, where he asked a porter to help him locate his wife. Just as the plane was ready to leave,

Mrs. Scott came up and, to use her expression, said, "Are we ready? I'm all cheery and bright." I was so glad to see her that there was practically nothing I thought to say except that she had worried me all night. She gave no explanation for her absence, did not want to discuss it, and, from the point of discretion, I decided to drop the matter.

But then, Scott began noticing his wife's "overtures" to other women, which he said usually occurred just prior to one of her periodic, never-explained absences. He recalled one such occasion while they shopped for groceries in a Bel Air supermarket.

While I had a cart in one aisle inspecting the merchandise, she was in another aisle when I heard her talking to a woman customer. I heard the same remark being made about beautiful legs and the woman told Mrs. Scott to stay away from her. . . . Sometime after this, Mrs. Scott left in the morning . . . she was gone all day . . . and when she returned, she refused to give any explanation for her absence.

Suspicious too, to Scott, were Evelyn's long, private conversations with Marguerite Watson whenever she visited her old friend in New York. Evelyn personally took Marguerite's letters from the mailbox as soon as they were delivered and shipped boxes of clothes to her friend. Scott never pressed Evelyn about it because she "resented" his questions.

Even Vera Landry, Evelyn's former maid, noticed something terribly wrong with her employer, Scott said. He quoted Vera as saying that "she stepped into one of the bedrooms and found Mrs. Scott and Mrs. [Olive] Wright [Evelyn's secretary], both wearing nightgowns, with their arms around each, both were crying, and, Vera stated, it was hard to tell which was the man and which was the woman."

From early in their marriage, the couple's social activities were curtailed by Evelyn's health problems—diverticulitis, cancer, and Evelyn's constant drinking—leaving her confined to her bed for days. Scott set up a card table in Evelyn's bedroom and ate his meals there to keep her company. She lost interest in the house, and ignored Scott's repeated requests to see that the household was properly maintained: New curtains in his dressing room were needed, along with a higher-quality set of venetian blinds in his bedroom.

Even Evelyn's friends, Mildred Schuchardt, in particular, noticed her troubles. Mildred, in fact, called *him* regularly to voice her concerns over Evelyn's health with him. "[She] stated that she 'knew that Evelyn was not inclined to discuss her physical ailments with even her closest friends.'"

As her health remained uneven, Evelyn announced that she was liquidating her stocks and brought up the subject of her safe-deposit box:

> It was decided . . . that a signature of admittance to the safe-deposit box in the Security First National Bank in Westwood be prepared and two sets of signature cards for joint deposit in some branch of the Bank of America, to be used for the receipts from The Edgewater apartments in Milwaukee, should an emergency or a necessity of any kind arise. These cards were kept in the upper left side drawer of the desk in the study at the house. . . . I [later] found only one set of these cards and never have, as of this date, been able to locate the second set.

After Evelyn vanished, Scott at first never left the house longer than the time it took him to run an errand or eat his meals. He left notes for her under a vase in the front hall. When he did go out, lights were turned on and off by a timing device; a loudly playing radio or television set, or a note put out for the milkman, was left to give the impression that he was at home. There were, Scott said, "a few calls during this period from some gossipy friends and I gave them as little information as possible, as I deemed it my duty to protect Mrs. Scott in every way and did not propose to put her in a position of being a source of critical conversation."

As time passed, Scott decided that it was silly for him to sit around the house and worry. He started going to dinner with friends such as Harriet Livermore and Patricia Deadrick, who eventually introduced him to Marianne Beaman.

Since certain bills had to be paid, Scott said he took $1,000 in cash out of a safe-deposit box for the checking account he opened in his own name at the Bank of Los Angeles. Then, hoping to reach an agreement with Charles Contreras over the publication of *How to Fascinate Men,* Scott took the pre-signed joint-tenancy cards from Evelyn's desk drawer on May 19, 1955, to see if his contract with Contreras was still in her bank box.

> I introduced myself to Mr. Mallory [whom Scott identified as head of the safe-deposit department] and explained my mission . . . on his right was a girl doing clerical work. Mr. Mallory took the card, and said that

the last time Mrs. Scott was in, she stated that I probably would come in before very long with the card for admittance to the box. . . . In view of the statement of Mrs. Scott to expect me to present [the joint-tenancy card], that he assumed it would be all right for me to have admittance to the box. . . . I expect[ed] to find the agreement from Mr. Contreras, but, on opening the box, found it gone. There were some small items, to the best of my recollection, and also a money bag with the imprint of the name of a bank in the eastern part of the United States. This bag appeared to have something in it but, inasmuch as it was none of my personal property, I did not open the bag.

Scott said he found Evelyn's traveler's checks already signed with both sets of signatures in a drawer.

I debated what to do with these checks, retained them in the house for awhile . . . [then] deposited some of these checks in the joint account but was undetermined whether to deposit them all at one time . . . because upon Mrs. Scott's return I assumed we would proceed to Germany. . . . I endeavored during this period to return to the Security First National Bank in Westwood to place these checks in the safe deposit box but at that time I was refused admittance to the box without any explanation being given.

About the same time, he encountered Evelyn's brother in front of the home on North Bentley Avenue.

Mr. Throsby came to the house early one morning and asked me where Evelyn was. In replying, I stated that she had been doing more drinking than usual, that she had left, and that I was worried beyond words. It had gotten to the point where I could not take it much longer and if she did not return soon I was giving consideration to obtaining a divorce.

Raymond, Scott charged, had much more to gain by Evelyn's disappearance than he did.

Mrs. Scott informed me that she had a will prepared, in which she left her brother an income from her estate but did not desire to leave him an outright bequest because he had gotten into trouble many times and cost her money. . . . [H]e was threatening to commit suicide. . . . [S]he

175

[said] that under no circumstances should I ever have anything to do with him. . . . [S]he knew that my financial situation was such that there was no especial [sic] reason for her to make a bequest to me in her will.

Then, once Throsby's suit made Evelyn's disappearance public, the harassment from authorities became unbearable. After he was run off the road near Bishop—"I was injured but fortunately, not very seriously"—Scott concluded that he would be a "sucker" to return to Los Angeles. "I turned around and headed for Chicago and eventually crossed into Canada."

Lambros, bolstered by Scott's unemotional and rational chronicle, was certain that the state's circumstantial evidence wouldn't hold up if the case ever made it into court. It was the state's burden to prove Scott's guilt beyond a reasonable doubt, and nowhere in the record did Lambros feel that the essential elements establishing the corpus delicti were present. He saw no proof that death had in fact occurred; even if Evelyn's death was presumed, Lambros saw no evidence that proved death had been brought about by criminal means or, separately, that it had occurred within the Superior Court's Los Angeles County jurisdiction. Lambros considered legal precedent as well: Only five "no body" convictions for first-degree murder had ever been obtained in California's history, dating as far back as 1880.

Though Lambros believed that Scott's chance for outright acquittal—not to mention a hung jury—was excellent in a jury trial, when the proceedings resumed, Lambros filed a pre-trial motion for dismissal of all the charges against Scott. No corpus delicti had been established, and "not one shred of evidence" absolutely confirmed Evelyn's death, the attorney argued, or established a motive for her husband to kill her. The grand jury's findings were invalid too, since the court had no authority to indict Scott for a crime the panel couldn't prove had taken place within its venue.

"What a travesty on justice," Lambros argued, "if this man should be tried for her murder, be convicted and sentenced to the gas chamber—just because someone found her glasses and her teeth—and have her walk in the day after the execution."

But Judge Lewis Burke, pointing out that it was not his function to determine Scott's innocence or guilt at this stage of the proceedings, ruled against a dismissal. "There was reasonable and probable cause for the indictments to be returned," he ruled, and Scott's arraignment was rescheduled for July 2.

That Tuesday afternoon then, found Scott back in Judge Burke's court, where Evelyn's errant husband pleaded not guilty to each one of the fourteen counts against him in a loud, firm voice. Scott seemed mildly amused—bored, even—as he listened at the counsel table to the proceedings. Afterward, Scott mentioned his preoccupation was with who should play his part in the movie of his life: "I'd like to see Ronald Coleman in my role. I don't know who would be exactly right for Mrs. Scott—perhaps an older Peggy Lee or Mary Astor."

Scott was optimistically nonchalant about his future. "I have gone through the transcript twice," he said, smiling. "I find nothing in there where I am accused of doing anything except taking a few individuals out to dinner, and I'm not apologizing for that."

Two weeks later, Judge Burke's ruling was appealed to the District Court of Appeal. Lambros' petition for a writ of prohibition—an order issued by a superior court that commands a lower court to cease from the prosecution of a suit because it belongs to some other court's jurisdiction—was based on the same three arguments he presented in his motion for dismissal of all charges against Scott: that no corpus delicti had been established, that there was no evidence to connect Scott with any crime, and that the grand jury proceedings were invalid. On August 5, Lambros' arguments were answered by Leavy in a 112-paged prosecution brief, a thoughtfully written document that painted a much different picture of the Scotts' life together.

□□□□□□□□□□□□□□□□□□□□□□ **28**

Avarice [Leavy's brief began] is one of the most basic motives for murder. Scott is not the first fortune hunter to marry an older wealthy woman, learn all he can of her resources, murder her and then appropriate them to his and younger women's use and, unfortunately, he will probably not be the last.

Scott, with no income to report, owning nothing, married Mrs. Scott, a wealthy older widow. . . . Immediately upon her disappearance he took control of her assets and income and started spending them on himself and women. . . . In every respect, Scott's actions were those of a penniless fortune hunter who had married an older wealthy woman, gradually taking charge of her affairs (theretofore in capable professional hands), seizing and converting to his own use her assets and income, as soon as he had done away with her. . . .

Scott's own actions, the backdrop against which Leavy laid Evelyn's disappearance, demonstrated Scott's consciousness of his guilt, the brief alleged:

> Telling Mrs. Scott's friends, falsely, that she was an alcoholic, mentally deranged, a lesbian and that she was in a hospital in Baltimore, whereas he told the police that she had suddenly disappeared; telling friends, who inquired as to why they had no answer on the telephone, that he and Mrs. Scott had been at home and that she was ill, this at a time occuring after the date he told the police that he last saw her. . . .
>
> Telling the police that he saw her write her name on bank documents, which were forged (and on another occasion that he found the documents already signed); never reporting her as a missing person to the police. . . .
>
> Repeatedly denying that he knew the name of her oculist, although he had met him twice and had asked him to find a certain type of glasses case for him (obviously because he didn't want her glasses identified); burning her clothing (either to cover up bloodstains or to make it appear that she had taken them with her). . . .
>
> Planning and requesting reservations for an expensive tour, for one, although he had no income to report and "owned nothing"; failing to deny an implied accusation of her brother that he had done away with Mrs. Scott; refusing to answer the door when friends and relatives came inquiring for Mrs. Scott. . . .
>
> Denying writing a letter canceling insurance on her jewelry until confronted with that letter, then giving a lame explanation for his contention that he gave her the jewelry, which she had insured three years before she met him. . . .
>
> Lavishly entertaining other women, buying a car needed for an "emergency" under a false name, significantly measuring the trunk compartment's capacity, expressing great concern for the car's ventilation sys-

178

tem and dependability at high speeds, registering it to the salesman's address, asking that the temporary registration of the car be fastened so that it would blow off immediately. . . .

Then, citing *Tisdale* v. *Connecticut Mutual Life Insurance,* an 1868 Iowa case holding that the seven-year period required for presumption of death could be shortened by circumstance, Leavy applied it to the Scott case:

> An honored and upright citizen, who, through a long life, has enjoyed the fullest confidence of all who knew him, prosperous in business and successful in the accumulation of wealth, rich in the affection of wife and children and attached to their society, contented in the enjoyment of his possessions, fond of the associations of his friends, and having that love of country which all good men possess—with no habits or affections contrary to these traits of character—journeys from his home to a distant city and is never afterward heard of.
>
> Must seven years pass, or must it be shown that he was last seen or heard of in peril, before his death can be presumed? No greater wrong could be done to the character of the man than to account for his absence, even after the lapse of a few short months, upon the ground of a wanton abandonment of his family and friends.
>
> He could have lived a good and useful life to but little purpose if those who knew him could even entertain such a suspicion. The reasons that the evidence above mentioned raises a presumption of death are obvious; absence from any other cause, being without motive and inconsistent with the very nature of the person is improbable.
>
> We submit that the evidence before the grand jury shows reasonable cause to believe that Mrs. Evelyn T. Scott was a wealthy person of excellent moral character, leading a well-ordered life and with absolutely no motive suddenly and voluntarily to leave her comfortable existence and her home, her friends, business associates and advisers whom she had invariably advised of any departure, failing to keep her regular weekly appointments at the beauty parlor, leaving all her personal effects "as though she was living there" and without her essential glasses and denture, or to take her own life. . . .

A week later, the District Court of Appeal denied Lambros' petition and ruled that the former fugitive would have to stand trial for

179

Evelyn's murder as scheduled on October 7, 1957. The court's brief order made no comment on whether the circumstantial evidence presented to the grand jury was sufficient to establish the corpus delicti of murder without direct evidence of Evelyn's death: The issue would have to be decided in court.

With eight weeks to prepare for the start of Scott's trial, Leavy and Alarcon went to work, mastering the complicated evidentiary sequence and memorizing the dates and details punctuating the lives of Evelyn and Ewing Scott. Despite—perhaps due to—a twenty-three-year age difference, their talents meshed together nicely: Leavy, the courtroom showman and chief strategist in the prime of a winning career, and Alarcon, the promising young prosecutor whose thorough research produced the meticulous, detail-oriented testimony crucial to a circumstantial evidence case.

Leavy was pleased to be trying the case before Superior Court Judge Clement Nye. A scholarly man with handsome, regular features, Nye was strict about the way his courtroom was run, especially when it came to needless delays. But Judge Nye understood the problems inherent in presenting circumstantial evidence cases, and Leavy knew that he would be open-minded about the proof admitted into evidence in his court.

Yet Leavy was only too aware that the case had to be airtight, with each essential element in the chain of circumstantial evidence against Scott clearly inferred or established by supporting proof. At least one-third of the testimony was expected to trace Scott's paper trail, requiring almost thirty witnesses, including eight employees from three different banks able to identify Scott and testify about the accounts he opened and the transactions they witnessed, two American Express representatives with records of the traveler's checks purchased by Evelyn, the accountant who customarily did Evelyn's taxes and the one Scott hired for the first time to prepare her 1955 return, and state and federal tax officials who would testify that a records' search found no indication that Scott had filed returns of his own for at least eight years. For Tom Doherty's testimony on the Scotts' respective assets, Leavy ordered a series of charts. And, although Leavy planned to call Donn Mire, he also asked Clark Sellers, arguably the world's leading

180

authority on questioned documents, to testify. As competent as Mire was, Leavy wanted no questions left unanswered about the perpetrator of Evelyn's forged signature. For Sellers' testimony, Leavy ordered enlargements of Evelyn's genuine and traced signatures.

Friends, associates, and former members of Evelyn's household staff, including Olive Wright, Vera Landry, Camilla Hanson, and Frank Justice, made up another third of the witnesses, subpoenaed to testify from firsthand observation about Evelyn's character and morals. Seven health professionals provided the state's proof that Evelyn's physical and mental health were excellent, and Jim Boyle, subpoenaed by Leavy, was expected at last to turn over Evelyn's wills.

Cunard and Thomas Cook Travel Agency representatives were asked to outline Scott's travel plans, while Leavy arranged for another dozen witnesses from Bishop, Detroit, and Windsor, Canada, to detail Scott's north-of-the-border sojourn, since, under state law, evidence of flight was admissible as evidence of guilt. Firsthand testimony of Scott's extramarital romancing was planned from Harriet Livermore and Marianne Beaman. Leavy assumed that Raymond Throsby was a key target for the defense, but Throsby had a solid alibi: He was working an extra part-time job, and Leavy was prepared to call Throsby's supervisor with his time card for the night of May 16, 1955, if necessary. Ulrich Quast, whose brush with Evelyn as a potential client for a Mercedes-Benz was the most casual of acquaintances, pinpointed the last known moment Evelyn was seen alive on the afternoon of May 16, 1955, by anyone other than her husband.

In all, the prosecution planned to call 98 witnesses and offer 304 separate pieces of evidence; they would make Scott's nine-week trial one of the longest in California legal history. By training, Leavy and Alarcon knew they could bank only on facts, not on luck, but nonetheless, the prosecutors were treated to an astonishing windfall of unexpected evidence. First came a telephone call to Alarcon from Sidney Laughlin, Marianne Beaman's new criminal defense attorney.

Marianne, painfully aware that she would be subpoenaed again and forced to replay her bit part in Evelyn's life as Scott's paramour, had reluctantly agreed with her attorney's advice to volunteer to testify for the state. On her behalf, Laughlin telephoned Alarcon. "We would very much like to talk with you," he told the startled prosecutor. "We know you know about Vegas."

Alarcon *didn't* know about Vegas, but he answered the attorney quickly, as though he did. "All right," he said evenly, "where do you want to talk?"

"In my office. Mrs. Beaman has two stipulations, however, in exchange for her complete cooperation. She wants *you* to question her in court—she doesn't know Leavy—and she wants your word that you won't ask whether or not she has had sexual intercourse with Scott."

"All right," Alarcon agreed, "I can guarantee Mrs. Beaman that I'll question her and that I won't ask her specifically about her sexual relations with Scott. If the other side asks—and I can't see why they would—I will object, though I can't promise how the court will rule." But, Alarcon thought to himself as he hung up, if she admits she spent three nights in the same room alone with Scott at the Kona Kai Club, the jury is going to draw its own conclusion anyway.

By the time the prosecutor arrived at Laughlin's Los Angeles office, Marianne was already there, dressed demurely in a neat suit, her eyes veiled behind a pair of black angel-winged sunglasses. Despite a situation she clearly found humiliating and embarrassing, to Alarcon, Marianne was as gracious and poised as possible.

"Tell me about Vegas," he suggested first. He was pretty damn curious to find out what the hell her attorney was talking about.

"Over Thanksgiving weekend in 1955, Mr. Scott and I spent an extended holiday in Las Vegas," Marianne said. "We bumped into some friends of his on the steps of our hotel. He introduced me to them as his wife."

"Do you remember who they were?"

"Yes—Roy and Polly Whorton—they live in Tarzana. After that, I went to their home several times with Mr. Scott."

Alarcon wrote down the name. Not a bad lead, he thought, if the Whortons will back up Marianne's story under oath. "You were asked about the trips you made outside of Los Angeles with Mr. Scott during the grand jury hearing," he said. "Why didn't you mention this trip at that time?"

"I guess I was trying to protect Mr. Scott and myself from public criticism."

"Did you go anywhere else with Mr. Scott?"

"Just the two trips to the Kona Kai in San Diego—I think you already know about them. But Mr. Scott did invite me to spend the night at his home and I accepted several of his invitations."

"You're kidding." What kind of man, Alarcon thought in shock, would bring another woman home to his marital bed if he was expecting his wife to return? "When?"

"The first time in September 1955. Then, I guess, one night in each of the next three months."

"Did he give you any indication that he was expecting his wife to return?"

Marianne shook her head. "Nothing other than what I've already testified about. He said she'd tried to poison him, that's why he thought she left him. He thought she was a sick woman and drank a great deal. Her mind slipped on occasion, and he thought she needed psychiatric treatment.

"There is something else I think you'll want to know about," Marianne continued determinedly. "Mr. Scott gave me some jewelry that he told me belonged to Mrs. Scott—I think some of it is quite valuable. Here"—she opened her purse and pulled out a soft pouch—"I brought it with me." She held it out to Alarcon; inside he found two ropes of pearls, a set of pearl earrings that matched the larger strand, a second pair of earrings with the unmistakable water colors of high-grade aquamarines, a sterling silver diamond-studded chain, a heavy brooch encrusted with a hundred diamonds, and a wide gold bracelet set with semiprecious stones and pearls.

Alarcon looked up from the jewelry at her in amazement. "When did he give you this?"

"On the morning of my testimony before the grand jury." A slight flush threatened her poise.

"I see. Did he give you anything else?"

"Yes. There were some household items—a bathroom scale, a heater, and a night-light—and several other things that belong to Mrs. Scott—a black wool coat, some luggage, and three leather purses. I think that's all."

"You expected to marry him, didn't you?"

Marianne nodded slowly. "Well, Mr. Scott did asked me—twice, once matters were settled with his wife, but—" Marianne shrugged with a wry, pained smile.

"Did you hear from Mr. Scott while he was a fugitive?"

"No. Not a word." She shook her head with a tight smile. "You know," she said quietly, "I've lost four jobs in the last year."

"Have you heard from him since?" Alarcon pressed her gently.

"Yes." Marianne hesitated for a brief moment. "He sent me a short note from the county jail. But that's all."

Leavy sent an investigator out to interview Roy and Polly Whorton. Not only did they confirm Marianne's story, but, before the conversation ended, Roy handed over the thick white envelope Scott had left with him only hours before Evelyn's disappearance became page-one news. Leavy perused its contents with great interest, for the envelope held an unforeseen, but potentially valuable, piece of evidence. It was Scott's will that Leavy was reading, and of particular interest to the prosecutor was Scott's handwritten codicil dated March 5, 1956, and the bequest Scott had made to his absent wife.

Leavy made one more fortuitous evidentiary discovery as Scott's trial neared. Gifted as he was with a phenomenal memory for trial detail, Leavy similarly took note of the inessential minutiae of daily living. Like Evelyn, his own wife of nineteen years wore a denture, and, though he never discussed it with her, Miller knew that Violet left her plate discreetly wrapped in tissue paper on the bathroom sink at night. Leavy knew further that she would never think of leaving their home without it, and neither, he reasoned, would a society woman such as Evelyn. So, Leavy ordered two enlargements of a picture of Evelyn, which he personally drove out to Evelyn's dentist. At his request, Dr. Coldwell agreed to alter one of the two enlargements to show the jury how Evelyn looked without her plate in place.

As his interview with the dentist ended, Dr. Coldwell casually asked Leavy if Evelyn's "gadget" had ever been found.

"What gadget?" Leavy asked, his attention instinctively aroused. "You mean she had something else other than a denture?"

184

"Oh yes," Dr. Coldwell said, "I sent her to the orthodontist who made it for her. She wore it at night to keep her teeth in place."

"No," Leavy said, shaking his head slowly, "I'm sure that nothing like that was ever found."

Fortunately, Evelyn's orthodontist, Dr. Spencer Atkinson, was located in the same medical office building as Dr. Coldwell, and Leavy stopped by his office the same afternoon. Dr. Atkinson remembered making that gadget, a retaining device designed to keep Evelyn's loose upper fore anterior teeth from spreading apart.

"Could she wear this thing, this gadget, at the same time as she wore her denture?" Leavy asked, still not entirely certain why she wore the device.

"Oh, no," Dr. Atkinson said, "she couldn't have both in her mouth at the same time. I instructed her to wear this one only at night."

Leavy could hardly believe his ears. In absentia, Evelyn's missing gadget was a weighty piece of inferred evidence that narrowed down the time of Evelyn's murder to evening, probably sometime after she retired to the privacy of her own bedroom. When he cross-examined Scott, Leavy planned to grill him about its absence.

There were a lot of other things Leavy planned to ask Scott under oath. Why did he alone believe that Evelyn was an alcoholic and ridden with cancer? What proof did Scott have of her supposed lesbianism? How did her teeth and glasses end up in their neighbor's yard? Why did Scott avoid Evelyn's well-meaning friends? Why didn't he ever look for her and file a missing person's report with authorities? He planned to live pretty well over the seven years he told Harriet Livermore he expected to wait until Evelyn was declared legally dead, didn't he? What about the cruise for one he arranged and the other women he romanced? Why did he propose to Marianne Beaman if he expected Evelyn to return? Why did he close out her checking account and give away her clothing and jewelry? What about the "coincidental" timing between Evelyn's disappearance and the liquidity of her stocks, bonds, and bank accounts? Why, if he was innocent, didn't he answer the questions asked by the grand jury? Where did Scott get the hundred-dollar bills he used to pay his bail, to buy the new car in Detroit, to live for eleven months on the run?

What did he plan to do when he ran out of money in Canada? Why was his version of events so different from everyone else's?

Leavy knew that Scott's only defense was his attack on Evelyn's character, morals, and integrity. Leavy, however, intended to see that it was Scott, not Evelyn, who was put on trial.

Though Lambros firmly believed that no jury could—or would—convict Scott without absolute proof of Evelyn's death, he still had to offer plausible alternative explanations for her long absence. So, let Leavy weave his web of circumstantial evidence, Lambros decided; he planned to unravel the loose ends he saw dangling on the fringe of the prosecution's version of the Scotts' marriage instead. What Lambros needed were eyewitnesses to confirm Scott's rendering of Evelyn, and with all the publicity surrounding Scott's trial, Lambros didn't have far to look. Girded with a handful of intriguing suggestions about Evelyn's own activities since May 16, 1955, largely offered by citizens who volunteered to testify on Scott's behalf, Lambros was certain he would convince Scott's jury that Evelyn was the sick, secretive woman her husband said she was.

As outlined in his agreement with Scott, Lambros invited Al Matthews and Tom Williams, partners in a small Los Angeles law firm, to join the defense team. Though Lambros had faced Leavy in court before, most notably as one in the series of attorneys who defended James Merkouris of the double murder that twice resulted in a sentence of death—perhaps only Matthews truly understood the enormity of the challenge presented in the person of one J. Miller Leavy.

Matthews had run up against Leavy many times before, most memorably for Matthews in the Caryl Chessman case. Leavy was a brilliant lawyer, though, Matthews thought, absolutely prejudiced in favor of the state. Yet, he knew Leavy was an honorable lawyer: Despite a judge's stern order, Matthews once watched Leavy refuse to prosecute a man he believed to be innocent at the risk of his job and reputation. But when Leavy was convinced of a defendant's guilt—as he believed in Chessman's culpability—Leavy was relentless.

Matthews, a slight, mustachioed man, had liked Chessman; he was bright, gracious and, Matthews found, easy to get along with. But sexual assaults against women were rare in 1948, and Leavy refused to plea-bargain with Chessman. One of Leavy's first witnesses had been especially damaging, Matthews remembered grimly, a young girl who described the act of oral copulation Chessman forced her to commit and how she watched his semen drip down her coat afterward. It had been an uphill, ultimately unsuccessful, battle from there. Though he had fought Leavy for Chessman's life, Matthews gave no credibility at all to Chessman's charge of Leavy's complicity in preparation of the transcript since his personal observation showed Leavy to be incapable of such a dishonesty.

Matthews faced a painful, personal irony on the day of Chessman's execution: Within hours of Chessman's death, another young man was arrested for an almost identical assault. This tragic coincidence succinctly articulated Matthew's argument against capital punishment, that Chessman's death was no deterrent to other like-minded individuals.

Though Evelyn's continued absence hardly ran in Scott's favor, Matthews, like Lambros and his own law partner, Tom Williams, a ruddy-complected, round-faced man, believed that Scott's rendering of his wife contained enough truth to appear reasonable to a jury: Evelyn wouldn't be the first rich woman who liked to forget about Bel Air once in a while and sample the fruits forbidden by her elegant life-style. That strategy allowed Scott's defense to suggest several scenarios, including the possibility that Scott's words and actions were his own method of protecting his wife by hiding her offenses against her own elite social class.

Too, could not Scott's statements be perhaps nothing more than small white lies from a humiliated husband, too ashamed to admit that his wife deserted him? It was not unthinkable, either, to imagine that this sort of woman might leave her husband for another man, maybe even for a woman. Didn't anyone else, especially her debt-plagued brother, have a motive to engineer Evelyn's absence? Wasn't she just cruel enough to know that her husband was standing trial for her murder and do nothing to save him?

As October 7 approached, Lambros dropped a meaningful hint to reporters. "Definitely," he said, "our investigation shows that Evelyn Scott is still alive."

187

On Monday morning, October 7, Alarcon met Leavy in his sixth-floor office, and together, the prosecutors caught an elevator to the courtroom two floors above. They shared the ride up with two of their legal colleagues. "C'mon, Miller," said one, needling Leavy slightly, "you don't really think you'll pull off this Scott thing, do you?"

"Yes, frankly, I do," Leavy answered him earnestly; as the elevator doors closed behind them at the eighth floor, he glanced at Alarcon. "From now on, we'll take the stairs," Leavy said as they headed toward Judge Nye's chambers. "There might be jurors in the elevator next time."

Inside the courtroom, Leavy spotted Scott immediately, though Scott, if he noticed the arrival of the prosecutors, ignored them. He was clearly in marvelous spirits, however, as he magnanimously pointed out the brown dress shoes he wore with his new $185 gray pinstripe suit of imported English woolen. His black shoes, really the proper ones to wear with a gray suit, he explained, were not checked through the jail in time to reach him before he left for court.

At the request of the defense, Judge Nye called Leavy and Lambros for a brief pretrial conference in his chambers. Was the state willing to sever Scott's murder charge from the thirteen other counts of forgery and grand theft? asked the judge. Leavy agreed instantly, eager to avoid a possible "compromise" verdict: Leavy knew that it was conceivable a vascillating jury might convict Scott on the lesser charges but acquit him on the more serious one. The other counts were put off calendar until after Scott's trial for murder.

Since the case had captivated the city's headlines for eighteen months, the court had called an unusually large panel of 350 prospective jurors. Judge Nye's foresight was fortunate. "Is there any of you," he asked the group, "who has not read or heard about this case?" Not a single hand was raised. To select a panel of Scott's peers thus required one full week: Not until Friday was a seven-man, five-woman jury—two accountants, a supermarket manager, a PBX installer, a couple of salesmen, a retired city worker, and five housewives—seated. During the proceedings, Scott often dozed.

On Monday, October 14, Leavy started his opening statement, acquainting the jurors with this "keen, intelligent woman" and her very agreeable life-style. Speaking without notes for more than an hour, Leavy kept the force of his monologue moving toward the moment when she waved good-bye to a foreign-car salesman and disappeared forever into her home with her husband:

"The charge against L. Ewing Scott is for the murder of his wife, Evelyn Scott. We will not produce any witness who saw either the body of Evelyn Scott or any portion of it." But if Leavy couldn't give the jurors the when, the where, or the how of her murder, he believed he could give them the why: "We expect to prove that after the defendant married Evelyn, he entered into a long, well-planned, preconceived plan of deliberation and premeditation to do away with Evelyn Scott and to appropriate her vast estate. We will prove with circumstantial evidence that Evelyn Scott is dead and that she came to her death by a criminal agency."

Leavy called his first witness that afternoon, the bank teller who sold Evelyn her traveler's checks. Before Leavy's questions started, however, Lambros rose.

"Your Honor, we move that no testimony be allowed in this trial until the matter of jurisdiction has been satisfied. . . . There is nothing in Mr. Leavy's opening statement that indicates that they will prove venue or jurisdiction, and any testimony in our opinion is not proper, . . ." the lawyer said. "In view of the fact that there's no proof of death and that an essential circumstance of the chain here is the fact of death, why, we feel it would be grossly unjust and a miscarriage of justice to allow this thing to proceed until they have proven where this alleged death occurred and under what conditions it occurred. . . . Being armed with the presumption of innocence, and the presumption that a woman lives [on] for seven years, I think that the district attorney's office is far off base here."

But the court overruled Lambros' objections, and Scott's murder trial was at last underway.

Ulrich Quast was the state's second witness, and he replayed the events that had earned him his chilling footnote in Evelyn's life.

189

Evelyn seemed sober, composed and gracious on the afternoon of May 16, 1955, and her warm smile, the salesman was certain, lacked no teeth. "She was just like any other normal lady," Quast said, "any other lady of that age." The Scotts' car purchase was never consummated, however. "He said he was very sorry to disappoint me, but his wife took ill suddenly and he was taking her east for treatment."

Evelyn's orthodontist took the stand next. "She wore this every night—it kept her teeth from spreading," Dr. Atkinson explained, gesturing with the replica of Evelyn's retaining appliance he'd created at Leavy's request. "I had to take her denture out of her mouth and show her how to wear it—she could not wear both at the same time."

Dr. Coldwell followed Dr. Atkinson to the stand, and the dentist positively identified the denture found by Captain Hertel as the same plate Evelyn wore in his office on May 13, 1955. Alarcon then showed Dr. Coldwell a photograph of Evelyn, her face lit by a full, spontaneous smile. "The last time you saw her," the prosecutor asked, "were her teeth as they appear in this picture?"

"She certainly has teeth in that picture. I don't think it would be anything else but her bridge."

Alarcon held up the identical photograph again, Evelyn's broad grin spoiled this time by the black gaps usually filled by her five false teeth. "If she was not wearing her denture, would there be these empty spaces?"

"Oh yes," Dr. Coldwell said. "The missing teeth would be quite noticeable."

The defense hammered away on an old denture Evelyn had not used in fourteen years as Dr. Coldwell admitted that she could even eat steak without any denture, old or new, in her mouth.

"Would it be impossible for Mrs. Scott to wear that first plate now?" Williams asked.

"No."

"Mrs. Scott could be wearing that first plate today?"

"If she had it, it would be possible, yes."

"You don't have that first plate, do you, Dr. Coldwell?"

"No, sir, I do not."

"We were looking for a buried body," said Captain Hertel during the first of two days of testimony on his discovery of the denture, eyeglasses, medicines, cigarette holder, filters, hairbrush, and the tube of Ultrasol home hair-care treatment. "Tossed is not a good word. Thrown is not a good word. Placed is not a good word. They were just there."

Those articles were never shown to the Scotts' neighbors for possible identification, Hertel admitted. "Had you already decided that Mr. Scott was guilty," Lambros asked, "and that it was the job of your department to find evidence to back it up?"

"No, sir."

"Nevertheless you didn't check with the neighbors?"

"Object to that as argumentative." The court sustained Leavy's objection. But it was Lambros' turn to object as Leavy offered the very items in question into evidence.

"They have not been tied in to the problem that faces us with corpus delicti—they are immaterial, incompetent, and irrelevant," Lambros argued. "There is no proof of how they got there. It would be just as easy to introduce Mrs. Scott's hat and say it was found in the yard. The prosecution is saying that because these things were found on one side of the wall, ergo Mr. Scott killed his wife, which is utterly ridiculous."

Lambros' objections were overruled. Though the court's action was not an indication that the corpus delicti was yet adequately established, Judge Nye's ruling did allow further testimony about Scott's statements and conduct in connection with his wife's disappearance, a point the prosecution underscored as Opal Mumper was called as the state's twelfth witness on Friday, October 18.

She'd shared a pleasant, unremarkable lunch at Scandia's in March 1955 with her former sister-in-law, and, Opal testified, Evelyn sipped on a single glass of sherry throughout their meal. In April, they planned by telephone to meet again soon for lunch, but that conversation was the last time Opal spoke to Evelyn.

"How would you describe her physical condition when you saw her in March of 1955?" Alarcon asked.

"I would say she looked very well," Opal, a well-dressed woman with delicate features, said, "especially nice that day."

"Did you, either in March of 1955, or at any time, ever notice any signs of any mental aberration?"

"Never."

Opal was unable to reach the Scotts after Ewing's telephone call to her on June 16. In July, Opal drove to Bel Air with Maxine Davis, only to see Ewing staring at her from the den window after the doorbell had been ignored. That encounter intensely interested Lambros.

"Did you tap on the window to attract his attention?"

"No, I didn't."

"Why didn't you do that?"

"I could hardly reach it from where I was standing."

"Could you throw a pebble or holler at him?"

"Oh yes, I could have done that."

"Any reason you didn't do that?"

"The only reason is that I didn't want to."

"You didn't want to?" Lambros wanted the jury to know that Opal didn't really try to talk to his client, that she couldn't really be certain it was Scott she saw.

"No. I mean, he was sitting there in the window looking right at me. I don't think I would throw a rock at his window."

Lambros persisted. "Did you wave to him?

"No, I didn't. He just sat there . . . doing this"—Opal twisted her wrist in tight circles—"with his glasses."

At the counsel table, Scott, his right hand idly whirling his plastic horn-rimmed glasses in midair as he listened to her testimony, quickly brought his wrist down.

Evelyn's attorney followed Opal. Boyle, advised by the American Bar Association that he should produce Evelyn's last two wills if subpoenaed, finally turned over the documents to the court, which Leavy promptly offered into evidence. But Judge Nye, saying he needed the weekend to study the issues involved, dismissed the proceedings, promising to rule on the wills' admissibility on Monday, October 21.

By habit, Leavy and Alarcon waited around their offices until the day's transcript was ready; frequently, they were joined by a reporter or two, for whom Leavy might pour an informal glass of bourbon from a bottle he kept tucked in a desk until the end of the day. Today, it was Lloyd Emerson of the *Examiner* who joined them. Emerson, a pleasant, reserved man, always followed Leavy's cases with great enthusiasm.

"You think you'll see what's in her will?" Emerson asked. "You know Scott says that Throsby's her only beneficiary."

Leavy shrugged and shook his head. "What's in her will is really immaterial. I can argue it either way. If she did provide for him, she might have been considering rewriting her will. If she didn't, well, all the more reason he'd want her out of his way. Say she decided to divorce him—he didn't want her around to interfere with his plans."

"You think you can prove Scott knew what was in it?"

"He was into all the rest of her business, wasn't he? Besides, Boyle doesn't have Evelyn's copy in his files, and he'll testify that his standard office procedure is to mail it to his clients at home."

On Monday morning, the court placed Evelyn's wills in sealed envelopes, marking them as joint exhibits of the prosecution, defense, and court. The wills would not be opened, Judge Nye stipulated, unless the proper foundation was laid for their admission as evidence. In addition, the judge ruled that Boyle could no longer invoke the right of attorney-client privilege since the trial was primarily for his client's benefit.

Testimony resumed with Boyle still in the witness chair, and Leavy questioned the attorney about a conversation he had with the Scotts in 1953 or 1954 on the liquidation of Evelyn's securities.

"Mr. Scott said he felt the market was quite high," Boyle said, "and there was greater risk in holding common stocks than in converting to cash. I told [Mrs. Scott] it was a matter that no one could be sure about but in my opinion the market wasn't high."

The Scotts both expressed their fear that there was "a danger of atomic bombs dropping on this area and [that] it was a good idea to deposit cash in various banks throughout the country," Boyle said. "I said I thought it was an unnecessary precaution but that it couldn't do any harm." Boyle also remembered Scott's desire to oversee Evelyn's assets: "I recall Mr. Scott saying he thought he could do a better job than her professional investment counselors. He was proposing to take over management himself."

Despite his advice to the contrary, Boyle said Evelyn refused to file a joint tax return even though that action would have saved her a substantial sum of money, and juror number 3, Otis Embree, an accountant, wanted to know why.

"She told me that Mr. Scott didn't have a separate income of his own," Boyle said, "and she didn't want to embarrass him."

Dr. Rudolph Schindler saw Evelyn as a patient six weeks before she vanished, and testified that she was "a perfectly healthy woman." In fact, the physician had encouraged her to make another trip abroad and, should her diverticulitis flare up, prescribed Aureomycin and Sulfadiazine for her. That trip was the same one Evelyn mentioned to Gladys Baum, who testified later the same day, Tuesday, October 22.

On May 14, 1955, Evelyn "seemed as normal as any woman could be," Gladys said. But, "Mrs. Scott was a very peace-loving woman. She made remarks to me that little things didn't matter, that it was easier to give in in the interest of harmony. I don't know whether they were happy or not."

"You figure you are a close friend of Evelyn's, is that right?" Lambros asked under cross-examination.

"I *was* a very close friend of Evelyn's."

The attorney let her hint go by. He was laying the groundwork for something else, a trip the Baums made to New York City with Evelyn two or three months after the death of Norris Mumper. Lambros drew first from Gladys that Evelyn visited alone with Marguerite Watson during that trip.

"Did Evelyn ever tell you how her friendship developed with Mrs. Watson?"

"No."

"Why she went to see Mrs. Watson?"

"No."

"Did you go up to her hotel room?"

"I suppose I did, maybe half a dozen times."

"Mr. Baum go with you?" Lambros strolled toward the defense table.

"Sometimes he did not."

The attorney picked up a picture of Evelyn and Gladys from the table. What interested Lambros was Gladys's inscription, which, written with an arrow pointing at her own bosom, he felt supported Scott's claim of his wife's lesbianism. Lambros read the inscription aloud: "For Evie privately and personally, with love, Gladie." When

Gladys confirmed the handwriting as her own, Lambros's cross-examination was over.

To the prosecution then was left the task of explaining that suggestive inscription, and Alarcon asked the witness first to describe what she wore in that picture: a long-sleeved satin dress with a scarf artfully draped over the bodice. Delicately, Alarcon asked about its neckline.

"Immaterial!" objected Lambros. "That photograph speaks for itself."

Leavy appealed to Judge Nye, who dismissed the jury to hear the prosecutor's argument.

"Along with other questions asked of Mrs. Baum," Leavy said, "the implication with this photograph is that there would be some unnatural relationship between Mrs. Baum and Mrs. Scott. . . . In order that the defense may not rely on this kind of evidence . . . we should have the right to remove any such implication, since the evidence will show later that Scott, in attempting to explain the absence of Mrs. Scott, said Mrs. Scott was a lesbian, implying that she might be away with some such person. And in attempting to explain who the lesbians might be, he said Olive Wright and Marguerite Watson. What else? Some photographs. . . . We intend to disprove Scott's false utterances that Mrs. Scott was a lesbian."

"If and when the matter becomes an issue, then we'll have evidence on the subject," said the judge. "But I'm not going to permit counsel to anticipate something not in evidence. The court rules against the proof at this time."

But Leavy did manage a partial explanation of that provocative inscription during redirect questioning: "I felt there was a slight embarrassment in the picture," Gladys testified about the dress's plunging neckline. "That's the reason I wrote on it that it was privately and sincerely for her—I didn't care particularly about having it shown around."

That night, the Leavys stopped for a quick dinner at Bob's, a coffee shop not more than five blocks from their San Fernando Valley home. Miller, preoccupied with the trial, sat lost in his own thoughts until a spirited debate in the next booth roused his attention.

"You just wait—Scott'll never do a day's time in jail," predicted a man's voice confidently. "They'll never get him—not in a million years."

Miller looked at his wife. "Oh yes, we will," he said, just loud enough for Violet to hear him.

Though he was the defense's key target, this time, Raymond Throsby refused to be intimidated or confused by Scott's attorneys. From the witness stand, his eyes every so often slid toward Scott and something cool flickered across his face, as if Raymond could take great pleasure in squeezing the breath from Scott's neck. As he had already testified at the trusteeship hearing, Raymond said that his unkind letter to Evelyn over his debt to her was an emotional reaction to the accidental death at his work site in the Marshall Islands. He had located his sister's April 16, 1952, reply to that letter, and Alarcon read it to the court:

> Dear Raymond,
> I received your letter today. It was at Mr. Boyle's suggestion that his letter was written to you in order that I make some semblance of collection for income tax purposes. That was the only reason for it and be assured, at no time, would I enter judgement against you. My wishes are only for the best of everything for Trudy and you.
> Always, Evelyn.

Told by Brawner of his sister's disappearance, Throsby confronted Scott outside his sister's home: "I said, 'Where is my sister?'"

"We object to any conversation that Mr. Throsby may have had with Mr. Scott," Lambros interrupted. "Anything that Mr. Scott may or may not have said to Mr. Throsby at that time could conceivably be construed as an implied admission. In view of the fact that we don't feel that the corpus delicti has been established—there is no evidence here yet that there has been a death by criminal means—we don't feel that this conversation should be allowed."

"On the authority of *People* v. *Spencer*," Judge Nye said, "the objection is overruled."

Leavy smiled in satisfaction: The ruling cleared a major hurdle for the prosecution by indicating that the court would not rule on whether the corpus delicti had been established until after the state rested its case. The legal precedent was the thirty-six-year-old trial of John Spencer, who was convicted of drowning his wife and trying to pass off her murder as an accidental death. The court had allowed testimony of Spencer's statements and conduct that proved not that death occurred, since Mrs. Spencer's body had been found immediately, but that she died by a criminal agency. If testimony was admissible to prove death by a criminal agency, Judge Nye indicated by his ruling, then testimony was permissible as proof of the death itself.

Defense attorney Williams read Throsby's original letter for the jury: "'When I am a little bit more rational,'" it ended, "'I will answer this letter and you too.' That was a threat, was it not, Mr. Throsby?"

"No, sir, it was not," Raymond answered firmly.

"Where were you on May 16, 1955, Mr. Throsby?" Williams demanded.

"I was working in Desmond's," Throsby said calmly, referring to his sales job at a men's clothing store. "I worked there as an extra."

"Did you ever have occasion to throw, toss or place anything on the property adjoining the Scott property?" Williams persisted.

"No."

"What do you know about your sister's disappearance?" the lawyer demanded.

"Objection!" Leavy, nearly shouting, was on his feet.

"Objection sustained."

Leavy had planned Mildred Schuchardt's courtroom appearance with all the drama he could muster. When her name was called, a uniformed nurse wheeled the frail, mink-draped arthritic into Judge Nye's chambers and up to the witness stand, leaving her prominently and conspicuously seated in her wheelchair. She was handed a microphone that would carry her soft voice through the room. Leavy knew this delicate woman, her physical discomfort and emotional pain obvious, was a unspoken tribute to the kind of woman that Evelyn must have been. Tenderly, he led her first through a recitation of her friendship with Evelyn, whose marriage to Clem Pettit gave her a special understanding of Mildred's condition.

"During the many years that you knew Evelyn, as this friendship grew, as you were less able to get around, did you and Evelyn always keep in touch with each other in some way?"

"Yes, sir, by telephone, literally every day. We talked—oh, about various things—she was able to go to parties that I was not and she would tell me the names of the guests and the things they did." But their last conversation was on May 5, 1955, the day Mildred left Los Angeles for a six-week trip to London accompanied by her nurse. Despite the distance, a beautiful bouquet of flowers and a note from Evelyn arrived at Mildred's hotel on May 12, her birthday. Mildred planned to call Evelyn as soon as she returned to Los Angeles on June 15, but the trip home had been tiring, and Mildred put off that telephone call until the following day. Instead, Ewing's early morning phone call woke her.

"Mr. Scott told me that Evelyn had been very ill mentally and physically during the time we were away and that he had had to put her in a sanatorium—shall I go on?" she asked hesitantly.

"Go on, yes," Leavy prompted her gently.

"He said that there were only three sanatoriums," Mildred said, the trembling in her voice magnified by the microphone, "that would take care of her neurosis and they were in the East. He said that he was taking her there at once. I asked him if he knew where and he said no, he did not. And then I asked if I might speak to her. He said no"—Mildred hid her face, sobbing—"I am sorry. . . . He said she was standing in the middle of the bathroom with a bottle of whiskey in her hand using obscene language. I asked him if he would please be kind enough to let me know where he was taking Evelyn and from time to time to let me know how she was."

"Did he ever do so?"

"No, sir."

"Ever?"

"No, sir." Mildred was crying softly.

"Never?"

"No, sir."

"Is that correct?"

"How many times he is going to ask that question?" Lambros interrupted.

"She has answered it sufficiently, Mr. Leavy," Judge Nye said. "The court will take an early recess."

When court reconvened, Mildred, calmer now, finished her testimony about Scott's previous comments about Evelyn's health: "He told me that she was mentally ill, physically ill, and that he was greatly worried about her."

"What did Evelyn say about her health when you inquired of her about it?"

"That she was feeling very well, with the exception of once or twice she told me she had had a little trouble in the night with the diverticulitis. She said she took some pills and felt wonderful in a short time."

"Did you ever see Evelyn intoxicated?"

"No, sir. Never."

"Did Evelyn mention anything to you about her brother?"

"Yes, she told me that he had wanted to borrow money from her and she did let him have it two or three times. The last time, she said she didn't know what to do. She was very upset because Mr. Scott and Mr. Boyle objected to her doing it and she felt she shouldn't lend him money under the circumstances. . . . [Then] she called me one morning and she had a dreadful letter from Raymond. She said, 'I am just heartsick, but I know that he did not mean what he said, that it is just not true—after all he is my brother and I love him very much.'"

Matthews cross-examined Mildred carefully. She was a very sympathetic witness, and Matthews knew that he must win her over, or, at the very least, not appear to offend her. He didn't have much of a chance to discredit her testimony but Matthews knew he had to try. "I have a little difficulty standing too long, so I'll join you in a tête-à-tête," Matthews said conversationally, seating himself in a high-back wooden chair a comfortable, still intimate, distance away from her. "Can you tell me what sort of a personality you thought Mr. Scott had?"

"I thought a very pleasing one. And he was very, very kind to me."

Matthews was pleasantly surprised. That answer was the sort he'd hoped to elicit from her. "When you had dinner with the Scotts, did he ever talk to you about Mrs. Scott?"

"Yes, sir. He would first always say, 'Doesn't my bride look beautiful tonight?' And then he'd tell me how ill she'd been before they had come to the party."

"You're in your early sixties now, aren't you," Matthews asked, appearing only slightly interested in her answer.

"A little later," Mildred said modestly.

"A little later than that," Matthews repeated. "Well, you have known Mrs. Scott since—oh, it's been more than twenty years, hasn't it?"

"Yes, sir, twenty-one years, I think."

"Now, Mr. Scott did tell you that Evelyn had done a couple of things that he thought were—well, that indicated to him that she might be a little ill mentally, isn't that true?"

"He told me about some artificial flowers that she said to have taken out, that they were wilting. But I didn't think much about that because she had such a wonderful sense of humor and she would have said that as a joke. . . . He told me that she came downstairs one morning in her dressing gown with her hat on. I didn't think too much about that either because—"

"That's never happened to you?" Matthews eagerly finished Mildred's statement for her. "Has it happened to you?"

"Well," said the witness a little wistfully, "not that I can remember. It's been so many years since I have been able to put on a gown like that."

"He seemed to be in love with her, though, didn't he?"

"I thought so."

"And she was in love with him?"

"I thought so."

"Was Mr. Scott trying to break up your friendship with Mrs. Scott?"

"I didn't think so but we met more and more rarely."

"They say that a lady who would lie about her age would lie about anything else. All the time that you knew Mr. Scott before all of this gossip came up, it never occurred to you that he was the type of man

who would kill his wife, did it?" Matthews rose abruptly before the
stunned witness could answer. "Mr. Bailiff, the chair, please. That is
all, Mrs. Schuchardt."

□ **30**

If the prosecution called many more sympathetic witnesses such as
Mildred Schuchardt, Matthews knew that the defense might have a
rough time of it. But what worried him was the prospect of Leavy's
questioning Scott on the witness stand, and Matthews brought his
misgivings up to Lambros.

"Leavy is probably the greatest cross-examiner around," Matthews
said. "He's got a way of lulling his witnesses to sleep just long
enough to slug 'em with a sandbag full of evidence."

"You don't think Scott can handle Leavy?"

"What's he going to do, get up there and say that the rest of the
world is lying?" Matthews demanded. "Look, I don't believe any of
that 'dear Evelyn Scott' business any more than you do—she might
have been a whore before she got so damn respectable, for all I know.
But that doesn't change a goddamn thing here. Leavy'll tear Scott
apart."

"I'm in charge of the defense. I'll be the one to make that decision."

"All right, I get it," Matthews said. "We're just like two guys in a
bar: The only thing we've got in common is that we both like whiskey. Well, I've got my fish to fry here and I'll do everything I can to
keep Scott out of the gas chamber. But if Leavy gets ahold of him, it's
going to make my job a helluva lot tougher."

The prosecution busied itself next with some of the slight, but
essential, details of Scott's paper trail. Among the witnesses called
was Odgen vice president Helen Bellman, who identified twenty-one
canceled checks as the ones issued to Evelyn for her share of The

Edgewater's monthly income. Until June 1955, every check bore Evelyn's personal endorsement, with one exception in October 1954, when Evelyn had asked Bellman to deposit the check with a typewritten endorsement while she was abroad. But in June 1955, Odgen's check was cashed with a typewritten endorsement and deposited in the joint account Scott had opened; thereafter, Evelyn's endorsement was always rubber-stamped.

Lambros countered Bellman's testimony with Scott's correspondence file with the management company, though, at the court's request, he read only half of the ninety-three-letter-long file into the court record. Those letters, Lambros believed, written about the routine aspects of the property, showed that Scott had Evelyn's blessing to oversee her affairs.

Then Vera Landry, the maid who said she had refused Scott's order to eavesdrop on Evelyn's phone conversations, silenced the courtroom with her recounting of one of the Scotts' first battles. "Mrs. Scott came down with a bruise on her cheek," Vera testified. "I went to the refrigerator and got a piece of raw beef and applied it. During the night I had heard a noise from the Scotts' bedroom. It sounded like someone fell on the floor."

Later, Scott told her what had occurred. "He asked me if Mrs. Scott had told me what happened. I told him 'no,' and he said he had 'slapped the wind out of her,'" Vera said.

As his former mistress took the stand on Monday, November 4, Scott's face was impassive. Marianne Beaman wore a blue jersey dress with a wide, scalloped-brim hat and dark sunglasses; her tongue nervously traced the outline of her upper lip during much of her testimony. Alarcon asked for a list of Scott's gifts to her: three leather purses, a leather hatbox, a train case, a bathroom heater, a scale, a night-light, a fingertip-length black lamb's wool cape, and Evelyn's jewelry.

"He asked me if I would like to have them and I said I would. They appeared to be used . . . . Some of the things he said had belonged to Mrs. Scott but she didn't use them."

"Have you ever been at 217 North Bentley?" Alarcon asked.

"Yes, about four times, with Mr. Scott."

"Were you an overnight guest?"

"Yes."

"What name did he use in introducing you?"

"Mrs. Scott."

Alarcon turned to their trysts at the Kona Kai Club. "Do you recognize that writing?"

"Yes. It is my writing."

"How were you registered?"

"I don't know."

"Were you in the same room with the defendant?"

"Yes, I was."

On the evening of May 1, 1956, Marianne met Ewing for dinner at Chip's a restaurant on Santa Monica Boulevard.

"When we left the restaurant, I started to turn to go into the parking lot and Mr. Scott told me the car wasn't there, that he would be walking me home. . . . I asked Mr. Scott where the car was but he said it was parked a short distance away. He didn't tell me where."

"Did you see Mr. Scott or talk to him the next day?"

"No, I didn't."

"Did you ever see him again?"

"Never."

Lambros was less gentle with Marianne. He read her denial of Scott's marriage proposal before the grand jury aloud, forcing Marianne to admit that she had lied under oath. Marianne had clarified her answer later the same day, but, she admitted, "I was trying to save both Mr. Scott and myself from public criticism."

Marianne testified that Scott came to her apartment on the night of February 14, 1956, after his interview with the district attorney's investigators. "He looked like he had been bruised badly on one side of his face and his lip was cut."

But Bill Brawner, whose testimony followed Marianne's a day later, described his observation of Scott that night. "He was continually twisting the sides of his face with his thumb and finger, first on one side, then on the other," Brawner said, demonstrating with his long fingers pulling on the side of his own face. "He continued that very noticeably for quite a while. He had a cold sore on his lip and he was pinching that, pulling on it with his thumb and forefinger. He was also knuckling his eyes, first on one side and then on the other."

"At social gatherings as early as 1952, what did the defendant say with reference to securities and investments?" Leavy asked.

"He said that he was urging Mrs. Scott to sell her securities and to convert them into cash, that he thought [it] should be done at this time and that he thought that they should go to South America or Portugal or someplace to live and they could do very much better than they could staying here. He repeatedly urged that course on myself as well as on other people."

"What did Mrs. Scott say?"

"She said that the United States was good enough for her. She said she did not want to live in South America or Portugal and she did not care to sell her securities but she thought she would sell some of them to keep peace with her husband. . . . Sometime after their return from a trip abroad in 1954, she remarked to me that she was all ready for the storm, that she had sold all of her securities, and that she had to sell them if she was going to live with her husband."

Later that same year, Brawner testified he "noticed that there were black and blue marks on the side of her face and a tinge of purple around her left eye and on the side of the cheek," and the last time he saw her, at her May 12, 1955, birthday celebration, Evelyn "seemed constrained and worried."

During his cross-examination, Lambros tried to discredit Brawner with the charge that Brawner had been suspended by the California State Bar in 1955 after a "Mr. Jones" claimed Brawner stole money from him.

"I was never disbarred, never suspended, and the court dismissed the charge," Brawner answered Lambros cheerfully.

Lambros tried another tact: "Now, Mr. Brawner, why was it you chose H. H. Montgomery to front for you when you wanted to contact Mr. Throsby?"

"Well," said Evelyn's former neighbor and the friend who had urged the late Ernie Roll to investigate her absence, "I was deeply suspicious that Mr. Scott had done away with her and I wanted to divert this inquiry to some source where I didn't think it would attract his attention. I was deeply concerned in knowing what had happened to Mrs. Scott."

On Leavy's motion, the court ruled on November 6 that Evelyn's wills were accessible for inspection in a joint conference by all counsel. But the wills would not yet be an official record and were to be returned to the court for sealing. The prosecutors and the defense lawyers spent their lunch hour looking over the documents; Leavy prepared to introduce them into evidence. But in a hasty conference at the bench called by Lambros immediately after lunch, Evelyn's wills were unexpectedly admitted as joint exhibits.

Evelyn's latest will, dated September 10, 1954, was essentially identical to her earlier will, which was dated November 25, 1949, changing only a few minor bequests to friends. But Raymond was not her principal beneficiary, as Scott had publicly insisted; rather, Throsby and Scott were to share equally in her estate upon her death. One-half went directly to Scott, with the remaining half in trust for Raymond, who was to receive income every month from her estate. When either Scott or Throsby died, each one's share would be distributed to the survivor. Evelyn's final beneficiary, when both her husband and her brother were deceased, was the La Vina Tuberculosis Sanatorium in Pasadena.

Testimony resumed later that afternoon as Lambros pursued the subject of Evelyn's securities with Brawner, scoring, in the process, a point for the prosecution. "On May 12, 1955," Lambros asked, "you said that Mr. Scott told you that he had induced his wife to sell some stock and convert them into cash?"

"Yes," Brawner said. "He said she had it in a safe-deposit box—whatever she got from the sale of the securities—and that he had her do that."

Clark Sellers, elegant and bespectacled, brought more than forty years experience as a questioned-documents examiner to the stand as the state's seventy-second witness. From a study of Evelyn's genuine signatures back to 1940, Sellers had concluded that the twenty-six questioned signatures—two on the co-renter's agreement taken from one model of Evelyn's handwriting, twenty-three traveler's checks countersignatures, and one on the joint-account form—were diligent copies.

"Did you reach an opinion," Leavy asked, "as to whether her handwriting had deteriorated through alcoholism or some other reasons?"

"I could not find any definite evidence that her signature had deteriorated. Her signature has been quite consistent."

Handwriting, like the voice, Sellers continued, has a natural range of its own, its form paced by the speed of the hand as one letter flows proportionally into the next. The traced signatures were exact duplications of Evelyn's writing, yes, but with none of the careless flaws of her own hand. The tracings "significantly violated" the idiosyncratic turns of her hand, and replaced it with the unmistakable characteristics of the tracer.

But, Matthews questioned him on cross-examination, "simulation of another signature doesn't necessarily imply fraud, does it?"

"Not necessarily, no," Sellers agreed. "A person may be authorized to sign someone else's signature."

"And to avoid the inconvenience of explaining to virtual strangers your authority, you might simulate the signature, let's say, of someone like your wife, isn't that right?"

"If I understand the implication of your question, it is, did I find it to be a fact that Mr. Scott simulated Mrs. Scott's handwriting?" Sellers said. "My answer is that I cannot definitely identify him as the writer of the questioned signatures."

Leavy countered with another question. "Within limits," he asked, as Sellers' second full day of testimony ended, "can you identify who was the tracer of the questioned signatures?"

"Under certain limitations, yes," Sellers said. "If the inquiry were limited to two persons—did Mrs. Scott or did Mr. Scott write the questioned signatures?—I would say—with that limitation—Mr. Scott wrote the questioned signatures."

Sellers' testimony took the trial into its fifth week, and so far, the prosecution showed no sign of resting. "This trial has gone out of the realm of being a lawsuit," Judge Nye observed wearily to all counsel. "It's becoming a way of life."

Testimony in the trial's sixth week dealt with the specific allegations that Scott's wife was a cancer-ridden lesbian. In August 1947, testified Dr. John Wirth of the Pasadena Tumor Institute, two benign lesions were removed from below Evelyn's right eye. The treatment was successful, and Evelyn had returned to Dr. Wirth religiously every six months until July 1954, with no sign of recurrence.

Olive Wright, a prim matron with two grown children of her own, gave a matter-of-fact accounting of her eleven-month employment with Evelyn. She went to work for Mildred Schuchardt almost immediately after Evelyn's marriage to Scott.

"Was there ever any conduct on your part or on Mrs. Scott's part of an unnatural kind?" asked Leavy.

"No, absolutely not."

On Thursday, November 14, Leavy moved to an analysis of Evelyn's financial affairs to show how some of her liquidated assets were fraudulently used by her husband. The prosecutor called Tom Doherty to the witness stand for two-and-a-half days' worth of detailed testimony about Evelyn's $600,000 in assets.

Doherty, leaning close to his work sheets to read his rows of figures with his poor eyesight, gave his accounting of Evelyn's holdings as Leavy followed along with a pointer on the charts he'd had made. Most important to Leavy was the timetable Doherty presented illustrating Evelyn's cash withdrawals, which totaled $57,177, and her parallel safe-deposit-box entries between March 10, 1952, and August 9, 1952. To support Leavy's inference that that cash went into her safe-deposit box, Doherty testified that *all* of Evelyn's deposits into her checking and savings accounts over that period were by check, never cash. But on Lambros' objection, the court cautioned Doherty not to tie her withdrawals, specifically to Evelyn's box entries: "That's an inference to be drawn by someone else, not you," Judge Nye said.

Doherty also produced records dealing with Scott's finances, which consisted of four bank accounts that Scott jointly shared with his mother before her death in 1950 or maintained in his own name. There were two joint accounts: one, opened January 28, 1944, and closed January 3, 1950, that had had as much as $10,000 on deposit for two brief periods; the second, opened with $15,000 on July 8, 1948, that dwindled until it was closed on October 27, 1950.

Slightly more than $3,000 was on deposit in the two accounts when Scott married Evelyn in 1949.

Another account, opened October 26, 1950, with $1,670, had as much as $3,000 at one time on deposit, which included funds given by Evelyn to her husband, but that account was closed on February 17, 1954, when its balance dropped to zero. The fourth account was still active; it was the one Scott had opened at the Bank of Los Angeles in his own name just after Evelyn vanished.

As he readied for the sixth week of testimony, Leavy was anxious that every element in his chain of circumstantial evidence was set in place. Two minor cases of the flu—the first patient was a juror, the second the defendant—put the court in recess until Wednesday, November 20. Scott, recovering in the hospital ward of the county jail, was visited by his three attorneys, and he managed a bit of humor for them: "Everyone else was getting the flu and I didn't want to be different."

Harriet Livermore's testimony ended the trial's sixth week; Scott's onetime companion, dressed stunningly for court in a black suit, white hat, white gloves, and a fur stole, repeated Scott's comment that Evelyn had deserted him after five years of marriage. Later, on August 15, 1955, Harriet and Ewing drove to Santa Monica for dinner. As they drove home over Mulholland Drive, an area she said Scott seemed to know quite well, Harriet was told about Evelyn's poor health and lesbian tendencies.

"I said, 'If you feel so dreadfully toward your wife—as you must—why don't you just get a divorce?' He said, 'No, I am going to wait seven years and she will then be declared legally dead.'"

Under cross-examination, the defense hinted that Harriet repeatedly tried to entice a reluctant Ewing into an affair. "Is it not a fact, Mrs. Livermore," Lambros questioned her, "that you put on a hostess gown which zippered down the front and you opened and closed the zipper three times?"

"No," the witness replied firmly. "In fact, I don't possess a hostess gown."

On Tuesday, November 26, Leavy rested the state's case with the ninety-eighth and final witness, Hallam Mathew, who served as trustee of Evelyn's estate on behalf of the Citizen's National Trust & Savings Bank.

"Up to this moment," Leavy asked, "has the defendant ever claimed any interest in the assets under your control in the missing person's estate of Evelyn Scott?" Leavy asked. He wanted to establish that only after his arrest did Scott show any legal interest in his wife's affairs. " I am referring to any interest of his own or any community-property interest."

"None at all," Mathews replied.

"But," asked Lambros on cross-examination, "have you ever asked Mr. Scott if he has or claims any community property?"

"I have not," Mathews admitted.

"Never asked him," Lambros repeated, certain of a small victory for the defense. ". . . You went ahead anyway, didn't you, with your rounding up of the assets . . . You are satisfied now, are you not, that you have marshaled all the assets that are available?"

Mathew's answer was not what Lambros expected to hear. "No, sir," said the estate trustee emphatically, "I am not."

For three hours on Wednesday, November 27, Lambros argued in the absence of the jury a series of defense motions to put a stop to Scott's trial, including an advised verdict of acquittal, based on a statement made by Judge Nye while overruling a defense objection to the testimony of a witness from the Internal Revenue Service. "I think, Mr. Lambros," the judge had remarked at that time, "that in view of the fact that this [case] is based entirely on circumstantial evidence [the fact that there is no record Scott had filed an income tax return since 1945] is one of the circumstances that should be taken into consideration by the court and the jury in the overall picture." The defense called the remark "misconduct" on the ground that the judge had invaded the province of the jury by saying what "should" be considered. But Judge Nye, pointing out that his remark was directed at Lambros, not the jury, denied Lambros' motion.

Lambros tried other arguments, including the absence of proof of

Evelyn's death. Even should her death be presumed by the court, there was no evidence that death occurred by criminal means. And, again arguing the matter of venue, Lambros charged that the court had no jurisdiction to hear the case because the state offered no proof that death occurred in Los Angeles County.

"We have here an unaccountable disappearance. That's the only statement we have in the record. Unless they can prove Mr. Scott had anything directly or indirectly to do with the disappearance, they haven't proved the corpus delicti . . . I don't believe Your Honor could preclude the good possibility of Mrs. Scott returning to Los Angeles and into this courtroom . . . We have nothing but teeth, glasses, and a missing person . . . We are going to stretch the law too far if we are not careful."

Judge Nye denied these motions too, and Lambros moved to strike certain testimony concerning Scott's alleged statements on the ground that the corpus delicti had not been established, as well as alleged comments of Evelyn made out of the presence of the defendant, on the grounds of hearsay. The attorney admitted that some of Scott's conduct might seem peculiar: "I know everything he did will be explained at the right time." His motions to strike those pieces of testimony were not granted.

Defeated, Lambros announced for the first time that he might not even present a defense when the trial resumed after the Thanksgiving weekend. "Mr. Scott may very well not even take the stand," Lambros hinted. "There is not much he can tell that has not already been told."

□ □ □ □ □ □ □ □ □ □ □ □ □ □ □ □ □ □ □ **31**

Lambros was succinct: "We believe that what the defendant will present in his behalf will convince you beyond a reasonable doubt that there is no evidence that Evelyn Scott is dead; and on the contrary,

210

the evidence should point more to her being alive." With that abbreviated, one-sentence opening statement, the defense was ready to call its first witness, Sheyla Bergman, the neighbor on whose property Hertel made his discovery.

"I have here, Mrs. Bergman, a cigarette holder and 101 filters," Lambros said, showing them to her. "Can you identify any of those items?"

"This looks like a cigarette holder my husband threw away. He was watering the rose garden . . . and I remember him taking it out and throwing it approximately in the vicinity of the incinerators. . ᐟ . [Later] we threw out a bunch of filters."

"That's the Scott incinerator?"

"Ours was right above it—they're tiered things."

In June 1955, two weeks after Evelyn vanished, the Bergmans moved. "During the course of your moving, did you discard anything?" questioned Lambros.

"I cleaned out medicine chests. I threw away some pills because I didn't exactly know what they were for."

"Were any of them Aureomycin, do you know?"

"They could have been."

"Do you remember throwing away any [hair] brushes?"

"It's very possible we did. I do not remember that specific brush [but] someone else in the house could have thrown it out; my housekeeper or somebody of that sort."

"I show you here an Ultrasol solution, purportedly a hair fluid. Did you throw this away?"

"I can't answer for my housekeeper," the handsome, soft-spoken witness replied, "but I know my husband and I did not."

"Did you ever see any strangers working around Bentley Avenue—a little before or after May 16?"

"I don't exactly know what you mean by strangers."

"At any time did you observe three Negroes in the area?"

"No."

"Did you ever hear any screaming or shouting or anything unnatural taking place at the Scott household?"

"No."

"Everything appeared perfectly normal to you?"

"Perfectly normal."

Lambros called one of Scott's former civil attorneys next. "At the time that Mr. Scott talked with the district attorney," he asked Seth Hufstedler, "did he give the same story that he had consistently told you folks about the disappearance of his wife?"

"Object to that," Leavy said, "as calling for a conclusion of this witness; confidential privileged communication to which there's been no waiver; as well as a self-serving declaration."

Lambros tried another tact. "Mr. Hufstedler, in your presence, did Mr. Scott answer all questions put to him by the district attorney?"

"I would have to say no."

"Did you and Mr. Beardsley at any time advise him not to answer any questions?"

"Yes, we did."

Then Lambros, hinting that the cars that had followed Scott and his lawyers were the reason for Scott's flight, asked, "Did he at any time indicate to you that he was afraid for his life?"

But Leavy's objection blocked the witness's answer. The prosecutor, on cross-examination asked about Hufstedler's interview with a woman in Mexico, who was rumored to be Scott's missing wife. "I satisfied myself," Hufstedler said, "that [she] was not Mrs. Scott."

The defense had to counter the prosecution's image of Scott as a penniless fortune hunter with proof that Scott was what he claimed to be: a highly successful speculator, accustomed to the complicated workings of sophisticated finance. But that kind of testimony came not from Scott's fellow Jonathan Club members, nor even from other land developers who could attest to a colleague's expertise. Instead, Lambros called Perry Pasmezoglu, an insurance-turned-advertising salesman, as proof that Scott was a prosperous businessman with money and assets of his own.

As noted, Pasmezoglu had met Scott in St. Louis, when, in 1934, the two men negotiated a trade: Scott offered to swap Pasmezoglu some Canadian bonds he was selling as an independent securities broker in exchange for the annual $1,000 premium on a $25,000 life insurance policy. But their deal fell through when the state regulatory agency ruled that the insurer could not purchase that type of bonds. Despite the Depression that gripped the rest of the country, Scott

212

appeared to be a man of "considerable" financial means, Pasmezoglu testified.

After that first deal, Pasmezoglu and Scott toyed briefly with the idea of going into business together, though they never did. They lost touch until a chance meeting in 1939 in the heart of Los Angeles' financial district, when Scott told Pasmezoglu that he was still in the investment business. Soon after, Pasmezoglu received a postcard from the Fiji Islands, his last contact with Scott until now.

To the prosecution, Pasmezoglu's testimony was limited to his own vague impressions, the unchallenged source of which was Scott himself. On cross, Alarcon put a little perspective into Pasmezoglu's picture of a financially sound Scott. When the bonds were ruled ineligible, did Scott make a counteroffer? Alarcon asked, hinting that Scott was actually unable to afford $25,000 worth of life insurance.

"No," Pasmezoglu admitted.

"All right," said Alarcon, satisfied. "Now, the last time you had contact with the defendant personally, you saw him on the street here on Spring Street?"

"That's right."

"At that time, you asked what business he was in and you say, 'He told me he was in the investment business,' is that correct?"

"That is what I recall, yes."

"You have no other information other than what he told you as to whether or not he was in the investment business?"

"No, none whatsoever."

"You didn't make a check yourself at the time?"

"No."

"He didn't tell you he had an office somewhere?"

"No, sir, he did not."

On Tuesday, December 3, Chuck Beardsley took the witness stand, and Lambros zeroed in on the efforts to find Evelyn in Mexico, in the eastern United States, and in California. Testimony such as this was crucial to Scott's defense; at every opportunity, Lambros had to hammer home that—somewhere—Evelyn Scott might still be alive. The most intriguing tip, Beardsley testified, had been the report of a gardener, who was said to have seen Evelyn and a man resembling her brother putting suitcases in a car on the afternoon of her disappearance. But, Beardsley admitted, he had been unable to track down the gardener in question or trace the source of that rumor.

"And were there any other leads that you pursued?"

"There were a great many."

"Did Mr. Scott at any time stop the investigation?"

"Oh, no."

"Did he at any time attempt to limit the investigation?"

"Not at all."

"Was he at all times cooperative and desirous of searching out and finding his wife?"

"Completely so, yes, sir."

Pleased, Lambros moved on to the next phase of Scott's defense with the witnesses who were to confirm Scott's rendering of Evelyn as a drunk. The first such eyewitness was Maxwell Rozan, a Russian-born, retired independent oil operator. Rozan, who said he considered it was his duty to volunteer to testify on Scott's behalf, said he met Evelyn and her husband in July 1953 at the Beverly Wilshire Hotel bar. "She was drinking while I was present. She got up from her seat and seemed wobbly on her legs as though she were indulging in too much liquor," Rozan, a slight, bespectacled man, said.

He said he saw the same woman at least twice again, once in 1954 and then around May 11, 1955; on each occasion, Rozan testified that she was accompanied by a man other than her husband. "I would say she was intoxicated on every occasion I saw her," Rozan said.

"Is there any doubt in your mind that the woman you saw was Evelyn Scott?" Lambros asked.

"There is no question in my mind," the witness said firmly.

To courtroom observers, Leavy's cross-examination of Rozan seemed irrelevant, as the prosecutor grilled the witness, a resident of North Dakota, on where he spent his time in Los Angeles. But in minutes of relentless questioning, Leavy elicited some surprising information from the witness, which the prosecutor knew eroded whatever credibility Rozan might have otherwise enjoyed. "As a matter of fact, you served three months up in the county jail, didn't you?" Leavy asked.

"Yes, sir," Rozan admitted reluctantly. "Out at the farm."

"That is a cheap way of trying to impeach a witness," Lambros interrupted. "He was not convicted of any felony. That's not a proper question to ask—he has nothing to hide—it has nothing to do with the issues involved here."

But Judge Nye overruled the objection, and Leavy continued. "How do you fix the month of July of '53 that you claim you saw Evelyn Scott in a bar with Mr. Scott?"

"It was shortly after I was arrested and charged with assault with a deadly weapon," Rozan said, a charge he testified grew out of a physical altercation with the attorney handling his wife's divorce petition. Rozan served a seventy-four-day term for that offense, and, he admitted next under Leavy's questioning, he was convicted in Canada of false pretenses, a felony offense in that country, for which he served time in a Canadian reformatory.

But all Lambros needed was the whisper of doubt in a single juror's mind, and he called Havilah Eames as the defense's next witness. To a rapt courtroom, Eames, manager of the Sprouse-Reitz dime store in Santa Paula, a California town near Santa Barbara, identified pictures of a customer he saw on May 21 or 22, 1955, as Evelyn. She was with two other women, Eames said, one of whom purchased a moss rose-patterned cup and saucer; with a dramatic flourish, Lambros introduced an identical cup and saucer into evidence.

"I bumped into this lady and I said, 'Excuse me, Mrs. Bellkamp,'" Eames said. "I thought she was one of my steady customers—this woman resembles one of my steady customers so much. Then I recognized that she wasn't . . . the only part that I can recollect of our conversation was that she stated either she had just arrived in Santa Paula from Ojai or that she was just leaving for Ojai."

"Is there any question in your mind whether this"—Lambros gestured with the photograph Eames had identified—"is the woman you saw in your store?"

"Well, all I can say is that I feel she is the same woman beyond a reasonable doubt," Eames said, adding that the same customer came in again during the holidays, sometime between November 15 and December 15, 1955. He had not seen the woman since; only when Lambros jogged his memory did Eames recall the incident.

"Was the story you related here today suggested to you in any way?" Lambros asked. "This is your own testimony? No suggestion [was] made to you about how to testify?"

"No, no, sir."

"Have you," Leavy asked the witness, "ever seen a person as you are walking about the street or whatever you might be doing that might look like some other acquaintance or some other personality you knew?"

"Without a doubt," Eames agreed.

"You have had that experience a number of times in your life?"

"I think everybody has had that experience."

"I am asking you."

"Yes, without a doubt I have."

"After this incident in the store, the next day, did you forget all about it?"

"Yes. It didn't mean anything to me."

"You forgot about it until how many days ago?"

"Well, I never even thought about it anymore until Mr. Lambros brought it back to memory."

"And you'd say that's how many days ago?"

"I don't know how long—" Eames hesitated. "How long ago was it, Mr. Lambros?" he asked.

Leavy smiled as the courtroom, Judge Nye included, erupted in laughter. "I'm sorry," the prosecutor said, "you can't ask him questions." Eames was unable to fix the date asked for by Leavy.

Ladya Sanborn, a prim, self-assured widow, was Lambros' next witness, and the one least shaken under cross-examination. Sanborn, smart in a tailored suit and pillbox hat, identified two pictures of Evelyn as the woman she saw trying to board a plane at the Mexico City air terminal on August 18, 1955.

"I was in Mexico City on business," Sanborn testified, an employee of California's Department of Employment, "and I was leaving in the morning around eight o'clock. The lady came in with another lady in the foyer of the air terminal and she was, to say the least, very highly stimulated."

"When you say she was highly stimulated, what do you mean?" asked Lambros.

"She had been drinking or something. She was very—gay. It created a great deal of tittering. . . . I didn't see her again . . . until oh, probably twenty minutes before we embarked. She was being escorted by someone down the ramp to the airplane. She was still pretty high and the attendant started questioning her and she said, 'There's nothing wrong with me at all—I just took a pill for my heart and I'm all right.' The attendant took her by the arm and ushered her back up the ramp and that was the last I saw of her," until, Sanborn said, she saw Evelyn's picture in the paper late that winter.

But under Alarcon's cross-examination, Sanborn refused to be pinned down on when exactly she did see Evelyn's picture; Evelyn's disappearance, after all, did not become public news until the following spring.

Emelyn Routhier testified that she met Evelyn as Mrs. Pettit at a USO in 1930. On May 19, 1955, a date she remembered because she withdrew money from the bank to buy a pair of shoes, Routhier said she saw Evelyn again.

"I saw her on Wilshire. I was going down Wilshire one way and she was coming up the other with [another] woman. . . . She came over to me, caught me by the arm, and squeezed it very hard. She asked me where the Beverly Hills Hotel was. I wasn't quite sure and this other woman called to her in a very abrupt, rough, coarse manner. I said, 'Are you in trouble?' and she said, 'Yes, yes,' and tears came to her eyes. The woman called her a second time . . . [and] a third time and in a rough way pulled her toward the sidewalk and then they went up into a building."

"Will you please tell the court and the jury how you happened to be here today, Mrs. Routhier?" Lambros asked.

"I felt very guilty and responsible that I didn't go into the hotel that day because she told me she was in deep trouble."

As testimony ended for that Tuesday afternoon, Leavy's cross-examination was nothing more than a gentle test of Mrs. Routhier's memory; the witness, an elderly, obviously forgetful woman, had trouble recalling dates, addresses, and names.

As testimony resumed on Wednesday, December 4, Lambros announced that Scott had been advised by his three lawyers not to take the witness stand in his own defense, and that Scott had agreed to their recommendation. The defense was banking on Lambros' belief that the prosecution would fail to prove its case beyond a reasonable doubt to avoid the risk posed by exposing Scott to Leavy's cross-examination.

Though keenly disappointed, Leavy knew he could turn Scott's failure to testify to his advantage. "Well, we'll just make sure that the jury remembers that Scott didn't take the stand," Leavy told Alarcon later. "They didn't hear Scott himself deny that he killed her."

Lambros called Julian Warnack, a ticket seller for the Santa Fe Railroad at Union Station, to the stand next.

"When did you see [Mrs. Scott], sir?" Lambros asked.

"The only time that I can say that I saw her is when I sold her a ticket to New York City on the Super Chief, on July the 20th, 1955."

"Will you tell us the circumstances surrounding that purchase?"

"She asked me for a reservation [for] the train leaving that evening. . . . She said her name was Scott and I was just a little particularly interested because that is a family name. She said she just married the name . . . and finally, she told me, 'I am leaving Mr. Scott, but he doesn't know it.' I was amazed at that quotation because I very seldom ever hear anything like that from an elderly woman."

"Mr. Warnack, how do you remember Mrs. Scott as compared to the thousands of other people you must have coming there every day?"

"Because of that amazing statement, I looked at her again . . . and I pointed her out to Mr. Williams," a fellow railway employee, Warnack said.

Warnack reported his suspicions later to the police, and Lambros asked, "Were you ever called by the prosecution or the police department, and asked to come here to testify?"

"No, sir."

That last point was of intense interest to Leavy, and he asked the witness to identify Howard Hudson, the LAPD detective who did, in fact, interview Warnack about that ticket sale a day after Warnack's call to the authorities. Warnack failed to recognize Hudson, however, and Leavy reminded him of the substance of their meeting:

"Didn't you tell [him] that you were sure you had sold a ticket to what you believed to be Mrs. Scott around May 16, 1955?"

"No, I did not say that."

"Was there another employee there?"

"There were quite a few of us there, sir."

"Didn't this occur: While this gentleman from the police department was down talking to you in 1956, didn't the employee who was there tell you in the presence of this officer that there was no use looking for your sales around May 16, 1955 . . . and reminded you that you were off for about a month and in the hospital? Didn't that occur?"

"Yes, it did," said the witness.

"You never told the officer you sold the ticket in July of 1955, did you?"

"No, I didn't," Warnack admitted.

Next came Gordon O'Bannon, a TWA redcap at O'Hare Airport in Chicago. O'Bannon testified that in July 1951 he met Scott in the airline office, where he was waiting for his wife. When Evelyn arrived, she appeared to have been drinking, O'Bannon said.

"When he [Scott] asked her where she had been—we told her we were holding the bus for her—she said, 'Hell, I have been away before. That is nothing new. None of your damn business,'" testified the witness.

"How do you remember this incident back in 1951?" Lambros asked.

"I remember the incident so clearly [due to] the language she used and by being intoxicated," and, O'Bannon admitted later under Leavy's cross-examination, when his supervisor reminded him of the incident.

"In my profession and in my business, two things I remember: nasty people and nice people," O'Bannon said.

"Those are the things you remember, when you hear a woman use profanity?" Leavy asked.

"Especially if the lady was dressed like [Evelyn] was and looked like she looked—aristocratic—that type of woman."

"Was she wearing glasses?"

"Yes, I believe she did have on glasses."

"She wasn't reading anything, though, was she?"

"No," O'Bannon said.

But Leavy had made his point. Earlier testimony had indicated that Evelyn's glasses were for reading only.

Next, Lambros called Carl Vernell, the part-time actor and construction worker who had tried vainly to collect his fee from Scott.

"Now the Bank of America wanted you to do something for them and Mr. Scott, is that correct?" Lambros asked.

"That is correct. They wanted me to contact Mr. McGovern [of the FHA] and see if I could get a commitment, which Mr. Scott had asked for, for $535,000 for the construction of thirty-five homes in Santa Ana."

Scott promised Vernell 10 percent, or $8,200, of what he said he expected to earn on the project, plus a superintendent's job for Vernell at the construction site. Vernell's intervention was successful, but almost immediately, Scott sold out his interest in the tract for $15,000. "I think I probably chased Mr. Scott all over for the following year and I wasn't able to accomplish anything," Vernell said. "I didn't get any of my money out of it, which was very annoying—I could have used it."

By chance, Vernell spotted Scott on the Huntington Hotel's dance floor. Though Scott was clearly upset at Vernell's interruption, Evelyn, not Scott, suggested that Vernell visit them at home to reach a solution. Vernell did so twice, first in 1950, then again in 1954.

"She said that Mr. Scott was financially sound and they had invested their money in some real estate," Vernell said. "I don't know exactly where—I think it was a middle western city—it could have been Milwaukee."

"She said that she had invested her money in some property with Mr. Scott?"

"No, that Mr. Scott had invested his money with her."

"Did she say how much?"

"No [but] she said he had invested all his funds because they decided to do their financial activities as a team."

"What else did she say?"

"She said that she had every respect for his business ability and that especially when it came to real property she felt he was an expert."

On both occasions, Evelyn served stiff drinks, her own, Vernell said, consisting of "three fingers of bourbon and less water. . . . I thought she was pretty gay and a very lively woman and I think the bourbon made her feel a little gayer."

Vernell continued: "She told me [Scott] was a very conservative man, that he didn't like drinking or smoking. . . . She said she was the type of woman who was just vain enough to want to walk into a dining room with the best-looking man in the crowd. She said that she had always been like that, even when she was a young girl —why, she always wanted the best-looking boy in school and if she made up her mind she was going to have him, that's all there was to it."

To Leavy, the weight of the testimony of friends who knew Evelyn well far outweighed Vernell's observations of Evelyn, and on cross, the prosecutor questioned the witness about his never-paid fee. "Have you, to this moment, ever gotten your $8,200, or 10 percent?" Leavy asked.

"Nothing, absolutely nothing," the witness said.

"Still have hopes, is that right?"

"No. I don't think Mr. Scott can afford it," Vernell said.

The defense called Kenneth De Remy, who said he'd worked as a chauffeur for Evelyn in 1936 and in 1937, when she was married to Clem Pettit. "Were you in a position to observe Evelyn Pettit's condition of sobriety at any time?"

"Well, all I got to tell you is this. Her sobriety wasn't very good. She either had a mental aberration or she was drunk, that's for dog-gone sure. . . . One time, I drank some of her wine, to tell the truth. She tried to measure with her index finger and thumb to see how much was gone and she got hysterical," De Remy testified.

Leavy's cross-examination of De Remy was swift. "Weren't you out here waiting to be a witness before the twelve o'clock noon recess?" he asked.

"Yes, I was."

"Weren't you under the influence of liquor at that time?"

"No, I wasn't," De Remy said.

Leavy asked the court bailiff to stand up and De Remy's answer changed. "You want me to tell the truth? I had some liquor last night—"

"All right, now," Judge Nye interrupted the witness. "It seems to me you are going to get yourself into trouble if you keep talking."

Alarcon subsequently called the bailiff, Henry Akard, to the stand. "What was your opinion as to Mr. De Remy just before the noon recess?"

"In my opinion, he was under the influence of alcohol," Akard said firmly.

To Leavy's surprise, he was the next witness, called by Lambros to demonstrate that authorities were still not convinced that Mrs. Scott was dead. "Have you received various communications, various leads, from people who have indicated that they have seen Evelyn or heard from her?" Lambros asked.

"Oh, about every other morning I get a letter either telling me how to try the case or some kind of a lead," Leavy said.

"Did you turn over any of those leads to the police department?"

"Oh yes."

"And to your knowledge did they follow through to check them out?"

"Yes, though they are usually so vague and mixed up that it is very difficult."

On cross, Alarcon, somewhat bemused, questioned his colleague. "Mr. Leavy, would you say that most of the letters that you have seen are the type we would label 'crank' letters?"

"I would say that most of them fall into that category. The others are people who want to help—they give ideas where we can find the body of Evelyn Scott, that sort of thing."

"[The police] have eliminated whatever information was contained in [each] letter?"

"They have," Leavy replied firmly.

Leavy was followed to the stand by the defense's final witness, Sergeant Howard Hudson, who acknowledged that authorities were still pursuing possible leads to locate Scott's missing wife.

"And if a lead came in tomorrow, would you follow that up?"

"I would say we would, yes," Hudson said.

"Some of the leads," Leavy countered on cross-examination, "included ladies who themselves thought they were Mrs. Scott, didn't they?"

"Yes, they did," Hudson said, adding that none of them, of course, proved to be Evelyn.

On Monday, December 9, Leavy recalled Sergeant Hudson as a rebuttal witness, to refuse the defense's assertion that Scott had a community interest in Evelyn's holdings. Leavy was brief:
"Do you have an envelope in your pocket?" he asked.
"I do," Hudson said, handing it to Leavy.
"May this envelope, which contains a copy of a will and handwritten codicil of a Leonard Ewing Scott, be marked next in order of identification."
Stunned, Lambros leaped to his feet to object. But despite strenuous argument, Scott's will, dated July 5, 1951, and his handwritten codicil, dated March 5, 1956, were admitted into evidence. Not only did Scott clearly state that he held no community property with his wife, but he acknowledged the existence of "cash in a safe-deposit box," the rightful owner of which, alleged the prosecution, was Evelyn.
Leavy read this part of Scott's codicil aloud to the astonished courtroom:

"I revoke all bequests to my wife Evelyn Scott with the exception of $1, because she has ample financial provisions for her needs. I leave the rest . . . as follows: 50 per cent of the remaining sum shall be given to Marianne Beaman of Santa Monica, Cal., and the remaining 50 per cent shall be given to Roy Whorton of Sherman Oakes [sic] Cal. . . . I furthermore state as part of this codicil that all cash in a safe-deposit box was acquired before my arrival in California; that required taxes were paid at the period of acquisition of same and that no taxes of any kind are required or payable for these funds prior to their distribution under the terms of my will."

□ **32**

On Wednesday, December 11, "court" reconvened in the driveway of the Scott home, where, for an hour and a half, Scott's jurors toured the house, peered inside the incinerator and over the retaining wall, and wandered through Evelyn's flower beds. Scott, under the close watch of two sheriff's deputies, basked in the winter sunlight in a patio deck chair.

A day later, Scott was back in a courtroom chair, listening as Alarcon presented the prosecution's opening argument: "The law does not give a person a reward for disposing of his victim," Alarcon said. "Otherwise, a person could kill and hide or dispose of his victim, then sit back smugly and be immune from prosecution. . . . He was brainwashing Evelyn's friends for the day when he would murder his wife. He could then say she was ill and going to a sanatorium to account for the fact that she was no longer among us. . . ."

The prosecutor pulled up a chair and seated himself center stage in the courtroom. "He sat there," Alarcon said, recalling Scott's refusal to acknowledge Opal Mumper, "smugly confident, twirling his glasses"—Alarcon whirled his own horn-rimmed pair in midair for effect—"just as he has done in this courtroom, hopeful that you will not convict him because we cannot find out what he did with Evelyn. . . . It would be fantastic, impossible, ridiculous," Alarcon emphasized, "for this type of woman to walk out, to simply vanish, voluntarily."

A day later, Friday, December 13, Tom Williams offered the first phase of the defense's three hours of final arguments: "If your husband or wife disappears," Williams warned the jury, "you had better stay home. Do not go anyplace or the district attorney will file a murder charge against you . . . I can't convince myself with all of these witnesses that a crime of murder has been committed. I will defy anyone to find a corpus delicti unless there is a body someplace—whether you can see it or not.

"If Mr. Scott is clever enough to murder his wife and conceal her body so that it has not been found for two and one-half years, then that man is not stupid enough to leave anything on the surface of the ground. I can think of a thousand ways he could have gotten rid of them. Besides, where is Mrs. Scott's other denture?" Williams demanded. "In my opinion, she is wearing it."

As for Scott's failure to take the witness stand in his own behalf, Williams referred to the many times Scott appeared for questioning by police, district attorney, and grand jury.

"Objection," Leavy interrupted. "He most certainly did not testify before the grand jury, and there is nothing in the record to show that he ever testified under oath on any occasion."

"I'll put the transcripts [of Scott's official interviews that were not under oath] in the record," Williams offered.

"No, we would rather have him take the stand," Leavy retorted.

But Al Matthews, in the second stage of defense arguments, had his answer for this very point, that Scott did not take the stand in previous court actions on the advice of his civil attorneys. The reason? Not due to fear that Scott might implicate himself of murder, Matthews charged, but to forestall incriminating himself on forgery or income tax evasion:

"This is just one leg of his journey through the courts. They aren't interested in murder—they're interested in something else, forgery or tax evasion. . . ."

Matthews continued: "There is no violence in this case. They haven't told you *how, where, when,* and *why.* You can't even visualize what is supposed to have happened to this woman. . . . Tell me," he demanded, painting Scott as a man pruning trees, waiting to retire, and maybe dabble a little in the stock market, "what was his motive? You don't shoot Santa Claus. What was he going to do with the money? He's no gambler, no drunkard. He told different stories to friends to hide his humiliation—that she would leave him—to get them off his back until she returned.

"No overt act by Scott has anything to do with murder. Even if everything the prosecution has brought into this courtroom is absolutely true, it still doesn't stop Mrs. Scott from walking in that front courtroom door—and you know it."

"If you," Lambros said, concluding the defense's argument on Monday, December 16, with an impassioned appeal to the juror's emotions, "think you can look yourselves in the face for the rest of your lives on this evidence, go ahead. Convict him. But you'll find yourself living through agony when she comes back here and Scott is gone. You'll find yourselves subconsciously looking for Mrs. Scott as you walk down Broadway or Wilshire Boulevard. . . .

"What is so inconceivable," Lambros asked, "about someone else entering the house while Mr. Scott was out getting the tooth powder? Why is it so impossible Mrs. Scott walked off, was kidnapped, or was involved in a conspiracy? One thing a guilty man would have done was report Mrs. Scott missing the next day. How simple. How logical—for a man who has planned to kill his wife for years. . . .

"Don't come back with any compromise verdict of second-degree murder," Lambros urged. "Mr. Scott is an innocent man. Don't put him in an institution because you are not sure. . . . Nothing is more certain that death. If they are so certain that Mrs. Scott is dead and Scott is their man, why do they waste a minute of their time checking? There's a doubt in their minds, that's why."

Lambros paused. He looked levelly at the jury, weighting his words with soberness. "God rest all of our souls, ladies and gentlemen, if Mr. Scott is convicted and she walks in. The pillow will not be comfortable at night. You'll twist and turn with the rest of us."

With might and thunder, Leavy pounded home again and again Scott's failure to testify in the prosecution's closing argument on Wednesday, December 18. "The defendant did not take this witness stand"—Leavy smacked it hard with his palm—"and tell you under oath that he is not guilty. I want you to keep in mind that Scott and his attorneys expect you to come back into this courtroom and by your verdict tell the defendant he is not guilty, but the defendant *did not take this witness stand* and tell you with his own lips that *he is not guilty.*"

Scott wasn't the first murderer to make mistakes, bobbles, Leavy called them, not the least of which was his serious underestimation of Evelyn's friends. "Had not the Brawners, the Schuchardts, Jim Boyle, Marguerite Watson, and all of those people been breathing down Scott's neck as they did, had he been able to keep them off his back and keep out of sight, had they not been preserving people who loved Evelyn Scott and would find out where she was and what happened to her. . . . Yes, Scott misjudged the friendship and loyalty of Mrs. Scott's friends, the fact that they would pursue this matter until they knew what had happened to Evelyn Scott. Another mistake he made was that he never knew until this that there are police officers, district attorney's investigators, and prosecutors who would someday put this case together in a courtroom. . . . Scott thought he was smarter than everybody else. Well, not this time."

226

If Scott was really smarter than everyone else, Leavy said, then he wouldn't have "bobbled" Evelyn's denture and eyeglasses, carelessly leaving them to be discovered months later by police in what had to be "an act of God."

"He isn't the first one to make bobbles. It is likely that Mrs. Scott had someplace she kept her denture at night—in a drawer or someplace, perhaps with her glasses and other things. Mr. Scott must have bobbled the denture somehow when he was disposing of her things. Perhaps a box set on the retaining wall tipped and fell over unbeknownst to him. He was oblivious in his haste or in darkness. We do know that some girdles were burned in the incinerator. . . . If Mrs. Scott wanted to absent herself voluntarily, she would never toss her denture and glasses over that wall."

"All," Leavy continued, his extemporaneous argument punctuated by his booming voice and constant movement, "was not sweetness and light in the Scott household. She consented to a change in the management of her Milwaukee property because she was 'continuing to live with her husband.' She liquidated her securities to keep peace with him. He conned her, all right. She didn't know what was coming [though] she perhaps was aware she had made not too good a bargain in this marriage. Nevertheless, she provided for her husband. But you know a will doesn't take effect until death, and it can be changed anytime before death."

Though the defense argued that Scott was simply "too nice a man" to commit murder, Leavy had his own version of Scott's character to offer the jury. "The woman whom he has asked to marry him when his troubles are over, the woman with whom he has been to bed, he drops her just like that," he said, snapping his fingers, "just as he did away with Mrs. Scott. He goes to Canada, stays out of sight for nearly a year, and Marianne Beaman never hears from him again. He leaves her here to humiliation and embarrassment. . . .

"Are we supposed to believe that Evelyn Scott's ghost came back and signed her name?" Leavy asked. "No, the defendant traced her signatures [on] the traveler's checks and bank documents. The forgeries and grand theft are a part of his motive—avarice and greed. . . . If he can't take the stand here and face cross-examination of the very things that constitute the motive, he can't explain or deny

227

them, then that brings the crime home to the defendant just as surely as any eyewitness."

The defense appealed to the juror's emotions, but Leavy asked them to use their own good sense to return their verdict:

"In no circumstantial evidence case does one bit of evidence stand alone in establishing a corpus delicti of murder, establish the essential elements of murder, or the guilt of the defendant. You have to take one circumstance which may be meaningless standing alone, then you take another circumstance that may be meaningless standing alone, and the two together may not give any meaning. But maybe there's another circumstance, a fourth circumstance, maybe a fifth. . . . When you take all of the circumstances together, they are a mosaic, a picture, of the corpus delicti of murder. They establish together each link in the chain of circumstances that is inconsistent with any rational hypothesis of innocence. By your good reasoning, by your good judgment, you will come to the conclusion that Evelyn Scott is deceased by some criminal agency and that the defendant is the perpetrator. No, we can't say that she was suffocated, chloroformed, poisoned, or whatever, but that by some criminal agency she met foul play. And there is only one person, with the exclusion of all others, that the evidence points to," Leavy said, "and that is L. Ewing Scott."

For another thirty-six minutes, the jurors listened to instructions read to them by Judge Nye. At eighteen minutes before noon, they began their deliberations, to be interrupted only for meals and rest.

"Aren't you glad it's over?" Scott asked reporters outside. He was relaxed, jovial, and confident about his future. "I'm certainly looking forward to my last nights in my present accommodations," he said. Over the next three days, he flipped through magazines while his attorneys ordered champagne and rented a hotel suite to hold a party for the jury Lambros was certain would be unable to return anything but a verdict of not guilty.

That verdict clearly was not the one Leavy expected to hear. After more than a million words' worth of testimony, Leavy, too, was glad that Scott's long, exhausting trial was over, though he was restless and preoccupied as he waited for the verdict. The trial ceaselessly returned to his thoughts. What more might he have done? Had he missed some vital link in his chain of circumstantial evidence? What would carry the jury, the weight of factual proof or the possibility that Evelyn might somehow still be alive? Over those three days, Leavy rested only intermittently.

The women prisoners in the county jail were rehearsing Christmas carols when the jurors' signal came just after noon on Saturday, December 21. By 1:15 P.M., the trial's participants were assembled in the courtroom, which seemed somehow larger than usual on this chilly weekend afternoon. To the strains of "God Rest Ye Merry Gentlemen," Scott heard the jury's decision: "We find the defendant, L. Ewing Scott," read the clerk, "guilty of murder as charged and find it to be murder in the first degree."

Scott coughed once. He looked at his attorneys. "Well," he said, his voice flat and even, "I guess some people like Lincolns and some people like Fords." With that ambiguous remark, Scott folded his long fingers in a neat, two-handed fist on the counsel table and looked at the three lawyers expectantly. Lambros, thunderstruck, sank back in his chair and stared back at Scott in silence.

Five feet away stood Leavy and Alarcon, both hiding tight smiles of elation. But Leavy soon slipped away from the courtroom and back to his office, for he still had a little more of Scott's business to which to attend. When the proceedings resumed a day after Christmas, Leavy intended to demand the maximum penalty for murder: death for Scott in the small green chamber just inside the walls of San Quentin State Prison.

□ **33**

To Scott, Christmas Day was just another day of waiting: no visitors, no gifts, no church service. He ate his holiday dinner of roast chicken, dressing, potatoes, and gravy in his cell, alone, except for the twenty-four-hour "suicide watch" posted over anyone convicted of a capital crime. A day later, he listened impassively as Al Matthews eloquently pleaded with his jury to spare Scott his life.

"If you give him life imprisonment, time is your ally," Matthews said, his voice quiet and solemn. "Every day that Evelyn Scott doesn't show up, people will come up to you and say that maybe you were right, she still may be alive somewhere. But if you sentence him to death, time is your foe. Believe me, you will inject yourselves into a controversy that will never leave your lives. To kill, to condemn to death a murderer is a left-handed way of accepting his poison as a remedy."

Matthews's voice was stronger, louder. "Mr. Scott may be a psychological casualty, a man born without a feeling of love. But *pity* is the *eye* of *mercy* and *mercy* is the *heart* of *love*. Don't let *anyone* force love for another human being out of your hearts."

"When God"—Matthews was shouting now—"caught Cain redhanded, He didn't kill him. He banished him. He said, 'I put a seven-fold curse on anyone who kills. . . .' If there is any possible doubt in your mind," Matthews pleaded, "in the name of God, give this man life imprisonment."

But Leavy turned Matthews' plea into a question. "Examine the evidence," said the prosecutor. "Is there anything that entitles him to life imprisonment? This was not an impulsive crime, not a crime of passion. This was a carefully well-laid plan to do away with Evelyn Scott for one purpose only—greed. He planned it for months and years. Little did Evelyn Scott know that every day she went to her safe-deposit box, having withdrawn cash from her accounts, she was one day closer to her end. It was carefully, coolly, coldly, and cruelly outlined. Every day, as he helped her out of the car, that was only his veneer. In the back of his mind he was scheming. That is why he didn't take the witness stand. He knew you would see through his veneer. You would see he had the coldness and coolness to do what he did to that frail, innocent woman.

"L. Ewing Scott has earned for himself capital punishment. He ran the risk—through greed—of facing this day. There isn't a single thing in this evidence which calls for life imprisonment," Leavy said. "He has earned his sentence of death."

But four hours later, the jury that found Scott guilty of murder sentenced him to life imprisonment. Scott blinked once as his sentence was announced, and Lambros smiled tightly. For his part, Matthews felt grimly gratified; at least, he thought, this once, he'd won life against death against Leavy.

Though disappointed, Leavy thought he understood why the jury returned the verdict it did, a thought he shared later with Alarcon. "My own feeling is that we got as much as we could out of the case. When you try a man who has no prior police record on purely circumstantial evidence, there aren't many juries that will give him the death penalty."

Lambros, still stunned by the verdict, promised to present new evidence, showing that Evelyn was still alive, if granted a motion for a new trial, which Lambros requested before Judge Nye on January 24, 1958. Lambros' motion contended that the Superior Court had no right to try Scott without proof that Evelyn died in Los Angeles; his request was denied by the judge, who instead formally sentenced Scott to life imprisonment. At Leavy's request, the thirteen remaining charges against Scott for forgery and grand theft were left off calendar.

For months, the back pages of the city's newspapers carried postscripts to the case that formerly so gripped the headlines. Scott's parting with Lambros—Matthews and Williams resigned after Scott's sentencing—was mercifully brief, as Scott angrily denounced his former attorney for "rolling roughshod" over his desire to testify at his trial. Lambros retorted that Scott had agreed with and even supported the decision when it was made.

Within days of Scott's conviction, actor Leo Carrillo, the popular sidekick on television's "The Cisco Kid," informed police that two men had approached him and asked him to help Scott by claiming he saw Evelyn in Rio de Janeiro after May 16, 1955. One of those two men was Richard Mowery, a thirty-two-year-old amateur private detective from Ohio, who, when questioned by police, revealed an even more bizarre effort on Scott's behalf: a plot to plant the detached arm of an elderly woman injected with Evelyn's blood type and wearing

231

her wedding band in the Corona del Mar beach home of Bill Brawner, where Evelyn had been an occasional guest. Mowery claimed that Scott had provided a sketch of the house and told his alleged partner in the scheme, Frank Massad, where Evelyn's wedding ring could be found inside 217 North Bentley. Though Massad, who had worked as an investigator for Lambros during Scott's trial, was found not guilty of conspiracy in a jury trial, Mowery pleaded guilty to the same charge and was sentenced to the 166 days he had already served in county jail.

A rusty, black humpbacked trunk belonging to Scott found by janitors in the basement of the Jonathan Club was immediately seized by police. Amid much public fanfare, the trunk was opened by authorities to reveal an ancient prayer book and three long plaits of brown hair. From his county jail cell, Scott identified the braids as the hair of his late mother. Since Evelyn's short hair had been gray, officials accepted Scott's explanation.

For the first time in the nearly two years since Throsby's filing for control of Evelyn's fortune, Scott, with plenty of free time on his hands now, suddenly took an intense interest in the settlement of her affairs. On Scott's plea that "she'll want it when she gets back," Hallam Mathews, as trustee, agreed to place Evelyn's prized $2,400 mink stole in storage for one year. But Matthews denied Scott's petition for a $600-a-month allowance to defray the cost of hunting for his wife and Scott's contention that it "would be [Evelyn's] wish that petitioner continue to occupy and care for the home pending her return."

Scott remained in county jail awaiting the outcome of his appeal. On December 21, 1959, the District Court of Appeal handed down its lengthy, eloquent ruling by presiding Justice Clement L. Shinn, who wrote in conclusion:

> In our study of the evidence we have found no reason for questioning the correctness of the verdict. Although, as we have said, the case is factually without precedent, it is not without precedent in principle or in the law, which allows death to be proved by circumstantial evidence. Appellant wove about himself a web of incriminating circumstances that was complete. He has evolved from the evidence no theory of innocence;

the jury could not find such a theory, nor can we. Appellant merely says, and others may say, "But Mrs. Scott may still be alive." They would have to rest their belief upon some mythical or miraculous hypothesis, since it could not find support in any reasonable deduction from the established facts. But the law is reason; it does not proceed upon fantasy or remote and unrealistic possibilities.

The undisputed facts point unerringly to a single conclusion. The evidence of appellant's guilt was convincing. The judgement is affirmed.

Through his new attorney, Morris Lavine, Scott announced he planned to appeal the ruling.

Soon after the district court's decision, Scott was transferred temporarily from county jail to Chino, a state prison near Pomona, then to his permanent home in California's oldest state prison at Point San Quentin on March 1, 1960. Ironically, tenants moved into 217 North Bentley Avenue that same month, paying $450 a month in rent for use of everything except the upstairs den closet holding what was left of the Scotts' respective personal belongings.

To Scott's bitter frustration, the United States Supreme Court refused, on December 5, 1960, to review his conviction. Only Justice Douglas dissented:

. . . . It was not even shown directly that his wife, whom he is now convicted of murdering, is dead. Proof of the *corpus delicti,* as well as proof of the petitioner's criminal agency, was to be inferred from his wife's inexplicable disappearance coupled with his unnatural behavior thereafter. A prominent aspect of this unnatural behavior was his silence. . . . Using a defendant's silence as evidence against him is one way of having him testify against himself. This would not be permitted, we have assumed, in a federal trial by reason of the Fifth Amendment. . . . The present case shows how utterly devastating the state rule which sanctions it can be.

A subsequent ruling by the court, written five years later by Justice Douglas, did hold that judges and prosecutors could no longer comment, as did Leavy, on the defendant's failure to testify in a state trial. But unfortunately for Scott, that "silent defendant" ruling was not retroactive.

Scott, though jailed in a maximum-security prison, was befriended by Ruth Maiorana, a forty-four-year-old legal secretary who firmly believed Scott to be innocent of Evelyn's murder. "Ruthie," as Scott called her, offered a $10,000 reward for news of Scott's missing wife, $20,000 if proof that she was still alive was offered before Evelyn's will was admitted into probate. But no one had stepped forward to collect Maiorana's reward by the time Evelyn was at last declared legally dead on March 10, 1961, and her will admitted to probate.

In May 1962, a superior court judge who played a bit part in the lawsuits over Evelyn's fortune, turned over to police a handwritten letter mailed to him from Redding, California:

"Sir [it said], I am not dead yet! Don't you think that L. Ewing has suffered enough at your hands? That brother of mine is a devil— watch him. I will return someday. Mrs. Evelyn Throsbey [sic] Scott." A handwriting analysis ruled the letter a hoax, probably written by an elderly woman who misspelled the middle name that Evelyn abbreviated in her genuine signature.

From time to time, other sightings of Evelyn were reported, most of them originating from Scott's 4½-by-9-foot cell at San Quentin. Scott churned out a relentless stream of letters to reporters, politicians, and elected officials, always proclaiming his innocence and filled with his ideas about where his wife was now. His reports variously located Evelyn "in a mental institution somewhere in the northwest" (a change from his earlier statements that she was in the northeast), in Mexico, where he said she was arrested twice on charges of drunk driving, and in northern California, where Scott said he had heard she was living with a Mexican family. As a gesture of friendship, Tom Williams, one of Scott's former attorneys, did check out that last report, a fruitless search.

As Scott publicized his efforts to find Evelyn, he bitterly fought against the settlement of her estate, becoming, in the best tradition of "jailhouse lawyers," quite adept at the law. But, despite his legal protestations, a decree of distribution was issued on February 5, 1963, and to Scott's fury, it held that his conviction made him ineligible to receive his bequest under the terms of Evelyn's will. Instead, Scott's half of Evelyn's estate, which, reduced by administrative fees and federal and state inheritance taxes to a total value of $344,815, was awarded outright to Raymond Throsby, whose own share was put in trust and paid to him monthly as his sister had stipulated. (Evelyn's ultimate beneficiary, the La Vina Tuberculosis Sanatorium, was eventually awarded about 20 percent of the estate's total value through a series of agreements reached between the sanatorium and Throsby.) Raymond and Trudy Throsby took up permanent residence at 217 North Bentley Avenue.

Several months after Scott's conviction had been affirmed, one of his prosecutors took a transatlantic telephone call from a woman who nervously added her own frightening footnote to the case. "Is the judgment final?" she asked Art Alarcon.

"Yes, ma'am," Alarcon told the woman, who never gave him her name, "but may I ask why you're calling from Rome to find out what's already been in the newspapers?"

"Well"—from half a world away, the prosecutor sensed her hesitation—"I was married to L. Ewing Scott briefly," she said finally. "The day after our marriage, he asked me to open up a joint bank account with him since his own funds were temporarily tied up. So, because I loved him, I opened a joint account, as he asked me, with $150,000 of my own money."

But within days, she was terrified to be alone with her new husband. "There were no direct threats, but there was—something— about his behavior that frightened me. After a few weeks, I told him I'd pay him anything he wanted to get out of the marriage. He asked for $50,000 in cash, which I gave him gladly."

Almost immediately, she notified her attorney, who asked if she had closed out the joint account. "I said no, I hadn't, I'd forgotten all about it. But it didn't matter anyway," she said ruefully to Alarcon. "My 'husband' had cleaned it out the day after it was opened. But, you know," the woman said softly, "it was worth $200,000. I'm alive."

Alarcon stayed with the district attorney's office until July 1961, when he moved to Sacramento to serve as Governor Edmund G. "Pat" Brown's legal adviser and clemency/extradition secretary; to his surprise, Alarcon received occasional letters from Scott asking Alarcon to handle his reinstatement as a member in good standing of the St. Louis Mason's lodge. Alarcon, struck by Scott's gall, passed the letters on for an official answer from elsewhere in the governor's office.

After serving as a Los Angeles Superior Court judge and as an associate justice on the California Court of Appeal, Alarcon was named to the U.S. Court of Appeals, Ninth Circuit, in November 1979.

Even in prison, Scott managed to enjoy the best accommodations, which were located in San Quentin's honor block, informally called "citizen's row." There, inmates enjoyed a few precious privileges unavailable to the general populace, including a bathtub and the right to furnish their cells with prison-made furniture and curtains. Scott's cell was typically spartan, however; his decorations were a few law books, his ever-present pile of current magazines, and boxes filled with files of the news clippings on his trial.

He was, for a time, a clerk in the prison hospital; when a slip on a stray handball broke his hip, Scott, who had charmed the hospital staff with his genteel manners, was treated with genuine affection during his recovery. That injury left Scott dependent upon a wooden cane, which he learned to wave threateningly at any young con who failed to make an adequately wide berth around the old man with shuffling steps. His fellows called him "old man Scott," and though Scott had made no friends among them, no one objected—much—to the hour of Lawrence Welk Scott liked to watch on the communal television set every Saturday night. On warm days, Scott sunned himself on a bench in the exercise yard.

But prison to Scott was only a temporary inconvenience, and he waged his own single-minded war for release. With two fingers, he pecked away at a prison typewriter, producing his letters and appeals, though, year after year, he accumulated only more boxes of polite rejections and denials. Every letter, every petition protested his innocence: Among the recipients of his letters were Presidents Eisenhower and Nixon, and then California Governor Ronald Reagan.

Scott, of course, was the atypical San Quentin con, and as the years passed, those differences only became more apparent; after all, a maximum-security prison system has little time to care for an aging, infirmed inmate such as Scott. In November 1974, he was given a release date, but adamantly and angrily, Scott turned it down. To accept parole, he said, was tantamount to admitting guilt for a crime Scott had yet to concede truly occurred. Prison authorities had no choice but to keep Scott installed in his San Quentin cell; Scott refused a second parole date two years later on the same grounds.

Scott's protestations aside, however, what he faced was really an ironic and terrible truth: As grim and unrelenting as prison was, Scott had nowhere else to go in a world that had changed beyond his recognition. He had $5,000 saved up from his social security payments, which would hardly return him to his former life-style of custom-tailored suits and long cruises to warm climates. With no friends, no resources, and no options, Scott was determined to stay in prison.

To his unhappy surprise, however, Scott was finally awarded the unconditional discharge—time served, no parole—he demanded. On March 26, 1978, with a crowd of reporters waiting at the prison's gate, Scott and his five hundred pounds of accumulated files were driven to the edge of San Quentin Prison, a short journey that every other inmate in the institution's history had to make on foot. At eighty-one years of age, Scott was again a free man.

Though he hinted that he was considering a move back to his former quarters at the Jonathan Club, in truth, Scott was dependent upon the charity of Midge and Chaplain Joe Katanick, a San Jose couple running a mobile worship center for truck drivers called Transport for Christ, who generously offered him a home. The Katanicks took Scott for his first meal outside the walls of San Quentin in almost two decades. It was a Big Mac, but Scott, apparently unimpressed, said it tasted "just like a hamburger." He also bought himself a new suit: Without so much as a glance at the more modestly priced polyester ensembles, Scott chose one tailored from soft, finished English worsted wool. His next move, Scott announced, was to "divorce Evelyn."

Scott did return to Los Angeles soon after his release, where he lived in a series of apartments in Santa Monica and in the Wilshire district. Hampered by his hip injury, Scott spent most of his time in a worn armchair, staring at a black-and-white television set and plotting new lawsuits against the state to recover *his* fortune.

From time to time, there were visitors, of course, though never very many. Among them was the crew of ABC-TV's "The Love Report," a short-lived news-style program. On July 27, 1984, Scott was the subject of a ten-minute interview, and he spoke the segment's final words with firmness and determination: "I did not kill my wife. That is the truth, the whole truth, and nothing but the truth."

ABC's interest in Scott proved that, even twenty-nine years after Evelyn disappeared, some people still question her fate. Dorothy Mumper, for example, Evelyn's daughter-in-law by her fourth marriage, still watches the papers for news briefs such as the one she saw in the *Los Angeles Times* on November 7, 1983:

> A pile of bones without a skull was discovered under an asphalt parking lot that had been paved at least twenty years ago at Leo Carrillo State Beach, near the Ventura–Los Angeles county line north of Malibu. The bones were exposed by ocean waves that had begun to undercut the asphalt, sheriff's deputies reported. Coroner's experts were conducting an examination to determine the age of the bones.

To herself, Dorothy wonders if those bones might be Evelyn's.

Even J. Miller Leavy, our conversation ending as summer's twilight paints the room in dusky hues, can't offer anything but his absolute and firm belief that only L. Ewing Scott knows where Evelyn is today.

"You know," Leavy tells me now, "I had a great disappointment in trying that case. He never took the stand. If I had had the chance to cross-examine Scott, they might have even given him the death penalty.

"I would never ask a jury to impose a death sentence if I, as a lawyer, didn't believe that the facts were sufficient to warrant execution. Actually, Evelyn Scott's alive and living on a beach in Bora Bora and I send her money every month just to keep her quiet." Leavy laughs and shakes his head.

"But you know," he says, suddenly serious again, "there's not a doubt in my mind he killed her. I *know* he killed her. He took that woman out, a woman he shared a bed with, and in some way or another, Scott got rid of every centilla, every piece of her body." Leavy's voice is a courtroom whisper. "She's never been found."

"Tell me what your full name is."

It is Monday, August 6, 1984. L. Ewing Scott called me at home yesterday to request what he said flatly would be our final interview. "I have a story to tell you," Scott told me gravely. "I think that this is something you'll want to hear." My curiosity was only modestly aroused—Scott's visitors are rare and he has enticed me before with "something" he must tell me only in person—but still, I agreed to visit him this one last time. His apartment is just off Wilshire in Los Angeles' Miracle Mile district, a once-grand stretch of boulevard now fallen on the hard times of urban neglect. Scott's efficiency apartment is furnished only with the functional necessities of old age: a hospital bed, a chair by a sunny window, and an electric clock that noisily rattles away his hours here one by one. He has been waiting for me, perched on the edge of his unmade bed, leaning on the walker that is his only means of transportation around the small apartment.

"Don't you know what my name is by this time?" Scott says. "My full name is *Robert Leonard Ewing Scott.*" His health has clearly deteriorated since my last visit in April, although, at eighty-nine years old, Scott is remarkably lucid and articulate. Today, he wears clothing that would fit him much better if he could stand upright: black trousers and a dull, pea-green long-sleeved shirt, both of which are made not of fine cloth from Europe but of polyester from Taiwan.

"Do you understand that I have a tape recorder and that the tape recorder is running?"

"Yes."

"Okay. What is the story you said you wanted to tell me?"

"Well," he says, and pauses for a long moment, "I arrived in Las Vegas about dusk." His words come slowly. "I waited until it was dark to point six miles due east of the Sands Hotel and I drove up to that point. I put four sticks in the ground so that I would not over-come anything—"

"Overcome what?" Is this story another of his endless tangents?

"The digging of the grave." He seems more intent on the pepper-mint candy he is eating than on the nature of our conversation. "I got down about six feet, which was not any hard job in sand, and when I got that far, I stopped, I went to the car, I got the remains of Evelyn, and I untied the piece of garment I had her in and I *dumped* her in the hole."

"What was she tied up in?"

"The gardener's tarpaulin, something like that. And after I dumped her in, I took the shovel and smeared it all over with grease so the sand wouldn't stick to it, and I shoveled it all over her, took up the four sticks I had planted. After I covered it up, I put the tools in the car, drove around and covered up my tracks, and went back to sleep in the car for a while, then I drove back to Los Angeles."

"Which car were you driving?"

"My 1940 Ford."

"What was Evelyn wearing?"

"Nothing."

"How did you kill Evelyn?"

"I hit her in the head with a mallet, a hard rubber mallet." His voice is as unchanging in its rhythm as the loud hum of the alarm clock on his bedside table. "Just once. On the head, right on top. . . . It was that day, the day we went for the test ride in the Mercedes-Benz—it seemed to me that that was about the best day to do it in, and so I just selected it."

"Why didn't Evelyn struggle? Did she see you coming with it?"

"Oh," he says, his eyes glinting, "she had ideas of struggling, but I cracked right through her hands."

"Where were you?"

"In our bedroom."

"Were you arguing?"

"No. I never opened my mouth. I never said a word, I never opened my mouth, and all she said to me was, 'But I haven't done anything.' She's a *liar* of the first order. I know."

"Did she say anything else?"

"No, she didn't have a chance to say anything else. Just one hard blow."

"Why did you kill Evelyn?"

"Why? Because she tried to poison me, that's why. Isn't that a good enough reason?"

"If Evelyn tried to poison you, why didn't you go to the police, and let her go to jail?"

"Why should I tell the police anything? If I went to the police, she would tell them a cock-and-bull story and turn the whole thing right on me."

"Did you ever regret killing her?"

"*No!*" His eyes, bright brown, burn. "Why should I? She sure in hell tried to take my life."

"You really believe that she tried to poison you?"

"Oh, I know it. I know it. Now what more do you want to know?"

"What else do you remember about that day?"

"Driving back home—I arrived before Frank [Evelyn's handyman] did. I put the car in the garage and I dusted off any sand that was on it. I threw the shovel in where the gardener kept the tools and I went up and went to bed."

"How did you feel?"

"Like I had justified a job that had to be done by five, no, six, other men."

"Why did you marry Evelyn?"

"Because she wanted me to—I didn't want to marry her. She wanted me to live with her—I said no, I don't believe in that, I will not live with you. She said, 'Then, you're going to marry me.'"

"Do you think you could have lived comfortably with Evelyn had she not tried to 'poison' you?"

"I don't think so because there was nothing between us that was comparable. Absolutely nothing."

"How did Evelyn's dentures and eyeglasses get up on the other side of your property? Did you throw them up there?"

"No, I did not. Some *dick* threw 'em over there."

"Did you think that you'd ever be convicted for your wife's murder?"

"I didn't care."

"You didn't care?"

"No. What did I have to live for? Nothing. I thought, I have had it, so let's get it all over with. But they never found her body in that grave."

"That's true. There's probably a hotel over it now."

"No," he says, "not six miles out from town."

"Is there any way to identify the spot where you buried Evelyn?"

"It's exactly six miles east of where the sun comes up from the Sands Hotel."

"Did you ever go back to her grave?"

"No. Why should I go back?"

"Why did you decide to tell me all this about Evelyn?"

"Why did I tell you all this? Well, it makes a good story, doesn't it?"

"It does make a good story. You had a lot of time in San Quentin to think it all over. Were you ever sorry?"

"No."

"What did you think about in jail?"

"Well, I thought there was no way for me to get out and I might as well stay here [in San Quentin] for the rest of my life and call it a day."

"Did you like San Quentin?"

"Well, I liked it better than the place where I had been living on Bentley Avenue. You have never been in prison and you don't know what a nice house is—you just think you do—so that's the conclusion I reached. Now, what more do you want to know?"

"Have you ever told anyone else this story?"

"No. Because they'd laugh at me—they wouldn't believe it. I'm sorry," he interrupts himself, "but I didn't shave for your visit—I just couldn't make it."

"Is there anything else you remember about killing Evelyn and driving her body out to bury her in the desert?"

He pauses. "No, I don't think that there is—I don't think so," he says, shaking his head.

"Did you think that you'd get caught?"

"Oh yes." He laughs. "What else have they got these goddamn dicks for?"

"Why didn't you leave town immediately?"

"There may be answers to that question, but you know, I really didn't give a damn—I really didn't care."

"Did you *want* to get caught?"

"Well, I thought it would make a nice story. The police all over the United States and Canada were looking for me and they couldn't find me. I made it as dramatic as possible. . . ."

"Go on."

"I didn't care. I didn't care if they caught me or didn't catch me—or if they executed me—what did I care? I didn't care. You know, they don't use the electrocution method at San Quentin—they use the poison-gas method. . . . I expected to go to the gas chamber. In some respects, I was disappointed that I didn't. What use did I have for living?

"Do you know what the cons in San Quentin said to me?" Scott continues. "That if I ever saw that woman again—their suggestion to me was to shoot her because they couldn't do a damn thing to me because I'd already served my time."

"But Evelyn was already dead. You knew you'd never see her again."

He laughs again. "Well, I *hoped* I wouldn't, anyway."

"Did you *hate* Evelyn?"

"No. I didn't hate her—I just—disliked—her. I think I'm going to have to lie down now." Scott swings himself back with the help of a ring mounted over the bed. "Oh, you son of a bitch!" he shouts at the stiff-legged pain he feels. "Wait till I get organized." He turns on his side toward me, tucking his legs up in a fetal half-curl.

"So now," he says, arranging his head on the pillow, "now, you've got a good story—you can put at the end of all that goddamn crap that that Jew lawyer put on—say, will you give me another candy, please?"

I unwrap a butterscotch and hand it to him. "What do you want next—what do you expect now from life?"

"Nothing."

"Do you want to die?"

"I'm ready."

"What do you think about when you lie here by yourself during the day?"

"I don't think about anything but sleep—"

"Go on."

"—so, I go to sleep."

"Do you have fear now? Any fear of God?"

"No. I believe in God. But how can I—why should I have fear of God when he's permitted that type of woman to continue to exist? Now answer me that. Answer me." He pauses only briefly. "Well, the answer is somebody had to do the job and it fell upon me to do it and I did it."

"Aren't you putting yourself in a godlike position when you say you thought Evelyn didn't deserve to live?"

"Not necessarily. Not any more than the fellow in the gas chamber of the penitentiary feels like God."

"Is there anything else you want to tell me?"

"Oh, that's enough." Scott is clearly tired. "There is nothing more I have to say, except when I went before the [parole] board, before they had time to ask me any questions, I said, 'Now, you gentlemen are supposed to be here to do your duty, and I want you to answer me: *Where is the corpus delicti?*' Because corpus delicti is the most important point, for the reason that until corpus delicti is established, there is no legal point in justice."

"You thought if they never found her body that you would never go to jail?"

"I didn't care whether I did or I didn't. I didn't care."

"You were just playing 'cat and mouse' with them, to see if you were smarter than they were?"

"Well, I was smarter than they were, wasn't I?"

"Because you hid her body and no one ever found it?"

"Well, wasn't that smarter?"

244

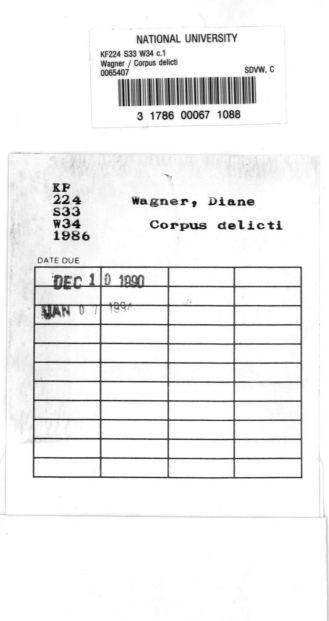